Financial analysis for development

In countries which are struggling to develop or floundering in economic chaos capital investment has to be conducted on the basis of careful investigation and logical analysis. This is advisable everywhere but in countries burdened with poverty, political instability and disrupted infrastructure it is especially hard to get good data and to make reliable predictions. This difficulty is further compounded when overseas investors are unfamiliar with local conditions and seek to introduce new technologies.

Those analysts who put together investment proposals seeking financial backing, and those who appraise these proposals on behalf of sponsors, bankers or indeed government authorities, need to take the methods of project appraisal used elsewhere and adapt them to this context. This will require a blend of technical, financial, economic, environmental and institutional skills. Michael Yaffey offers here some appropriate techniques in financial analysis. He shows how to plan, optimise and appraise within this difficult context using examples widely drawn from industry, transport and agriculture. A new type of cash flow analysis is introduced – beneficiary analysis leading to analytical sensitivity studies.

This book will be useful for practitioners dealing with these problems in Eastern and Central Europe, Africa, South America, Asia and the Middle East. It will be essential for academics and students seeking up to date methodology for developing countries everywhere. It will be a practical handbook for bankers and voluntary aid agencies.

Michael Yaffey is a lecturer at the Development & Project Planning Centre at the University of Bradford. He has worked as an economist in several countries and has had banking, accounting and financial experience chiefly in multi-national companies.

Financial analysis for development

Concepts and techniques

Michael Yaffey

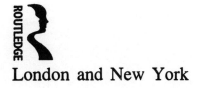

London and New York

First published 1992
by Routledge
11 New Fetter Lane, London EC4P 4EE

Simultaneously published in the USA and Canada
by Routledge
a division of Routledge, Chapman and Hall, Inc.
29 West 35th Street, New York, NY 10001

© 1992 Michael Yaffey

Typeset in Times by
NWL Editorial Services, Langport, Somerset
Printed and bound in Great Britain by
Mackays of Chatham PLC, Chatham, Kent

British Library Cataloguing in Publication Data
A catalogue record for this book is available from the British
Library

0–415–08095–9   M6

Library of Congress Cataloging in Publication Data
Has been applied for

Contents

Figures

Tables

Introduction

The making of business plans is an activity of growing volume and importance. Today, economic conditions change so fast and so radically that very few business operations are likely to jog along by repeating past years' experiences. Everywhere, perspectives are changing. Here we have a new nation state, requiring its own new currency. There we have a slump, requiring fresh survival strategies for core concerns. Elsewhere we have a rehabilitation programme following extensive hostilities. All of these demand the rapid revision of investment plans among those organisations which are already in place. They also encourage the creation of plans for new businesses which spring up in vast numbers, either in response to a genuine need in an under-supplied market, or driven by the desperation of otherwise unemployed individuals, who pin their hopes on profitable self-employment even with risky, flimsy or defective business plans for lack of an alternative.

The acronym 'LDCs' is used throughout this book. It stands for less-developed countries, an unfortunate phrase indicating less-developed economies, sometimes also known as the South, the Third World, or the Developing Countries. However, here it is meant to include also the Baltic States, the republics of the former Soviet Union, and the formerly centrally-planned economies of eastern Europe. Whereas once the United Nations' statistical publications contained the advanced economies in Category I, the centrally- planned states in Category II, and a Category III which came to be called the Third World, much of II has now transferred itself into III. Other than a higher level of literacy and a desire to be in some sense part of Europe there seems little to distinguish between the ex-Communist countries and the more advanced countries of the Third World. The former are LDCs too. They always were, economically, though their earlier category focussed on their political and institutional characteristics instead. China is still in Category II, but in many ways China too is an LDC and many of the techniques advocated in this book will apply in large areas of China also.

In the industrialised countries of the world, previous economic development has made it possible in most cases for those who propose to invest in normal business enterprises to collect the data, the know-how and the equipment needed to put together a business plan. This is not without cost, but can be kept down to an unimportant fraction of the total cost of the proposed investment, in all but the smallest cases. The data on product prices, for example, will be available if the intended product is one which is already on sale. The data on wage costs will be available if persons are already employed in large numbers in the same type of work. The data on equipment costs will be available if the equipment is determined by an existing technology which is already in place elsewhere in the country.

In LDCs, the detailed planning of economic activity is more difficult than elsewhere. Many plans propose to introduce activities which are new to the country, or new to the locality, so that local price and cost data are not available from published sources. Even for familiar staple products, the publication of official statistics is often found to be seriously delayed or disrupted. Managers and investors are relatively inexperienced with long-term business activities and therefore find it harder to conceptualise successful commercial strategies and to assemble credible business plans. For different reasons in industrial parts of eastern Europe, where a market economy is replacing centralised statism, price and cost data appropriate to a market economy are likewise not available from local experience.

Nor is the requirement simply one of obtaining straightforward factual information. The *structures* of competitively successful enterprises, which can be seen by shrewd interpretation of the financial and management accounting statements in mature organisations, and can be built upon to devise appro-priate expansionary investment proposals, are lacking. In LDCs, precisely because of the low level of development, there is a dearth of mature organis-ations, of meaningful and accurate management information within them, of proven structures, and of the ability to build wisely on past experience.

In these situations, advisers from overseas are often called in who can provide norms from their own specialised experience to incorporate in the plans. This is an expensive overhead cost, far beyond the reach of most small undertakings, and a considerable burden on the larger ones, but to some degree is probably unavoidable.

The task of financial analysis in this data-starved and structure-starved context is one which is very different to that faced in advanced, mature economies such as the USA. A different approach seems to be required, which can help to accelerate the planning and appraisal of investment proposals in LDCs.

A further characteristic of LDCs is that, in the very poorest, and in the least developed districts within some others, a high proportion of any new investment has to be financed by foreign aid. This means that the larger proposals must all be examined to see that they are *economically sound* according to the procedures and criteria of aid donors, and the consequence of this is that financial and commercial planning tends to be subordinated to economic appraisal.

That involves consideration of the effects of the projects – for that is what such investment proposals are commonly called – on economic growth, on the environment, and on poverty. The predicted impact on the poorest sections of the population may be taken to include that on women and female-headed households in particular. These economic and social aspects, to the extent that they are dealt with realistically and effectively, are of course highly important, but they should not be taken as all-important. The financial and commercial analysis has its own imperatives too; if these are not met, the investment will not achieve its intended results, or worse still, the organisation which undertakes it may collapse. Financial analysis ought not, therefore, to be perceived as a mere preliminary to economic appraisal, performing the donkey-work of putting up schedules of figures which can be used for economic or social cost-benefit analysis. In the following chapters, financial analysis is considered primarily in terms of its financial purposes, but with good hooks to which other aspects – economic and environmental – can attach themselves.

Separated from its companion economic analysis, it is debatable whether financial analysis may be considered as simply a branch of accountancy. It is certainly not the principal branch of that tree; most accounting activity is concerned with recording business transactions as they occur, and subsequently analysing them so as to produce a set of accounts which faithfully reflects what has occurred. This is a systematic procedure, under which the appropriate accounting actions *follow* the transactions. By contrast, the financial analysis of proposed investments is an unsystematic, partly intuitive, even visionary activity, in which all the accounting work *precedes* the transactions. Imagined accounting entries in imagined books of account do not lend themselves to routine book-keeping procedures from which a faithful set of accounts can be mechanically reflected. It is true that the treatment of any particular imaginary transaction should find its way into the final set of accounts according to settled rules and principles of accountancy, but the particular *figures* used cannot be derived from observing transactions which have already happened, and must instead be forecasted by a wide variety of estimating methods, sometimes rough and ready and sometimes sophisticated, depending on the specifics of the situation as it is perceived.

Success in this form of structured crystal-gazing depends to some extent on the wit and past experience of the analyst. Vision and imagination must be balanced by a healthy scepticism.

Success is relatively easier to achieve in that form of short-term forecasting which is known as budgetary control. Conducted within the structure of an existing business, this aims to produce and enforce a business plan or forecast for one or two years ahead, and of course the experience of recent past years is very helpful in making such predictions. Training in short-term planning of this kind is part of the standard training of accountants everywhere.

Any suggestion that accountants are meter-readers trained only to deal with events after they have happened is therefore incorrect. However, in budget accountancy, one has the advantage that most of the data is to hand, the structure of the budget is basically given and changes little from year to year, and last year's budget is available for easy reference together with a series of recent actual results in full detail. To plan ahead ten or twenty years starting from nothing with a brand-new activity and a brand-new organisation, as is quite common in the less developed economies, is much harder, and possibly more of an art than a science. This is not part of routine accountancy training; some will say that good financial analysts are born and not trained. Some accountants are never required to experience this particular specialism. Some other professionals, such as bankers, small business advisors, and consulting engineers, do it all the time. It therefore goes beyond accountancy.

How to go about this, conceptually, in the complete range of potential investment projects, has not been systematically treated in either the accounting or the economic literature. How to tackle this structured crystal-gazing in the special circumstances of the Third World, eastern Europe, the Middle East or China is the ambitious subject of this present volume. How to do so, that is, to the extent it can be achieved at all in LDCs.

In visionary mood, some new techniques are suggested here, including analytical cash flow. In sceptical mood, some old techniques are looked at afresh and specifically related to LDCs, including ratio analysis, break-even analysis and even the most fundamental concepts of discounted cash flow. Some insights are taken from seemingly unrelated disciplines.

I should like to acknowledge the support given me by the Development and Project Planning Centre in the University of Bradford in writing this book. Through this Centre, over the years, I have been able to meet with investment planners from many countries, and have tried out my ideas on many patient guinea-pigs. The Centre also released me from teaching and other duties for a period in order to write this book. I should also like to acknowledge the sympathetic contributions of three congenial multi-national corporations in which I have in the past acted as controller or financial analyst and from which I have learned much that could and should be made available in the poorer countries: Air Products and Chemicals Inc., Hermann Miller Inc., and Comshare Inc.

Chapter 1

The science and the project

'Doing your own thing', said an elderly woman to me, 'thinking of something you want to do, planning it, then doing it, watching over it, and seeing it come out the way you wanted – that's what life's all about, isn't it?'

'Well, yes', I said. When I use my photographic darkroom I get a kick from designing an enlargement and seeing it come out in the developing solutions. I try to create an object of artistic value, but what she had in mind was a bigger project – a Welsh Nationalist, she wanted to create a nation state.

Somewhere between modest and great ambitions such as these is the class of designed activities called investment projects. The formulation of purpose, the planning, the implementation, watching, intervening again if something looks likely to go wrong, the personal satisfaction with the result: these are the elements of creativity. Without this, a project will not thrive. There is a psychological aspect to this, a parent-like motivation, which provides the stimulus to effort and wraps the project in an environment of vigilant loving care.

WHOSE PROJECT IS IT?

Without personal creativity as a driving force, projects may fail from lack of effort or, when a challenge arises, from lack of vigilance. Unfortunately in LDCs circumstances are often not conducive to personal involvement. A project may be suggested by a visiting machinery salesman, taken up by a sponsor, fleshed out by a consultant economist, modified by a banker and a computer specialist, redesigned in detail by a team of consultants (engineer, accountant and market research specialist), translated roughly into government standard forms by a desk-bound administrator, approved by a committee or two, carried out by a manager hired for the purpose, and supervised by another banker. In this case, while the functions of design, decision-making, implementation and monitoring are shared, only the sponsor has a continuing personal role; for the other participants the parenthood is psychologically defective. Underdevelopment often prevents the sponsor from taking a more leading role, owing to (a) lack of the full range of necessary skills on the part of the sponsor, (b) a need to involve others to complement the finance available in-house, (c) hierarchical relationships which inhibit the whole-hearted sharing of the entrepreneurial function with subordinate managers, and (d) the strong supervisory function exerted by the state even over private sector activities.

PROJECT ACCOUNTS

The set of written papers known as the project accounts with notes make possible some continuity of intention through all these changes of personnel, and therefore some degree of control over the project by its creators. The project accounts are key documents. This is not to claim that accountancy is superior to the other disciplines involved – engineering, economics, marketing, banking, administration, computing, sociology, etc. Rather, information about the project must be kept in an organised, structured, robust system in which each discipline has a strong input and from which each can take its data; and the discipline which is most suited to provide a well-structured information system of this kind is accountancy. However, the design of project accounts has to bear in mind the needs of the other disciplines.

In this respect the requirement differs from the design of an accounting system which is to report on a project after the event (historic accounting), in which the principles of management accounting are conceptually most important while those of financial accounting and of commercial law may not be transgressed. Ex-ante (before the event) accounting is much more flexible, and much more a vehicle for personal and inter-personal creativity, than ex-post accounting (reporting what has already happened). In accommodating the other disciplines it has to respect the wishes of the various parties professionally involved. Not only is it technically essential to establish the inter-disciplinary communication of data, but it is psychologically important not to kill the parental instincts, as it were, on the part of the project's many progenitors.

The ready acceptance of teamwork is important here. In an LDC particularly, where accountants frequently lack training, experience and status, it is all too tempting for them to insist on a rigid form of financial statement which is established and well known, when another layout of the document would meet the team's needs more adequately.

Also, in countries where the state plays a large rôle, the use of government-ordained proformas is liable to supplant statements which address specific project needs, but in principle this can be overcome by writing both. For manufacturing projects, the United Nations computer program COMFAR has provided standardised financial statements, the use of which has become mandatory in several LDC ministries of industry, whether suited to the project or not. Here again the problem can be overcome by producing COMFAR printouts as well as custom-designed statements. The latter reveal much more information about the inner workings and weaknesses of the project and are therefore superior as a decision-making support if the decision-makers are versatile enough to handle them with full competence. Standardised statements are much better than nothing, but do much to kill personal creativity in projects, and are generally disliked. They will eventually be supplanted by custom-designed statements, of the kinds described in this book, as decision-makers learn more.

THE PROJECT CYCLE

The sequence of events as one project follows another in the endless stream of incidents during which an institution or a business grows and develops is often perceived as a repeating series or cycle. The concept is that experience drawn from the operation of one project is utilised in the design of another. As a project goes through the phases of identification, preparation, implementation and operation, each of these phases benefits from the experience of earlier projects. Of course, this feedback is particularly rich in economically developed countries where institutions and businesses are well-established and mature, and thus have more experience to draw upon, and better functioning information systems to conduct the feedback to where it is required.

In a mature, feedback-rich system, there are more sources of guidance available for the design of each new project. Moreover, as a new project proceeds through its phases of design and preparation, there are more new sources of feedback coming in from other projects, which call for last-minute changes of plan. Often these are reports of items, not previously perceived, which require additional expenditure. These become known to the designers when other projects, more advanced in their cycles than the project currently in design and preparation, encounter challenges and vicissitudes which require to be met at some cost. Even when a project is in its full operating phase, it can still receive useful feedback of this kind from an older project. Thus, news of a successful court case for injury at work, or for product liability, or for patent infringement, or for pollution damage, can lead to additional expenditure in sister projects on industrial safety, quality control, patent fees, or pollution control measures. News of the development of a rival product can lead to additional expenditure on product promotion or dealer discounts. Only in the post-mortem stage, after the operating life has ceased, when the project has died and its head, arms and legs are being cut off, is it no longer vulnerable to change, challenge and redesign.

Ex-ante financial statements are not, therefore, expected to be an unalterable design for the lifetime of the project. A military analogy may be helpful here. In mediaeval times cannon were used to fire lead balls at castles. The cannon was carefully aimed, but once the ball was fired its trajectory could not be altered. This did not matter as the castles always remained stationary.

When battle-tanks and personnel-carriers took the field, targets which could move at up to thirty miles per hour, a weapon was invented which fired a missile attached to a pair of wires, by which the operator could electrically steer the missile to its target. The movement of the target was acceptable so long as the operator, standing at the point of fire, could see it and correct the missile's course. Today, many military targets move too fast for this; they can move out of the operator's field of view, or they can move too fast for the operator to react in time to correct the missile's course. For such targets the missiles have to be self-guided. Within each missile is a computer which can correct the missile's course, anticipatively and without reference back to the operator. If a project is likened to a missile, that on-board computer is the autonomous project management.

Of course, reference back to base is a matter of degree. Only in a private enterprise project, managed by its owner and financed without outside borrowing, is it permissible to change course without reference to anybody. Most business circumstances do permit time for consultations. The two-wire system, in which the operator back at the point of fire retains a degree of vision and a degree of control, may be satisfactory if the target is slow-moving and large, as it is in some cases. But many LDC projects are set up and spoken of as though they were cannon to be fired at a stationary target, following a predetermined trajectory. This is because a set of ex-ante project accounts does define a single trajectory; that forecast and no other is approved by the authorising committees. It may contain some flexibility in the sense that the possibility of worse than expected costs has been discussed and recognised; if that possibility materialises, it will be understood. If managers react by introducing appropriate adjustments, that too will be understood. But it does not envisage, and does not authorise, pro-active changes in course and purpose. The parents of the child allow it to be fostered, but not definitively adopted, by the management which takes over the rôle of tender loving care later in the project cycle.

It is therefore insufficient to pass down the line a set of project accounts and footnotes alone. There has to be accompanying text which sets out the ultimate mission, the strategy, the tests of success. These will be the inputs of specific disciplines: marketing, engineering, cost accounting, economics. The financial statements with footnotes can provide only the framework which, with patient logic, links these together. The full document then represents the strategy for dealing with a specific investment opportunity, the *intention* of the project. As time passes, of course, the on-board management will feel itself less and less bound by this parental document. If it is perceived as poorly designed, or based on a very inaccurate forecast of the movement of the target (unexpected changes in the rates of exchange for foreign currency are notorious for invalidating planned trajectories) it will very soon be abandoned.

MAINTAINING THE STOCK OF CAPITAL

An investment project requires a capital investment. That is to say, it requires the amassing of sufficient money to pay for those resources – fixed assets, working capital, and early-year losses – which are needed to produce the desired results. This money is drawn from sources which are not limitless. At the micro level, a family business has access to funds consisting of its own money plus that which it can borrow. At the macro level, a country's investible funds consist of money which has been saved out of income or can be borrowed (or donated) from the savings of other countries. The project draws from this pool. If it is inherently profitable it will generate new resources – an excess of outputs over inputs, leading to a profit in the form of money – which will repay the investment. The repayment of the money to the pool permits other investments to go ahead in turn. Repayment with increase permits *more* investments and is a necessary though not sufficient condition for economic growth and development.

Consider a family business in which several children set up subsidiary businesses. One of those by mistake makes a loss: this is tolerable, if the others can subsidise it, though the loss of capital will slow down their growth and reduce the income of the grandchildren. It is not serious, perhaps not even embarrassing, since most business ventures involve risk, and so will occasionally fail. But it is a different matter if one of the businesses *deliberately* makes a loss. This can happen in either the public or the private sector. There are enterprises set up in unrewarding markets in order to deny market share to rivals. There are tax-loss companies whose main function is to operate executive yachts in the Mediterranean and the Adriatic. There are wild boutiques which are given to youngsters to manage as a learning experience. There are railways which serve the 'essential' transport needs of important regions but cannot cover their costs either from their own revenues or from regional taxes. There are public corporations which perform well in giving income to their chief executives but are grossly mismanaged in all other respects by deliberate policy.

Setting up a project which will diminish the pool of capital available to other projects must be a careful decision in which the specific reasons for wanting the unprofitable project are balanced against the damage thus done. A series of such decisions will ultimately reduce the pool of capital to zero and so bring to an end all new projects, profitable or unprofitable. This is the justification for the emphasis laid on profits and losses by the financial analyst. The intention of a project must therefore include the earning of a profit except in a limited number of special cases. The poorer the country, the more important this is.

In an LDC this emphasis may seem alien and so may encounter resistance or apathy. In the culture of a subsistence economy there is no conscious tradition of capital conservation, just as there is little or no tradition of maintenance of equipment. Nor is the pool of capital necessarily perceived as a common pool. Even after one or two generations after the swing out of the subsistence economy, these cultural values may still be lacking, needful though they are for national development. There is also the problem that the profits accrue to Government, or to private owners, and do not all go into fresh investments because some part, perhaps a large part, goes into consumption or into administrative overhead cost. It is therefore left to the specialist, such as a financial analyst, to preach that despite these problems the growth of the pool of capital and of the number and scale of investment projects is a pathway out of poverty. In LDCs this usually takes place in the context of the nation state: conservation and growth of the national capital provides a national pathway out of poverty.

Of course, there will certainly be project aims other than profit. Ultimately the application of profit to the financing of more investments to produce yet more profit must be pointless unless it produces some end result, such as additional   consumption.

Even in the poorest countries, it is unusual to find a project document where the intention is entirely expressed as one of profit. Thus, the intention of an investment in an arable farm will often be perceived as producing cereals for consumption, rather than as producing farm outputs in excess of farm inputs with the stress on the difference between the two, which is the surplus or profit. A school may be perceived as desirable for the purpose of raising the level of literacy and general education rather than to produce benefits in excess of its costs. The financial analyst may have to point out that in the long run the dietary benefits of farms, and the educational benefits of schools, will not be achieved unless inputs as well as outputs are taken into consideration: a development programme which requires inputs exceeding the outputs and thus reduces the pool of capital is not viable, and no such proposals should be entertained except in limited numbers and for special reasons, which rules out ordinary farms and schools. A development programme, to be sustainable, must comprise a series of mostly profitable investments. The information system provided by a set of project accounts with notes will disclose whether the project is profitable or not.

In this sense the financial analyst must claim the right to over-rule the other disciplines, those of the dietitian, educationalist or whatever. Of course the rule that outputs must equal or exceed inputs is not the sole property of the accounting profession. Many would call it an economic law, or a biological law, or sheer common sense, but in the multi-disciplinary field of project work, all sorts of mistake can be made by narrow thinking or by blind obedience to ideological paradigms, leaving the country worse off than before. Susan George actually goes so far as to say

It doesn't matter how many mistakes they make. Because mainstream development theorists are protected and nurtured by those whose political objectives they support, package and condone, they have a licence to go on making them, whatever the consequences.

(George 1988: 261)

If the consequence of a project will be to leave the country less able than before to support other development projects, owing to a reduction in the stock of capital which the financial analyst can objectively measure using project accounts as an acid test, then financial analysis can blow a whistle for foul play, even though the mistake may lie in a discipline far removed from finance.

THE INFORMATION SYSTEM

The accounting framework accepts numerical and other data about the project, organises them, performs calculations on them, and produces reports including an assessment of profitability. The framework consists of a number of tables of figures together with notes (text) with perhaps some graphs or charts to communicate the results pictorially.

If computing is available, this framework can be developed on a computer. Various computer programs may be used, typically a spreadsheet program for the figures, graphs and charts, and a word-processor program for the text. Many word-processor programs can extract numbers from a spreadsheet and incorporate them in text. There are also integrated programs which will do all these things. At the time of writing, the programs most generally used on small computers are the following:

Spreadsheets
    Lotus 1–2–3 (claims 70 per cent of the market)
    Excel (very powerful but has stringent system requirements)
    Quattro Professional (good for very large sets of numbers)
    COMFAR (specialised for industrial projects, not versatile)

Word-processors
    Wordperfect (claims biggest market share in USA)
    WordStar (claims biggest market share in Europe)
    Word (or Word for Windows, which fits with Excel)

Integrated programs, such as Framework, Paradox, Lotus Symphony and Integrated Seven, because they undertake so many tasks in the one program, tend not to be so powerful in each area, and in particular may not accommodate such large sets of numbers in their spreadsheets as do the specialist programs. For this reason, they are not favoured in project work. Project accounts for medium and large projects do tend to need big spreadsheets, although the examples used in textbooks are misleadingly small and simplified.

Project accounts produced on spreadsheets take their data from various sources. In complex projects, these sources frequently include special studies which require their own, separate computing programs. For instance, a project for a new highway will require traffic forecasts; spreadsheet programs are not suitable for the computation of these. A chemical process plant will require process calculations to establish its design; spreadsheets cannot produce these. Many projects have to calculate where best to locate their facilities; linear programming may be needed for this, and spreadsheets are not good at linear programming. In such cases, the specialised computing is treated as a *front-end* calculation which produces data as input to the project accounts in the main spreadsheets. On the other hand a project such as a farm or a sugar estate, where the location and process are known, will have a relatively simple front-end dealing with land usage, crop rotation, sugar-ratooning and so forth, which can be accommodated within the suite of spreadsheets leading directly to the project accounts.

The project accounts consist of a number of financial statements and economic statements – tables of figures. Although both financial and economic statements share the same sources of data and ideally should be parts of a unified spreadsheet, we are concerned here primarily with the financial statements, or *financials* as they are often called.

The front-end computation, financials, and economic analysis add up to a *model* of the project. It is a model in the sense that it is a simulation, on paper or computer memory, of something which may later exist in the real world. It is an imperfect model in the sense that it does not simulate every last detail of the real phenomenon but only those characteristics which are regarded as important for decision-taking. Computer programs which aid modelling are called decision-support software.

The modelling process deploys those sciences and disciplines which are perceived as relevant, to obtain data on cause-and-effect relationships. It quantifies those data which will have a major impact. It simulates causal relationships by expressing algebraic relationships between numbers in a set; that is the essence of a spreadsheet. It explores the possible effects of deviations from its own predictions. Finally it provides text and if necessary graphics which make it self-explanatory to the critical reader.

From a computing point of view the spreadsheet is the nub of the decision-support software. A spreadsheet program is one which makes the computer function in such a way as to mimic the operation of a large sheet of paper on which words and numbers can be calculated and written, i.e. multi-column analysis paper. The reason the paper is large is that one column is used for every year of the project's life. Several sheets of paper in A3 or double-foolscap size would be required for a project of moderate complexity and duration. Several thousand numbers have to be calculated.

Multi-column analysis without a computer is slow. Any delay in the decision-support calculations necessarily delays the decision itself and generally reduces the benefits which might be derived from the project by missing the 'window of opportunity' at which date the benefits will be greatest or by simply deferring the benefits. In cases of serious delay, the data themselves become out of date, unreliable and invalid, and the whole sequence has to be done again. For these reasons, non-computerised spreadsheets have to omit some of the most onerous calculations and the decision-making has to proceed in ignorance of certain facts. This is a bad deal, since the cost of computing is small in relation to the cost of medium- or large-scale projects, and indeed in relation to the cost of small projects where the latter occur in programmes consisting of many almost identical projects so that computing cost can be shared. However, some rough and ready simplified methods of analysis are available for use in the non-computerised environment.

FINANCIAL STATEMENTS

In ex-post accounting, the main financial statements are well-established by three hundred years of theory and convention and in many countries by mercantile law such as Companies Acts. Such statements report on the transactions, not of a project as such, but of a legal entity which is carrying out one or more projects. There are three main statements as illustrated in Figure 1.1. These are referred to as the principal financial statements because, in ex-post accounting, it is these which are required by law to be produced, for purposes of taxation or for publication. The order shown is the order in which they are most often produced by the line accountants. In the history of mercantile law, the requirement for the first two was introduced first, and that of the cash flow statement added most recently (for large businesses only). In the publication of annual accounts, it is often the balance sheet which is printed first, followed by the income statement, followed by the cash (or funds) flow statement if required.

In ex-ante forecasting, it is the balance sheet which is the hardest to get right. Some LDC project analysts omit the balance sheet completely. This is especially the case with small and very small projects (micro-projects) using simplified spreadsheet techniques; it is also the case with large projects carried out by government departments; governments (with one honourable exception) never publish their own balance sheets.

Whether the income statement or the cash (or funds) flow statement is drawn up first by most financial analysts working on LDC projects ex-ante is difficult to say. I have the impression that in agricultural projects a cash flow statement is usually produced first but in manufacturing and infrastructure projects we tend to begin with the income statement. It is arguable that the commercial shaping and designing of the project, in terms of the profitabilities of the various joint products, optimum locations, alternative pricing policies and similar tactical decisions may be best supported by looking at the Income Statements. More complex strategic decision-making such as the

Contents	Name	Notes
1 Report on the profit or loss made in the preceding year, with components contributing to it.	Profit and loss account, which may be preceded by a trading account in the case of a business which buys and sells.	Known in the USA as the income statement. May have to be produced quarterly as well as annually for critical early years.
2 Report of the assets (property) of the firm or other entity carrying out the project, and on the sources of finance which paid for them.	Balance sheet, or statement of condition.	The sources of finance consist of capital belonging to the owners, and sums borrowed from others.
3 Report on the money which came in and the money which was spent, leading to the amount of money in hand at the end of the year (or shorter period).	Cash flow statement or statement of sources and uses of funds. There is a slight difference between these two.	In ex-ante work there is a useful variant of these called an Analytical cash flow statement.

Figure 1.1 The main financial statements

timing of major investments may be better supported by cash or funds flow statements.

In practice there is no need to choose which to write first, since both documents remain under continuous revision and development as the data gradually flows in. It should be borne in mind that, as a project moves through its life cycle, from project identification through the stages of preparation for appraisal, preliminary data are replaced by more precise data, broad categories of expenditure or revenue are broken down into finer detail, assumptions replaced by knowledge. With every update, the full set of financials can and should be updated. Thus there will always be an income statement of some sort, a cash flow statement of some sort, and maybe some rudimentary forecasts of balance sheets, to consult for ongoing decision support. We do not strive to follow a linear sequence of (a) collect data, (b) make one key financial statement, (c) make improvements and adjustment decisions, (d) fill in the rest of the financials. *All* the financials are potentially available for decision support.

This is, of course, assuming a well-organised computer system. With a manual system, because it cannot react quickly to updates, a linear sequence may be insisted upon, with updates held pending if they arrive before the data are required, and ignored if arriving too late.

The laws which prescribe the three principal financial statements for ex-post accounting do not directly govern ex-ante financials. There is, however, good reason to produce ex-ante financials in a format which is directly comparable to that in which they will eventually appear ex-post. That preparation facilitates comparison between the two. It allows operating management to see how closely they are adhering to the intentions of the project's original designer-parents, and makes possible a *continuity of intention* without which the project may be regarded as having passed out of control.

In essence the three main financial statements all stem from the fundamental arithmetic of accountancy, the *double-entry system*, and are theoretically inseparable from it; this is a second reason why they ought to be incorporated in ex-ante work. However, it is in the details that the law imposes its requirements, and here we may depart from the ex-post procedures. For example, in an ex-post income statement, company law may require disclosure *only* of revenue, depreciation, directors' fees and net profit; an ex-ante income statement would include these within a comprehensive listing of all revenues and costs. An ex-post cash flow might or might not be legally required for a certain business, but ex-ante we might choose between a cash flow, a funds flow, or an analytical cash flow, as best suits the circumstances.

Most financial analysts consider cash flow planning, with its extension *discounted cash flow*, to be the basic tool of financial analysis. Indeed, some leading US authors put cash flow into such a pre-eminent position that income statements and balance sheets play no perceptible rôle in their calculations at all: see for instance Brealey and Myers (1984) or Franks, Broyles and Carleton (1985). That may be going too far, but certainly if ex-ante work is to be reduced to its simplest, minimalist form as is often necessary with micro-projects, that should comprise one single financial statement showing the flow of cash or funds. Indeed, very small loan applications are commonly handled by bankers using only the one document, which is a cash flow forecast showing payments into and out of the bank. That lends itself to easy monitoring by the bank. When the time comes for the client to declare business income for the purpose of annual taxation, the tax authorities may well accept a cash flow statement in lieu of an income state-ment, and waive the requirement for a balance sheet.

In ex-post accounting there is (if the double-entry system is used) a built-in device to detect and avoid arithmetical errors, the *Trial Balance*, which is a list of the balances on all the various accounts, added up together. It is from the Trial Balance that the three ex-post financial statements are prepared. In ex-ante work, there is no Trial Balance. Instead, to avoid errors, we have to depend on certain relationships between the three financial statements which allow us to perform certain other validation checks. This means that ideally all three financials should be produced, even for projects or entities which in their ex-post accounting would not legally require all three.

Given the arithmetical interrelationship between the three, and given a computerised environment in which updates are fed into all three at once, it is an over-simplification to regard the cash flow statement as primary. Rather, we should perceive the model as an integrated system.

Which is the most important financial statement for the purpose of *data input*? Project data are to be inserted, according to the nature of the data, into whichever statement is appropriate; this will depend partly on the way the questions are framed in eliciting the data, partly on the type of project, and partly on what kind of accounting arrangements are already in existence (if any) in the entity which will operate the project. In general, project data is fragmentary and will fall into all three financials. The available data are then used to calculate the missing numbers. This may mean that on the whole the cash flow is derived from the other two, or the reverse.

Which is the most important financial statement in the sense that it contains the *output of results* to support the decision-making? That depends on the nature of the decision to be taken. If it is desired to check whether the project is sound in all its aspects and will indeed produce the returns claimed for it, all three statements are useful but the income statement will be found most fruitful to elicit the commercial, marketing and technical aspects, and in fact all those aspects which bear on competitive success. If the decision-makers are generalists who disclaim any specialised knowledge of these aspects in this kind of project, and are willing to take these for granted, they are then reduced to financial analysis in its narrower sense of dealing only with cash flows and the management of funds. In that case, the interest lies in the statement of cash flow (or its near equivalent, funds flow) and its extension, the analytical cash flow statement. The balance sheet will be of limited interest and the income statement of little or no interest. Frequently, of course, the decisions are taken by committees including both specialists and generalists.

It is therefore impossible to generalise, and every project has its unique features. For the purpose of exposition it will be assumed that generally data input is to the income statements and balance sheets, that cash and fund flow statements are calculated from the others, but that for simplified models the cash flow statements can stand alone.

Of course, ex-post accounting is not confined to producing the annual financials which the law requires. It also produces additional reports, more frequently, as requested by management. This is called *management accounting* as distinct from *financial accounting*. Such reports might include a purchasing report, various reports on fixed assets and depreciation, labour cost reports, and unitary studies which deal with the cost and profit margin of a unit of output. In ex-ante work this information cannot be taken from a Trial Balance but must be calculated like any other spreadsheet numbers from data, from front-end calculations, and from algebraic formulae expressing causal relationships so that some numbers can be calculated from other numbers in a model.

THE COMPUTER SPREADSHEETS

The spreadsheets therefore form a sequence comprising perhaps a front-end dealing with physical aspects (which must be the basis of all calculations of value), several subsidiary calculations, the three main financial statements, perhaps an analytical cash flow which provides a link to economic statements in the context of national development, and then the economic statements themselves which, however, lie outside our present topic. In addition, a further front-end which is often required is one which sets out the price indexes to reflect the inflation, and probably also the foreign exchange rates to reflect the devaluations, which are expected to occur during the life of the project and will affect the values in the financial statements unless the study is required to be conducted entirely in fixed prices.

A back-end which is also often required is one which prints out the results in the format required by a government department. Such formats tend to be standardised in a way which prevents their use for sensible commercial decision-making; they therefore must be produced as well as, not instead of, the main statements. That is why they are produced at the end.

On paper, such a series of calculations cannot fit on a single sheet of paper. Likewise using a computer spreadsheet, they should be placed on separate imaginary sheets. Unlike paper, a computer spreadsheet *could* be large enough to hold all these numbers on one imaginary page (though most programs have severe limitations in this respect) but it is not wise to attempt to do that. A computer screen is limited in size and does not permit the whole spreadsheet to be viewed at once; if the sheet is very large, you can have trouble finding your way around it to the numbers you need. Instead, several spreadsheets linked together, in the sense that one sheet draws data from another as required, provide a better solution. Rosenkranz, on corporate modelling, says

> A corporate model is often likely to be a large model. In order to facilitate the control of such a model in general ... a structural and modular program is chosen ... Second, it is very likely that a larger industrial firm in a period of about five years undergoes changes of its internal structure ... A corporate model has to ... track and represent such changes. This together with the observation that a decentralised firm may want to build corporate models for different organisational subunits ... also calls for an extremely modular systems design.
>
> (Rosenkranz 1979)

LDC models do not normally cover such large and complex projects that require subunit models. It is as well to remember, however, that there are bigger brothers in the family. In particular, no rules should be issued governing the writing of spreadsheet models which would inhibit the addition of such further subsidiary statements as might be appropriate.

The main benefits of the systematic modular structure are as follows:

- You can find the part you want more easily.
- You can understand an absent colleague's work more easily.
- You can supervise and audit spreadsheets more easily.
- You can update the data more easily.
- You can change the project structure much more easily.
- You can use the same suite of spreadsheets for more than one project. The more general the framework, the larger the family of projects it will serve, changing the data while preserving the formulae. This is a major time-saver.

The planning of a spreadsheet therefore must begin with a plan of the modular structure. In a professional planning office certain norms or rules may be established in this regard to which all colleagues conform. These are, however, frameworks into which each project, with its own special features, must be intelligently placed – unless a specialised, rigid planning program has to be used, in which case the software has its own modules and there is no choice in the structure. Assuming that there is no such restriction, the following chapters offer some ideas of what can be put into modules.

Modular or not, spreadsheets are large pieces of paper, or their computing equivalent, and each sheet of paper has two dimensions. Putting together a pad of several sheets may give a third dimension in advanced modelling, but each sheet has two dimensions, horizontal and vertical. On this sheet we write words and numbers. The words and phrases needed for financial statements vary in length, so it makes sense to write them one on each line rather than as column headings. Numbers vary in width too, but not so much; in historic accounting you may need to record a figure with accuracy of twelve significant figures, but for looking into the future, we can happily work in thousands, lakhs, millions, crores, or billions, which allows us to use narrower columns than otherwise would be needed. What this leads to is that the successive years of a project life are forecasted across rather than down the page. This is generally the convention in both manual and computerised systems.

Spatially, therefore, a spreadsheet is organised (a) in columns, wide for words, narrower for figures, and (b) horizontally in chunks or blocks which represent the different financial statements and subsidiary workings. When there is so much organisation in a spreadsheet that it becomes troublesome to find what you want in it, we start another sheet, and that gives us our modular structure, but it is better to plan the structure from the outset than to slide into it unthinkingly by experiencing troublesome space problems.

THE BEGINNING OF THE PROJECT

The first columns of figures therefore represent, in each financial statement, the start of the project. In accordance with the project cycle, a project starts after the decision to start it has been taken, and it goes through a phase, known as the *implementation* or *construction* phase, when the physical and financial resources needed for its operation are being obtained and put together. The second phase is the *operation* phase; during this period the benefits will be obtained. The column headings represent years (more rarely quarters or months) running through both phases.

If the specific dates are known, or proposed, then each column header is a financial year, for example,

Years ending 30 June
1993/94   1994/95   1995/96   1996/97   . . .

for an enterprise which has its financial year from July to June. In general, as a proposal proceeds through its stages of preparation, its start date is initially unknown, approximately known, and eventually it is properly scheduled. Proposals submitted for Government approval in LDCs are often held up for years in a queue, awaiting funding; in such cases the start date clearly cannot be known, though it can be proposed, at the time of submission.

The convention most commonly observed when exact dates are not identifiable is this:

• Assume the operating phase starts on the first day of a financial year. The construction phase therefore ends on the last day of a financial year, but may start at any time.
• Call the first year of operation Year 1 and number the subsequent years Year 2 and so on.
• Call the last year of construction Year 0. If the construction phase requires more than one year, work backwards calling them Year 0, Year −1, Year −2 and so on.

An alternative convention is to call the first year of implementation (construction) Year 0 and proceed from there. This system is quite commonly found in agricultural projects, especially large plantations. In such projects, the clearing of forest or bush and the planting of pioneer crops may go on for many years before all the allotted land is used up; some of the area comes into commercial production while other parts are still in implementation. In any project where implementation and operation overlap like this, or are not clearly distinguishable for whatever reason, this alternative convention is recommended.

When the spreadsheets are computerised, it is an easy matter to substitute precise dates, as soon as these are known, or whenever they are revised, in place of notional years. However, when an investment is to be undertaken by an existing enterprise, its financial year will already have been determined, and cannot conveniently be made to coincide with the start of project operations. Thus, both the construction phase and the operating phase may commence mid-year. This calls for quite detailed recalculations, especially in balance sheets; it will have to be undertaken meticulously in organisations which impose high standards of controllership, but perhaps is left undone elsewhere.

THE END OF THE PROJECT

Is it true that every investment proposal must have a finite duration, a distinct end? Not always so, though you might get that impression from reading the literature on project economics. The planting of a permanent forest, as an amenity or as a wind-break, or to increase the oxygen in the earth's atmosphere, can be expected to bring benefits of infinite duration. Ex-post, we also find that dis-benefits, like the extinction of the edible dodo, can also be of infinite duration. Infinite duration causes problems for the analyst, but these are not insuperable. Obviously you cannot have an infinite number of columns on your spreadsheet. Fortunately, or unfortunately, when we come to look at the results, we tend to ignore the very distant future. This allows us to leave out years beyond a certain point, or to scale down their figures in such a way that we can apply algebra to arrive at a total. If we did not scale down the figures of later years, the net benefits of many agricultural projects (positive or negative) would be infinitely large, and there too we should be unable to reach a yes/no decision on the advisability of the project. In commercial projects, infinite duration is rare, since the commercial conditions for translating benefits into revenue may not last very long, and we have to apply the accounting principle of prudence, not to expect too much.

It is advisable for the analyst to consider specifically what event if any will bring the operating phase to an end. In an industrial project, it ends when the main fixed asset (machinery) comes to the end of its useful life (say, twelve years). There is no reason to suppose that it will be replaced with another, similar machine. Essentially we are judging the costs and benefits of that machine and its appurtenances. The same is true of a water project, where we may assign a life (say, forty years) to a reservoir or to piping. By contrast, an investment project which will set up an agricultural estate will have no particular dominant fixed asset other than land. The fertility of the land will be expected to rise rather than fall, and no clear termination date is obvious. In such a case, the project end is arbitrary, and may be put at a convenient time in the crop rotation pattern, typically after twenty years for arable farming or forty years for slow-growing nut and fruit tree crops.

Having selected the end-date, the analyst should consider whether the enterprise comes to an end at that date facing the fate of liquidation or as a going concern with a future.

A farm project would typically end as a going concern, since its termination is an arbitrary truncation of the arithmetical representation of activity which actually is likely to continue without the need to take another major investment decision. The value of any assets (and liabilities) which are present at the end of the final year can be deemed to be realised, i.e. assumed to be sold (and paid off) at that moment, in full. At the last moment of the last year of the operating period, assets and liabilities are deemed to be transmuted into cash values, and their physical forms vanish.

By contrast, an industrial project cannot be expected to go on beyond the life of its principal equipment; even if it is succeeded by more equipment, that will have to be decided on separately in due course and is therefore a separate project. The worst case, and therefore the most prudent scenario to assume, is complete liquidation. That means that whatever assets are left at the end of the last operating year should be assumed to be sold off, realising somewhat less than their previous book values because of the expenses of disposal, and this liquidation must take place in a phase following the operating phase, adding a year or two to the spreadsheet with additional columns.

To sum up, an investment proposal which creates a quasi-permanent enterprise has an arbitrary end-date and its assets and liabilities are deemed to be realised as cash on that date. A proposal which commits a very specific set of assets to a specific marketing scenario has an end-date associated with the useful life of the main assets (which may be that of the scenario, if that ends first) and liquidation is to be envisaged after the operating period has ended.

We have been considering the end-date of the operating phase in the context of a period of time when the assets, installed during the imple-mentation phase, produce their intended results. There are, however, some so-called projects which seem to live forever in the implementation phase. Examples are projects which aim to build institutions. Thus, a series of road-building projects may be accompanied by a separate project to create an effective road-maintenance organisation. Basil Cracknell (1991) has drawn attention to the importance of allowing a sufficiently long time-horizon in such cases, providing funding and technical assistance for up to fifteen years if necessary. In principle the output of such a project is an input to the road projects and this means that there is an operating phase simultaneous with the implementation phase, but in practice such a highly dependent institution would inevitably be providing its services within a Government accountancy system in which no revenues are recognised.

Chapter 2

The income statement

The spivs in London after World War II used to say 'When you're starting a business you've got to have an *angle*.' This is because, in a perfect market, competition between similar businesses will drive down net profits to unacceptable levels. So it will not do to run an innocent taxi-cab enterprise or an artless fruit stall in a market. There has to be some *angle* which will protect the business from competitive pressures, but since this will be unpopular with customers and possibly illegal, it has to be a *hidden* angle. Thus the taxi business may enter into arrangements on the side to obtain cabs for owner-drivers who privately would not be creditworthy. The fruiterer may have to find some special, privileged way of disposing of damaged and over-ripe fruit, perhaps by keeping pigs or by making 'mixed fruit' jam. The core business remains what is overt, but it is approached in a special way, from a special angle.

Medium-sized and large businesses are no different; even when an enterprise is mature and well-capitalised, its expansions and its quests for additional market share have to have an *angle* or they will not show attractive returns. Some few enterprises dominate the market in their core business area, but still seek some special protection for themselves, denying entry to others, or building quasi-permanent government contracts by subtle and possibly corrupt means. At this higher level, this is not called an angle; it is called marketing strategy. You can see how it works if you see their income statement (a detailed one, with notes, not the brief document which they file with the Registrar of Companies). 'Pile them high and sell them cheap' is another marketing strategy which is more subtle than it seems on the surface.

VOLUMES

The output of a project must have some upper limit. If this were not so, projects would be enormous, and economic development explosive (and catastrophic). The scale of the output clearly determines the scale of the inputs, including capital costs, and including the size of the labour force and managerial force. Everything is related to volume, so it is not surprising that volumes play a key rôle in the front-end of spreadsheets.

Volume, however, is not a single figure. In a project with a fifteen-year operating life, volume may differ from year to year, and typically starts at a lower level before building up to a maximum. Within a year, it may fluctuate seasonally, especially in agro-industrial projects such as sugar factories. We must also consider fluctuations within the 24-hour day, that is, the likely pattern of shift-working if any, the preparation time, the maintenance and cleaning time; what a machine can do in a day is not what it can do in an hour multiplied by twenty-four, and what it can do in a year is not 365 days' production. We must bear in mind too that the maximum achievable output, given steady working, might be briefly exceeded in short bursts for emergencies, but will not normally be attained in full for long periods, because of breakdowns and other unscheduled stoppages. We must also remember that if a stock of finished goods can be built up during one period while production exceeds output, it is possible in the next period for output to exceed production by consuming goods from stock. Finally, we must remember that most projects produce more than one product; indeed the single-product project is very rare. Each product will have its own volume figures; and an upward adjustment in the volume of one product may entail an increase in another, where they are joint products, or a decrease, where they compete for limited production capacity.

In short, the concept of volume can sometimes be quite complex, and probably is always significantly more complex than is apparent in ex-ante project appraisals, where inevitably some simplification is required owing to incomplete knowledge.

MULTI-PRODUCT VOLUMES

In designing the front-end spreadsheets the first step is to deal with the multi-product situation, if there is one. The products must be related together in some way, otherwise it is not one project but several which can be appraised separately. Some concept must be arrived at which relates the products to each other.

It may be that one product presents the main opportunity for profit and the others are by-products; in that case, the volume of the main product will determine the volume of the others. That happens when air is separated into its constituent gases to meet a demand for oxygen, but nitrogen is a by-product. On the other hand, it may be that customer requirements dictate a wide range of products. This happens in a furniture factory, which may offer just half-a-dozen ranges of furniture but which has a sales catalogue listing over a hundred separate items including replacement sub-assemblies and upholstery fabrics of different qualities. In such a case, the concept of volume cannot be based on one main product, nor on physical measures such as van-loads or tons, but rather on sales value. The amount of output is expressed in terms of its selling value, and since different customers pay different prices according to the discount structure, 'list prices' (full catalogue prices) are used for this measurement.

A third possibility is that the products are alternative forms of essentially the same thing, and the mix will be determined by commercial (market) considerations. For instance, a dairy can produce fresh milk, evaporated milk, condensed milk, long-life (UHT) milk, cream, soured cream, or butter, all using basically the same chief ingredient. If it is decided to sell two or three of these, the volumes can be shown separately, and there is no need to aggregate them except that the volume of input (litres of milk ex-farm) must be calculated. However, if it is decided to sell all seven of them, it might be a good idea to add them up in terms of fresh milk equivalent, or in terms of total solids content. Otherwise it will be difficult to work out the costs of processes which are common to more than one of the products, such as initial filtration of the milk.

THE MAXIMUM VOLUME

There are four main methods of putting a constraint upon the volume, in the spreadsheets:

1 Select a set of capital goods which has a limited capacity. Often in LDC projects the capital investment is limited by the sponsor's own limited wealth, or by the small market, and an attempt is made to identify the smallest sensible outfit. This is sometimes the smallest model selected from a catalogue by a machinery salesman. Alternatively, where some scarce factor such as raw material, electricity, or water will set a limit to the volume of production, the capital goods may be sized accordingly. A more sophisticated approach perceives the market as growing steadily and as requiring regular capital investments of a certain size, which can be estimated. In any case, the project will be capable of a certain volume of output and no more. Thus the volume of output depends entirely on capacity to supply.

2 A variant of this is one which changes from single-shift working to two-shift and even three-shift working as demand rises; this gives a step-wise increase in capacity. However, it is not easy to impose the most profitable shift pattern; family cultural aspects, passenger transport requirements, as well as machine needs are involved.

3 In its early years of operation the project may sell less than its production maximum, while efforts are made to achieve customer acceptance and saturate the market, but later the production ceiling is reached and no further sales are possible. Thus the upper limit of volume is determined in the early years by demand but in the later years by supply.

4 Where demand is expected to grow steadily in the long term, and where there is no constraint on inputs during the operating phase, it may be

envisaged that the initial capital investment will be followed by further investments, at intervals of five years or other appropriate stages, which will progressively expand the capacity. In fact, consideration of the long-term demand and the appropriate staging strategy is very useful as a front-end computation to determine the optimum size of the initial capacity to be installed. However, the inclusion of later expansion stages in the financial spreadsheets, showing staged increases in capacity, is rare. This is because later investments are separate projects. They are separate investment decisions which can be taken in due course, or refused. The initial decision should be justified in its own right and stand on its own. Only in rare cases do the series of stages form a single project; that would happen if the first stage alone was unprofitable but a necessary preliminary to an attractive long-term scenario. That would be a high-risk strategy. An independent first phase, if realistic, is preferable.

Thus the volume of any product is limited either by supply, which is fixed or possibly increasing by steps, or by demand, which usually is expected to grow steadily. Volume in any given period will be the lesser of these two. Many projects begin demand-limited and switch to supply-limited volumes in later years. A switch-over which is very late (say, half-way through the operating phase) implies significant unused capacity during the early years and is damaging to profitability. This does not mean, however, that it will be best if a project becomes supply-limited straight away; it may be more profitable to install a larger capacity, which is not immediately fully used, but when it is fully used becomes much more efficient, since a larger plant often has lower costs per unit of output. This is a trade-off which is a subject in its own right.

VOLUMES, YIELDS AND COST SAVINGS

An interesting argument arose when some Nigerian planning officers were examining the effects of a *reduction* in output, as part of a sensitivity study using a computer spreadsheet.

Some claimed that a 10 per cent fall in the volume of output should have exactly the same impact on the financial results as a fall in the price at which each unit of product was sold. They had in mind something like a farm, growing and selling cereals. If the yield per hectare is poor and output turns out to be 10 per cent below plan, that is just as bad as if the full output were sold at a 10 per cent discount.

Others had in mind something like a factory, manufacturing from various materials and selling into a market governed by supply and demand. If demand is weaker than forecasted, sales will be down, and the factory will react by making less volume. However, it will also buy less materials, and in general its *variable costs* will be less, which mitigates the damage to some extent. There is no such mitigation if the factory accepts a price reduction in order to maintain planned output.

The 'farm' scenario is one where yield is always uncertain, much more so than demand. The thinking is that you buy your inputs such as seeds and fertilisers and you are committed to them before you find out what your yield is, because yield depends very much on the weather from season to season, and only after the harvest do you really know your volume. And if there is a *long-term* reduction in volume below plan levels, that means that the land is not so fertile as had been expected, and you cannot remedy that by cutting down on variable costs.

The 'factory' scenario is one where yield is fairly certain (the outcome of a known technology) while demand is relatively uncertain. Output is essentially under management control and there are always some materials or other costs which can be reduced if output is depressed.

How can both of these views be correct? It emerges that volume is not an independent variable but depends on two or three other things. It may be wise to calculate it in different ways with the lowest figure prevailing. Then the sensitivity study can adjust, not volume directly, but the items it depends upon, by 10 per cent to see what will be the impact.

VOLUMES: FLOWS AND STOCKS

The relationship between output volumes and input volumes – the latter needed to calculate costs – is complicated by the fact that some volumes are put into storage, known as stockbuild. What is put into storage is not output, though it originated as an input. Consider the sequence of calculations shown in Table 2.1. None of these adjustments would be necessary if there were no stocks. There are no stocks, of course, in projects which produce services rather than goods; services cannot be stored.

These figures illustrate the evil rôle of the three main categories of stock in disrupting an otherwise beautiful relationship between inputs and outputs. The three categories are described in Figure 2.1.

Remembering that stockbuild means an increase in the holding of stock, as a global generalisation we can say that *input – stockbuild = output*. In spreadsheet terms, this means we have a choice of procedure, and the next step is to make this choice between the following options:

1 Decide on inputs and stockbuild, calculate outputs.
2 Decide on outputs and stockbuild, calculate inputs.
3 Ignore stockbuild and treat inputs and outputs as equal.

Where project output is determined by demand in the market, we proceed from the volumes specified in the market study, add stockbuild, and arrive at the inputs. Where output is determined by a scarce supply of inputs, we study the available input volumes, subtract stockbuild, and so calculate outputs.

Table 2.1 Stock adjustments

	Rupees
Raw materials purchased in 1999	1000
Raw materials left over from 1998 stock	200
Total raw materials available	1200
Raw materials left over for 2000	300
Raw materials consumed in 1999	900
Labour and other product costs, 1999	3200
Total production cost 1999	4100
Partly finished product at end of 1998	100
Partly finished product at end of 1999	200
Cost of finished product, 1999	4000
Finished goods left over from 1998	200
Total finished goods available	4200
Finished goods left over for 2000	800
Cost of sales in 1999	3400
Gross profit margin 20%	680
Sales (output) in 1999	4080

CATEGORY	ALSO KNOWN AS	AFFECTS
Raw materials stock	Materials inventory	Cost of raw materials consumed
Partly finished goods stock	Work in progress, work in process	Cost of finished goods made
Finished goods stock	Trade stock, finished inventory	Cost of sales

Figure 2.1 The main categories of stock

Where output is determined by the limited capacity of the capital goods, since this is *production* capacity, we work backwards adding stockbuild to arrive at inputs, and forwards subtracting finished goods stockbuild to arrive at outputs.

This is most readily calculated by setting up three different spreadsheets and using the one which is appropriate. Unfortunately, in a project where the early years are demand-limited and the later years are supply-limited, an all-singing and dancing model is required in a single spreadsheet which is fiendishly complicated to set up. Most people dodge the problem by either ignoring stockbuild or by setting up just one model and manually over-riding it in the year when supply-limited maximum volume is attained. After all, complicated models are error-prone and therefore to be avoided.

Nothing has been said yet about how to determine the stockbuild, other than mentioning the temptation not to do so. It will be more convenient to consider this under the heading of balance sheets (see p. 63).

CAPITAL COSTS AND DEPRECIATION

Buildings, equipment and other long-lasting assets will typically be bought during the construction phase of the project and used productively during the operating phase. The initial cost incurred at one moment in time thus produces benefits over several years. In order to follow the *matching principle*, which seeks to place the costs in the income statements of those years when the benefit arises, we spread the initial cost over the relevant years of the operating phase. This procedure is known as depreciation. In the great majority of cases the cost is deemed to be spread equally over the years when the assets are beneficially in use, and this is called straight-line depreciation.

THE BOTTOM LINE

The net profit, or as they say in the USA the *net income*, is the bottom line (literally) of the income statement: the outcome of the overt and covert processes of business, during the period reported upon. This figure, though it abstracts from the interesting details by netting them all out, is very important. As Mr Micawber pointed out to David Copperfield in Dickens's well-known novel, if it is more than enough, even by the slimmest margin, Result: Happiness. If not, Result: Misery, but we are confidently hoping for 'something to turn up'.

Since net income is the surplus of revenues over costs, the factors involved are the various sources of revenue and types of cost.

Net income may be positive (profit) or negative (loss). With an industrial project one would normally plan for a profit over most years of the project's operating life, though in the early years there is commonly a loss. Agricultural projects normally contain components which move into profit in the very first season, exceptions being sugar, bush crops such as tea, and tree crops such as cashew or rubber, which are relatively slow to reach commercial maturity. Virtually all projects make losses during their construction or implement-ation phase, when the fixed assets are being put together before they can begin to be profitably used. As stated above, this phase may be a matter of months for an agriculture project, such as a tube-well to irrigate an existing small farm, or indeed for a very small-scale industrial project such as a car repair garage, but it may take several years for an airport, railway or other infrastructural project. What matters is not the net income in any one year but the stream of net incomes over the life of the project including both construction and operating phases.

REVENUE: THE TOP LINE

Revenue means money-value earned by supplying goods or services in the ordinary course of business. It consists of such categories as sales, fees, fares, commission earnings, interest and rent receivable. Revenue excludes money obtained from events which are not in the ordinary course of business such as money borrowed, cash obtained by selling old fixed assets, investment grants received from Government schemes, and so on. Consequently it can be forecasted by referring to the volume of outputs which are to be delivered, and of course the prices at which outputs are to be sold. In general, where outputs are sold and can be measured, revenue equals output volume multiplied by price per unit. These figures are to be derived essentially from market studies, containing projections of physical volumes such as tons in which outputs are measured, and other front-end studies, which are calculated before the financial statements are attempted.

The selling price may be zero, as in the case of 'social overhead' projects such as free schools, free clinics, free roads, and so on. Strictly speaking these are not sold at all, and anthropologists will tell you there is a world of difference between a gift and a sale, but in spreadsheet arithmetic you get the same result by showing a sale with zero price; this is a handy device because the same spreadsheet can cope with both sales and gifts. In economic analysis, gifts have a value, anyway.

In an income statement, the various categories of revenues should be shown separately, e.g. values of goods sold ('sales revenue'), and services rendered ('fees and commissions'). Obviously with manufacturing projects the main source of revenue is sales (of industrial goods). In the income statement, sales revenue may be subdivided into sections, for example:

- Sales of different products (all of them itemised).
- Sales of different product lines (groups of products).
- Sales to different market segments.

Market segments may be differentiated according to geographical areas (including exports if any), or according to different types of customer. If the customers are themselves enterprises, as is the case when intermediate products or capital goods are to be sold, segments may be classified according to the economic sectors of the customers, or by sizes of customer enterprises, or according to end-use. Another common differentiation is according to channel of distribution, such as sales through dealers, sales direct, sales by mail-order. The differentiation chosen for the income statement should be that which is the focus of the main marketing strategy. Obviously, this presumes that data are available to support projections of sales volumes and prices for the various categories; if not, the marketing strategy is unsound.

A complex industrial project might well need to present its sales figures in two or three of these ways (in separate documents agreeing in their totals), and in combinations of ways, and will have a combination of dimensions to its marketing strategy. However, for financial rather than commercial decision-taking, the complexity of a multi-faceted presentation in which the total level of sales is forecasted might well be condensed into a summary financial statement, in which sales might appear as a single figure, or just a few figures.

For decision-making, the wise identification and separation of the revenue categories is indispensable. Thus, a furniture factory making both wood and metal furniture should show these two essentially different product lines separately: they differ in their methods of manufacture, in the skills of their labour forces, in their customer base, and in their profit mark-ups. A canning factory which sells several types of canned fruit would probably not show them separately, but it might well distinguish local sales from exports, or bulk (tank) sales from carton sales.

A dairy farm project should distinguish between sales of milk, milk products, calves, cows for slaughter, and miscellaneous; this last a euphemism for dead animals sold for pet food, which even if forecasted as nil in the ex-ante figures should still have a line of figures to itself so that mortality can be accommodated in the ex-post statements without distorting the main revenue components. Certain dairy enterprises, however, would need to break down milk into unpasteurised, pasteurised, and UHT (long-life) milk, or milk sold in bottles, in tetra-packs, in tins, in bulk, and in customer's own containers.

These examples show how a financial statement must suit the circumstances and should not be rigidly standardised, even for so homogeneous a group of projects as dairy units. There may be pressure to standardise, in order to follow a fashion or to provide figures directly onto official questionnaires. But in a competitive world, where one seeks to understand one's own commercial and economic environment a little better than the competitors, the innovatory insight offers a possibility of differential advantage, while standardisation denies it.

COST: THE BAD NEWS

Like revenues, costs need to be presented in meaningful categories to suit the circumstances bearing in mind the availability of data. Costs vary enormously in the way they are presented. The categories may be distinguished by reference to the following:

1 The categories of revenue which are being supported (but some costs, 'non-product costs', are not connected with specific revenues).

2 Simply by reference to the nature of the expense, i.e. what is being bought, e.g. electricity, depreciation, stationery, salaries, insurance, etc.
3 Behaviour, variable costs being separated from fixed costs; variable costs vary as a function of the volume of production (or of output) while fixed costs may be seen as *period cost* (essentially a function of the passage of time).
4 Function, according to purpose of expenditure viz. manufacturing, selling, delivery, administration, research and development.
5 Location, showing Head Office costs separately from branch costs.

Most businesses choose one of these five ways of classifying their costs for presentation in the income statement. The second method is perhaps the most common in small and medium enterprises and in Government projects. Some, using computers, use two or more classification methods for management's control purposes, but the actual presentation in the income statement must not be too complex or it will fail to communicate its contents to its readers.

A very small industrial project, such as a bucket-making workshop, would probably have ten or twelve separate kinds of cost distinguished by their nature and would show these as ten or twelve separate figures. In compiling this list, however, those costs which are variable (according to numbers of buckets produced), such as galvanized sheet, should preferably appear towards the top of the list and those which are not affected by product volume, such as monthly rent of workshop, should appear towards the bottom. This distinction (by behaviour as well as by expense) makes it easier to forecast or plan the costs, because they can then be related to the number of buckets which the market will absorb year by year; and break-even analysis may also be worked out to see how many buckets must be sold before the proprietor can make a living out of the scheme.

In a furniture factory the cost environment is different. Here, planning decisions are constantly being taken as to whether or not to make some new design of furniture, or spare part for a piece of furniture. Variable costs, fixed costs and break-even calculations are in the forefront of the planners' minds. The income statement might be structured as illustrated in Table 2.2.

In financial statements, it is common to use minus signs (or brackets) to indicate financial flows in the unexpected (reverse) direction. Costs are not shown here with a minus sign; both revenues and costs appear to be positive numbers, though in reality they are opposites. Unfortunately there is no fixed convention for this matter. While the accounting convention is generally as illustrated, the computing convention tends to show revenues as positive and costs as negative, which permits a straightforward addition of all the revenues and costs to arrive at the bottom line.

The percentage column illustrated in Table 2.2 is very helpful both for planning ex-ante and for appraising ex-post. Percentage here means percentage of revenues. In the furniture example, which is ex-ante, the

Table 2.2 Income statement for a furniture factory

	Million shillings	%
Revenue		
Wooden furniture	78,400	61
Metal furniture	51,000	39
Total revenue	129,400	100
Costs		
Manufacturing variable	58,230	45
Selling and delivery variable	12,940	10
Administrative and financial variable	6,470	5
Total variable costs	77,640	60
Manufacturing fixed	19,410	15
Selling and delivery fixed	6,470	5
Administrative and financial fixed (includes interest)	12,940	10
Total fixed costs	38,820	30
Net profit before tax	12,940	10
Taxation	5,176	4
Net profit after tax	7,764	6

percentages were chosen as commercial decisions, and the shillings were derived from them. The financial target here was 6 per cent on the bottom line; given the tax rate, this translates to 10 per cent return on sales before tax, which was confirmed as feasible in the study of competitors' behaviour. In this particular time period the sales volume was intended to reach such a level that fixed costs would fall to one-third of all costs, which translates to 30 per cent of revenue. Given the channels of distribution and other marketing plan details, salesmen's commissions and other variable selling and distribution expenses were decided at 10 per cent of revenue. And so on. This is a good example of an income statement being used to support commercial decision-making, in this case during the design of a project rather than in support of the yes/no decision.

TIMING OF REVENUES AND OF COSTS

Since an income statement covers a period of time, normally in project planning a period of one year, the revenues shown therein must reflect sales of goods or services actually achieved within that year. The achievement of a sales revenue within a particular time period has a legal meaning: each sale implies a legally recognisable contract of sale under which the seller's obligations have been carried out. Since some industrial products are large and complex, that degree of contract execution (manufacturing and if necessary delivery and commissioning) which is a prerequisite to the transfer of title from seller to buyer is implied here. Only then does production become output. Only then is it correct to recognise the revenue in the income statement for that particular year.

The costs shown in the income statement for a period of time must, like the revenues, be those which properly should be included in that period. In the case of period costs, such as depreciation or rent of premises, it is relatively simple to assign such costs to the period in respect of which they will be incurred.

In the case of product costs, such as raw materials, it is important to include only those costs which are to be consumed in producing those finished goods which can be recognised as output during the period; such product costs are usually known as cost of goods sold or cost of sales. By this means, we match the product costs against the product revenues for the period (an instance of 'the matching principle' in accountancy). As was mentioned above in connexion with volumes, we take care that our costs do not include the raw materials not yet consumed, nor any costs embodied in unfinished goods or in the stock of finished goods left unsold at the close of the period, which will be part of the cost of sales of some later period. In other words, we cannot regard all the costs incurred in production during 1999 as 1999 cost. The value of closing stock must be deducted in calculating cost of sales, just as the volume of closing stock has to be deducted to arrive at the volume consumed or sold. Likewise the value of opening stock, bought earlier but only now used and embodied in sales, must be added. Some presentations of the income statement actually show these adjustments (see Table 2.3).

Table 2.3 Income statement showing stock adjustments

		£
Revenue		758,000
Opening stock	22,000	
Production costs	458,000	
	480,000	
Less: closing stock	(30,000)	
Cost of sales		450,000
Gross profit		308,000
Selling, administration and financial expense		100,000
Net Profit before Tax		208,000
Taxation		98,000
Net profit after tax		110,000

In Table 2.3, there is a subtotal labelled gross profit, otherwise known as gross margin. It means the surplus of revenue above product costs (the costs of purchasing and/or making the products which are sold, that is, the cost of sales) before deducting those expenses which are regarded as of a different kind ('non-product costs', 'period costs', 'expenses of carrying on the business', 'head office overheads', 'central expenses', etc.). Sometimes this distinction is emphasised by using the word 'cost' for product cost and 'expense' for non-product cost.

Taxation of the kind in the table is not a cost. We mean here that share of an enterprise's profit which is taken by the competent authorities, variously called Corporation Tax, Income Tax, Zakat, Contribution to National Workers' Housing Fund, or whatever. Being a share of the profit (surplus of revenue over cost) it cannot be regarded as a cost in itself.

COST OF SALES

In the example above, assuming it is an industrial enterprise, cost of sales would include an allocation of the manufacturing variable costs, principally wood or metal, power, and the wages of operatives, and of the manufacturing fixed costs such as depreciation of plant and equipment and the wages of supervisory staff. Only an allocation, not the full amount, since some of these manufacturing costs may go into building up stocks of goods ready for sale in a later period, rather than goods sold. Costs which enter into stock values do not appear in the income statement at all; they are not actually costs in that period. They represent the formation of an asset and therefore go into the balance sheet which shows the position at the close of the period.

Manufacturing labour, both variable and fixed, is included in cost of sales, except that again we must deduct that calculated proportion which is regarded as embodied in the closing stock of finished goods and partly finished goods. Office and showroom labour cost together with depreciation of office equipment would be wholly in the category of selling, administration and financial expense.

Some industrial enterprises have a system in which the cost of sales (product cost embodied in goods sold) is clearly defined, while the second category (expense) merely represents all other costs, and is thus not a clear concept in its own right. Expense may include not only those costs which are clearly non-product costs, but also those costs which ought to be recognised as product costs if only there were a more sophisticated accounting system in operation. For example, a factory makes several models of radio receiver; the component parts are recognisable as associated with particular models, and therefore appear as cost of sales as and when those models are sold, but the wages of the quality control inspectors are not connected with particular models (though they could be, if their inspection reports were analysed for this purpose) and so appear as administrative expense. This is unfortunate since the true contribution of these inspectors lies in the manufacturing of goods and is not administrative. In other words, 'expense' means costs which either cannot be allocated to products or are too difficult so to allocate – central costs, if you like.

This system corresponds to that of most farms, where there are several products each with its gross margin, from the total of which a group of central expenses is deducted. Farms are even less inclined than factories to be pedantic about analysing their central expenses to reclassify them as product costs. It must be remembered that cost accounting by product is an innovation of within the last hundred years, while gross profit dates back three hundred years. This system whereby all costs which are bothersome to analyse or difficult to classify are treated as period costs is tempting to adopt, and may be 'good enough for the country', but it is not one which can be recommended for the planning of modern industrial projects.

Not all enterprises show cost of sales in their income statements. A taxi-cab company does not, because it does not sell goods in the course of its business. The furniture company used as an example above does not, because it prefers to stress the distinction between fixed and variable costs rather than between cost and expense. The surplus of revenue over variable costs is called contribution, not gross profit; in the furniture example where revenue is £129,400 and variable costs are £77,640, the contribution for the year is £51,760, and this has to cover both fixed costs and profits.

Gross profit is a very old accounting concept, and is used every day by many salespersons and marketing managers. Unfortunately some modern economists have chosen to use the same term, confusingly, to mean the surplus of revenue over all costs except interest and depreciation.

APPROPRIATION

The net profit of an enterprise belongs to the owners of the enterprise, whoever they may be, whether Government or private, one or many. When a profit is made, it is customary for the owners to take part but not all of it, leaving the rest in the business for expansion or for prudence. That part which the owners take is called dividend, if the business is organised as a company with shares, or drawings, if it is not incorporated. The account which shows the taking of the profit, and how much is left, is called an appropriation account.

This account is sometimes added to the bottom of the income statement, in which case the bottom line is no longer net profit, but that sum which is left in the business for future periods. It still belongs to the owners, anyway. However, it is probably better to give it a spreadsheet to itself. Dividends (or drawings) have to be paid in cash or by cheque, and so will have an impact on the balance sheets and on the cash flow or funds flow statements. Indeed, if the funds are insufficient to pay a dividend, it cannot be paid, no matter how

Table 2.4 Appropriation account for a furniture factory

	£
Net profit after tax as per income statement	7,764
Add: opening balance brought forward from previous year	352
Total available	8,116
Dividends:	
Preference shares	(1,000)
Ordinary shares	(6,000)
Closing balance of accumulated profit carried forward in balance sheet	1,116

large the net profit may have been in that year. Appropriation is therefore intimately connected with the balance sheets, notwithstanding that some of the numbers come from the income statements.

An example of an appropriation account for the furniture factory is shown in Table 2.4.

After these remarks on the general structures of income statements and the underlying concepts of the structures, we will now consider the subject in more detail.

Chapter 3

Income statement: details

Some of the categories of cost which appear in forecast income statements can be problematical. These include materials, labour, pre-operating costs, and research and development expense.

MATERIALS

Like labour cost, materials cost is determined partly by the chosen technique of production and partly by the unit cost of the input. The technique of production determines what material will be used, and how much of it will be used to produce a given volume of output, including wastage. It does not wholly determine how much should be held in storage; that depends partly on other considerations, and in any case is of no interest for the income statement – stocks go into balance sheets.

Materials inputs which are incorporated into outputs, like wood into wooden tables, can usually be quantified: each table requires a standard quantity, say 2.5m^2 of a certain type of wood, of known thickness and quality. The volume of the input of that type is a linear function of the volume of tables of that type. The cost of that wood is therefore a variable cost, i.e. it varies with the volume of output.

Many enterprises adopt accounting systems in which records are kept of the amount of materials embodied in the output. In such a system the cost of wood is not simply the cost of wood purchased in a period; some of that might go into stockbuild of raw material or of unfinished tables. It is the cost of wood embodied in tables finished and sold, the wood component of cost of sales. It is calculated ex-ante by multiplying the number of tables sold first by the standard quantity – 2.5m^2 – and then by the expected purchase price of the standard quantity. It is calculated ex-post by recording the actual volume of wood consumed in making tables (less an allowance for unfinished or unsold tables) multiplied by the actual price of wood per unit volume. Costs which are treated in this way – tracking the inputs through into the outputs – are known as *direct costs*.

Direct labour likewise is a quantity of labour for which there is a standard or norm in the making of an output. Each table may require, for instance, ten minutes of labour by an assembly worker, and that is a direct labour cost if the accounts so treat it. In any event it is a variable cost.

Another material used in making tables is glue. Factories do not, however, calculate a standard quantity of glue per table; monitoring glue volumes is a tacky business. Instead, glue is made available for use as required and can be used either for tables or for chairs without recording for which it is used. It is therefore not a direct cost. Nevertheless it has to be included somehow in cost of sales. The simplest way of dealing with this is to add together all such items, which are certainly manufacturing costs but are not direct costs, and label them manufacturing overheads. As with direct costs, we have to deduct that proportion which goes into unfinished or unsold product, and the rest goes into cost of sales. Unfortunately this simple procedure fails to distinguish between variable overheads, like glue, and fixed overheads, like rent, so that when volumes increase in the later years of the project we have no basis for increasing the overheads correctly.

A better way is to separate manufacturing overheads into two groups: fixed and variable. Thus we have three types of manufacturing cost: direct (variable), other (variable) and other (fixed).

This is a better procedure but it does not tell us how much it costs to make a table and how much to make a chair, and whether both chairs and tables are selling at a profit. It will suffice for a business which only makes one product, but such places are rare. Some formula needs to be chosen which will apportion the overheads between the different products. This may be done on the basis of the amounts of direct labour used by the different products, or the amounts of direct materials, or the amounts of metered power for the machines, or some combination of these quantified direct costs; and there exist other more esoteric formulae which are occasionally adopted.

Suppose that glue is put into a group of overheads which are apportioned between tables and chairs on the basis of the volumes of direct materials; this means judging that, say, 64 per cent of the glue used is for tables. Knowing that the annual cost for glue is planned to be X dinars and the annual production of tables is Y tables, the cost of glue per table is 0.64 X/Y dinars. We know this without measuring or weighing the glue put into every table or batch of tables, but it is based on a formula which is judgemental rather than precise. Costs which are treated in this way are called indirect costs; they can be variable or fixed.

Thus a modern costing system in a multi-product manufacturing environ- ment would show direct manufacturing costs; indirect variable, and indirect fixed manufacturing costs; and separately non-manufacturing costs which are those functionally concerned with selling rather than making, or with administering the enterprise and financing it. Materials may appear in any or all of these categories. But in LDC investment proposals it is rare that so sophisticated an accounting system is anticipated; manufacturing costs distinguish between fixed and variable on the basis of their behaviour but usually not between direct and indirect on the basis of their ex-post book-keeping treatment. As a result, little attempt can be made to apportion joint costs among products. Individual product profitabilities are therefore sadly omitted.

Similarly when we turn from a manufacturing context to farming, we find that direct costs are attached to specific crops, but farm overheads are not; so each crop has a gross margin per hectare, but no net income, per hectare or otherwise. Product profitability, which is net income per unit of capital employed in each crop, is unknown.

TECHNICAL COEFFICIENTS

The fact that a certain type of table-top requires 2.5m^2 of a certain type of wood is determined not only by the dimensions of the table as designed but also by the wastage including the way in which large sheets of wood are sawn up. The input volume, and therefore the input cost, depends on the technique of production. In investment planning, figures like this 2.5m^2 are called *technical coefficients*. Coefficient means multiplier. Such figures are crucial in determining the requirements for inputs of materials; for inputs of labour and of land, technical coefficients are also required but figure less prominently.

In general, the technique of production must be known before material costs can be calculated by spreadsheets. Financial spreadsheets do not lend themselves to calculating the optimum technique of production within themselves. It is true that two or more techniques can be taken and tested in turn so that spreadsheets calculations show up the financial and economic consequences of each, and the best can be chosen, but within each test, the calculation of details about choice of technique precedes the financial statements.

Figure 3.1 gives a few examples of technical coefficients used to derive material input requirements. They are not universal constants but have been found to apply to certain places under certain conditions. Some of these, such as the fungicide, relate to relatively unimportant inputs; though importance depends on the unit cost. Others however, like the feed conversion ratio, are central to the concept of the entire project. These will have been used at the beginning of project identification for back-of-an-envelope calculations, and the others added later as the project proceeds through its stages of preparation and appraisal. When we get to sensitivity testing, the key coefficients will already have been identified as prime candidates for testing.

Milk bottling (see Figure 3.1) offers an interesting example. In the UK, most cows' milk is sold as fresh liquid milk, and most of that is delivered to people's houses in re-usable glass bottles. Providing the bottles can withstand several round trips, this is much cheaper than providing disposable containers such as the waxed cartons used in supermarkets. The average life (number of

Cabbage growing	Kg of seed	1.2 per hectare
	Kg of fungicide	2.5 per hectare
Egg production	Day-old chicks	115% of survivors
Beef fattening	Daily weight growth	400 grams per head
	Feed conversion	4 times weight growth
Salmon farming	Feed conversion	5 times weight growth
Sugar cane	Kg of fungicide	0.5 per hectare
	Tractor fuel litres	2.5 per hour
	Tractor tyres	1 set per 2000 hours
Paper pulp	Cellulose in banana	46.7% of stems weight
Sun dried fruit	Fresh pineapple	11 times dried weight
Road mending	Graders diesel/hr	0.182 litres per hp
Milk bottling	Trippage	see text

Figure 3.1 Some technical coefficients

trips) per glass bottle, known as *trippage*, is a technical coefficient of great importance to the profitability of dairies. If you use 50,000 bottles and each bottle lasts ten trips, you have to buy 5,000 new bottles every day. In the south of England the trippage is around 7 or 8, in the north 12, and in Scotland about 20. Thus the national average is about 10. In other countries, the trippage would probably be under 5, so milk is not bottled at all. Any plan for a new bottling plant in a developing country, or even in the UK, if it relied on the UK national average trippage could go very wrong indeed. Here is a case of a technical coefficient which has a strong impact on all three financial statements and which must be taken from prior knowledge of a similar enterprise operating under very similar technical and cultural conditions.

Technical coefficients reflect the chosen method of production or (in the case of trippage) distribution. Other choices may be available, but the coefficient will be given in each case. For instance, the feed conversion ratio for salmon farming (Figure 3.1) can be altered if the operation is shifted from river estuary to open sea. Essentially, therefore, these coefficients are parameters (parametric constants).

It is useful to draw a distinction between these and other operating ratios which can be varied by management policies outside the technical area. Figure 3.2 gives a list of coefficients and ratios of importance in the bus transportation sector, taken from Stuart Cole (1987). The figures in any given case would emerge from a study of the income statement together with some other data (not entirely to be found in any of the purely financial statements). These are essentially variables. The number of bus passengers per bus, in a year on a particular route, is variable, depending partly on the level of fares, whereas the maximum number of passengers a bus can carry is a technical coefficient. The latter will strongly influence the former. Dead mileage (to and from depot) is a variable in that it depends on the operating timetables (number of visits to the depot per day per bus, and selection of route starting and finishing locations in relation to the depot), but the minimum dead mileage (distance

Cost per bus mile	Driver pay rate per hour
Revenue per bus mile	Fleet size by type of bus
Cost per passenger journey	Total passengers carried
Bus miles per employee	Total scheduled bus miles
Passengers per employee	Total operated bus miles
Employees per bus	Staff numbers by category
Passengers per bus	Revenue by type of service
Vehicles required at peak	Peak/interpeak ratio
Days operation in year	Hours operation in day
Number of routes	Dead mileage

Figure 3.2 Bus company ratios and coefficients (including both data and results)
  Source: Based on Cole 1987

to and from the depot once per day from the closest passenger point) is a technical coefficient. The latter will influence the former, but not strongly unless the depot is extremely poorly sited.

Bus transport differs from manufacturing, and is more like agriculture, in that there is a wide variety of management choices to be made which give rise to a wide range of results in terms of performance and efficiency, with technical coefficients acting as limitations, or mild influences, rather than as rigid determining factors.

With technical coefficients, which will be put in as data in the calculations, the art is to get the parameters right. With indicators of efficiency, which emerge as results from the calculations, the art is first to check that the indicators appear to fall within the range of what is good but achievable, and if not to go back and get the project design right, i.e. to give optimum results. For both of these purposes it is necessary to know *from previous experience elsewhere* what is an appropriate norm. For technical coefficients of critical importance in a project, ascertaining these norms (together with an appraisal of the market demand) is the essential starting point of project design.

LABOUR COST

Predicting the cost of labour in a project which will start a year or two ahead and run for many years is a crude, degraded version of the much more accurate forecasting work which a budget accountant does every year for a much shorter and more imminent period.

The budget accountant knows from the existing payroll data what groups of workers are employed, what their wages or salaries are, and what are their *payroll additives*. Payroll additives in developed economies are additional costs which the employer of labour has to pay but which are not paid as part of regular wages and salaries, or may not even be paid at all to the employees. They include productivity bonuses; employers' contributions to pension schemes, and similar local or national schemes and funds; taxes on payroll, if such exist; reimbursement of relocation expenses; the 'thirteenth month' additional salary which in some countries is payable every December; and an accrual for those 'holidays with pay' which, at the year-end, have not yet been taken, where employees are permitted to carry forward their holiday entitlements. In LDCs, payroll additives also include a plethora of allowances paid out to employees which in many cases exceed the basic wage: travelling to work allowances, medical allowances, schooling allowances, festival and holy day allowances, famine relief allowances, burial allowances and the like. Some senior employees, especially expatriates, also receive house and house servant allowances, entertainment allowances, car allowances, overseas leave allowances, overseas schooling allowances, and end-of-contract gratuities.

Two aspects of this require a decision as to the appropriate treatment in the spreadsheets. First, when is a labour cost not a labour cost but some other kind of expense?

'Travel to work' allowances are part of the cost of attracting labour, and so is the cost of overseas leave which normally includes travel, but overseas travel on business is usually not regarded as a labour cost. The cost of travel vouchers or tickets is not perceived as wages. Rather, it is an expense: administrative, selling or manufacturing expense according to the purpose of the journey. Travelling to attend training courses may be shown as part of course costs or may be included with business travel. Schooling allowances for employees' children are really labour cost, but attendance at courses and seminars for the training of the employees themselves is often treated as administrative expense, notwithstanding that it is necessary for obtaining skilled labour. The same is true for recruitment costs, including agency commissions, advertising, reimbursement of 'travel to interview' costs for all candidates and of relocation expenses for the successful appointee; all these are necessary to hire labour, and might logically be regarded as payroll additives, but are often treated as administrative expense.

Of course, this problem of perceived classification only arises when it is desired to show broad-brush cost categories such as *labour*, *materials* and *expenses*. If it is possible to show clearly and separately *labour including payroll additives*, recruitment costs, education and training (including related travel), business travel and subsistence, and so on and to do so separately for the various functions or departments, ambiguity disappears.

Obviously this needs much more data and attention to detail and does not suit the broad-brush approach, but the underlying problem may be, in truth, that certain people or certain ranks are perceived as having rights to certain allowances regardless of their business function, if any. It may be an unwarranted assumption to suppose that these perquisites have any precise business purpose which is capable of being elicited and classified. If the King of feudal Ruritania is entitled to a retinue of twenty-four armed knights, who are we to say whether their wine is for business purposes?

The second concern is that there is a mass of detail here which is available to the budget accountant in the operating phase but not earlier in the project cycle when we need it.

For instance, the wage rates. The budget accountant knows the existing wages; where these are age-related, the workers' ages are known, and if performance-related, the current and expected performance levels are known. If workers are paid on scales with annual increments, the position of each worker on the scale, including those who are lodged at the top of the scale, is known. The date in the year when the next increase is payable is known, and this is not usually coincident with the financial year used in income statements but part-way through the period. If trade union negotiations are involved in determining pay rises, these usually begin well before the date of each pay rise, and information can be confidentially drawn from the negotiators in order to decide what would be an appropriate assumption for the budget.

A much degraded picture is available before the project starts. Even if payroll details can be taken from similar projects which are in their operating phases at other locations – and that is not always possible in LDCs – the latest technical innovations may change the numbers of workers needed, the local position as regards availability of skills may be different, the local cost of living may be different, the local housing situation may require a different pattern of payroll additives, the new project intervening in an existing labour market may face cost challenges different from those of an established enterprise, and of course the ages and performance of individual workers cannot be known accurately before they are recruited.

Typically instead an effort is made to collect data on the 'going rates of pay' in the locality with special attention to the salaries of the highest-paid managers, and a safety margin built in by rounding the figures up or by adding an explicit contingency of between 5 and 10 per cent. Payroll additives are usually calculated as a simple percentage addition to the wage and salary bill across the board, as no further detail is possible.

Another area where detailed data are of necessity unavailable is education and training costs (including related travel). In practice these should be decided upon by the departmental managers in consultation with the employees concerned and with the head training manager if there is one, or in consultation with outside advisory services in the case of a smaller enterprise. We cannot do this job for them ex-ante and predetermine which courses they will attend and in which years. We can, however, allot sums of money for training, education and personal development in each department. All professionals need updating and refresher courses; who else is going to provide the funds for these? It is both inhumane and unprofitable to prevent people from keeping up with their subjects, fire them when they become seriously out of date, and recruit replacements. And the same applies right down to skilled and even unskilled workers, in whose area of competence technical progress is also underway.

A very large number of LDC project spreadsheets contain no expenditure at all on employee training and education. This may be an omission or it may be deliberate. Either way, the concept of taking people on to work in an unaltered way for the many years of the operating phase of a project is inconsistent with national development, with technical progress, with personal happiness, and probably with trade union realities, and in short will not work. It is therefore strongly to be recommended that all such spreadsheets contain a cost category 'education and training' (including related travel and subsistence) even if it is filled with zeros. This will draw attention to the matter so that the decision is deliberate.

The following three examples, taken from actual projects, will illustrate some key points. Table 3.1 is from a country in serious economic difficulties, with rapid inflation and a fluid situation, which adds up to poor quality data and an extremely degraded picture in the crystal ball. 'All employees will be given allowances and benefits worth 100 per cent of basic salary/wage. Salaries and wages are expected to be increased in proportion to production.'

You will notice the erroneous roster total, the designation of jobs and salaries by reference to ascriptive rights and perquisites rather than function-ality, the male-dominated payroll, wages and allowances expressed to one or at most two significant figures, and the absence of distinction between fixed and variable costs.

This second example (Table 3.2) sets up quite a different framework. The various field operations are listed; one of them is planting. For each operation the variable cost in currency units per hectare is estimated, according to the implement, if any, with which the labourer works. Table 3.2 shows the abbreviation codes used in Table 3.3.

You will notice that, where a vehicle is used, its cost is far more than that of its operative. The combined cost is expressed to one significant figure, and at this level of accuracy the labour cost is not significant; indeed it is not stated except for code MH. Where labour cost is stated, it too is expressed to only one significant figure. Table 3.3 shows the variable cost of planting per hectare.

It is noteworthy that this inattention to the exact remuneration of field workers, a matter of vital importance to them but of little impact on the profitability of this particular study, is not due to white-collar disdain for the lower orders. The same study expresses the salaries of the twenty-four 'permanent staff' to one significant figure also.

Aspects which fail to receive attention from this kind of treatment include the following. If the variable wage cost received by the field workers is expressed as an annual income, it emerges that the ratio between the lowest and the highest incomes is about 1:200; excluding expatriates it is about 1:18. Whether the poorest workers can survive or will be attracted to work on the project voluntarily is not examined. Needless to say there is no mention of education or training.

The next example (Table 3.4) is taken from a factory project which was to

Table 3.1 Crop farm labour

Manpower	No.	Monthly pay
Farm manager	1	5,000
Assistant farm manager	1	4,500
Lorry drivers	2	3,000
Tractor drivers	2	3,000
Mechanic	1	2,500
Headman	1	2,000
Farm hands	30	1,500
Total	38	71,000

Table 3.2 Planting operations: codes

Code	Meaning and unit	Cost per unit
TH	tractor hours (per hectare)	50
TR	truck hours (per hectare)	50
FL	fork-lift truck hours (per hectare)	30
MH	man-hours, for harvesting	1
	for other operations	0.5

Table 3.3 Variable costs of pineapple planting

	Per hectare
Cost of plants from local farms	2139
Collection of same 6 TR, 120 MH	360
Gathering and collection from nursery	
2 TH, 100 MH	150
Transport from the cannery	
2 TR, 40 MH	120
Fertilizing 30 MH	15
Planting 2 TR, 140 MH	170
	2954

make paper out of bagasse (sugar-cane waste). In this kind of situation the labour costs are typically derived from an organisation chart (organogram) which specifies the jobs of people in charge in some detail but tends to peter out among the lower ranks. The top four grades are recruited internationally and their pay is determined in US dollars. Others are determined in the local currency unit and converted to dollars at a stated rate. Payroll additives are to be added at 50 per cent.

It will be seen that the basic elements, call them data or assumptions, which are used here are the monthly salaries payable locally and these are expressed to one or two significant figures, to the nearest US$ 5. An appreciable margin

Table 3.4 Factory personnel: grades and salaries

| Grade | No. | Job description | U.S. dollars per month | | |
			Local	Remittable	Total
A	1	General Manager	150	500	650
B	4	Managers: Works, Finance, Sales, Procurement	135	400	535
C	3	Managers: Chief Engineer, Chief Accountant, Production	125	300	425
D	12	Mechanical engineer, Civil engineer, Electrical engineer, Instrument engineer, Personnel officer, other expatriates	100	150	250
E	9	Officers in charge of pulp mill, paper machine, drawing office, etc.	80	—	80
F	9	Foremen in charge of pulp mill, paper machine, etc.	70	—	70
G	70	Skilled labour, for production	55	—	55
H	111	Semi-skilled labour including clerks	40	—	40
I	128	Unskilled labour, peons, watchmen	30	—	30

of error may lie in the figures for grades H and I, which rely on very round numbers indeed, and contain such large numbers of persons that they may well have to be subdivided into subgrades. We should also remember that in LDCs (as elsewhere) there are typically quite large differences between the wages paid to men, women and juveniles, yet in this factory as in most LDC spreadsheets this is quite overlooked and grades are treated as all men or all women, with no trainees.

Despite the rough and ready basic elements, when you multiply by the number of people, add down, put in a contingency and add a percentage for inflation, the computer will print out a number with several significant figures and will give the impression of great precision – unless you deliberately introduce a rounding into the calculations. Rounding has the advantage that it communicates the true degree of precision. On the other hand the full set of digits allows readers to see more readily how each figure was arrived at, in case the notes do not make everything self-explanatory.

Pineapple canning, and many other agro-industrial and agricultural investment projects, are subject to *seasonal fluctuations* in activity. That means hiring and firing labour. This is not necessarily disruptive, since some such projects are put in place to provide employment for rural workers during the slack season – usually the dry season in a climate where only one harvest per year is possible. However, a clash between the peak demand for labour of the project and a strong demand for labour in the surrounding rural area can be disastrous. To expose this problem it is necessary to make a subsidiary spreadsheet with monthly estimates of the labour demand based on a job schedule, absenteeism from the permanent labour force, and net surplus or hiring requirement of labour. Hiring requirements during the busy rural season place a question mark over the success of the project. All temporary hirings and surpluses unless they are negligible in amount will require adjustments to the labour cost total. Fok Kam (1988: 74) has published a good example for the sugar cane industry, but none of the three examples cited above follow his procedure.

PRE-OPERATING COSTS

During the construction phase of an investment project, there is of course no revenue. There are, however, costs. Not only the capital costs of acquiring the fixed assets, which by the device of depreciation will be spread over the years of the operating phase, but ordinary costs, which if they occurred during the revenue-earning period would raise no eyebrows whatever. The enterprise which is to operate the project cannot wait until the construction is complete before coming into existence. It cannot abandon all its functions to consultants or suppliers. During the construction phase managerial work is essential. The reception, verification and caretaking of goods on site are necessary; procurement and accounting functions must be carried out. Operators needed on Day 1 of the operating phase have to be pre-trained during the construction phase. Customers who will buy products on Day 1 have to be persuaded beforehand. Interest will arise on borrowings, if any, during the months and years of the construction period. All these costs and expenses can be incurred before the flow of revenues begins.

In a mature enterprise which follows sound accountancy procedures and is regularly expanding its production facilities with new projects, costs arising from construction phases will normally be small in relation to revenues arising from earlier investments and so cause no problem. In that event, most of the costs described above would be treated as costs during the period of incurring them; in book-keeping jargon, they would be 'expensed', not 'capitalised'. Management, procurement and accounting would be booked as administrative expense. Operator training would be booked as manufacturing overhead expense (fixed cost), though not as cost of sales. Interest would be booked as interest, which is financial expense. Only the costs of receiving goods at site, goods which are destined to form part of fixed assets, would be regarded as adding to the costs of those assets and 'capitalised', i.e. accumulated in the balance sheet until the end of the construction phase, and depreciated over the operating life to match the timing of the benefits derived from operation.

Many LDC enterprises are immature; many projects are their first, or second, large investment, and the revenues of earlier investments if any are insufficient to cover the pre-operating costs of the new one. Management inexperience is not surprising in under-developed economies and it may show up as poor performance from the previous investments which fail to generate profits to cover the pre-operating losses of the current investments. In that context, if sound accountancy procedures are followed, significant overall losses may be booked during each new construction phase. This can be embarrassing, if shareholders and officials do not understand the causes. Many LDC officials express genuine surprise that a project can incur losses *before* it is operating. Such losses if correctly shown in the ex-ante financial statements of the project can damage the ability of the enterprise to attract capital investment and thus prejudice the project. The problem is compounded if further losses are expected during the early years of the operation phase too, owing to low output volumes as is common especially with industrial developments. Losses are damaging to the ability of the enterprise to attract capital from outside.

As John Richard Evans in commenting on a leading case in British accounting practice very wisely says

> In an unregulated environment management is free to select the account-ing method which best supports its chosen strategies . . . If the aim is to finance activity from internal sources, the capital accounting procedure which produces the lowest . . . reported profit, i.e. the immediate write-off of capital expenditure against revenue, is likely to be favoured.
>
> (Edwards 1989: 121)

In LDCs the boot is on the other foot. Capital is looked for from outside. The temptation is to defer the reporting of expenditure. It has therefore become commonplace in LDC investments to adopt accounting devices which defer pre-operating costs to the years of the operating phase. Everything tends to be capitalised rather than expensed; the very term 'pre-operating *expense*' is avoided or its true meaning disregarded.

This runs counter to the established accounting principle of prudence, whereby losses are recognised promptly rather than postponed to a supposedly sunnier day. International lenders and donors make no objection, however, and the practice is sometimes justified on the grounds that is accepted by the World Bank.

The device consists of adding all pre-operating costs either to the value of the fixed assets, to be depreciated later, or to a special class of notional asset, which is spread over an arbitrary period of years during the operating phase of the fixed assets. This is called amortisation rather than depreciation, though the arithmetic is the same. This notional asset is of a fictitious nature; it is not saleable nor tangible. It may be called 'pre-operating cost capitalised', which at least is clear, or 'preliminary expenses' which can cause confusion.

Genuine preliminary expenses are the expenses incurred in forming a company: registration charges, legal fees, hotel bills and so forth, sums laid out by business people before the company actually exists, but reimbursed to them by the company itself. It is permissible to amortise preliminary expenses over some years, presumably on the grounds that the benefit of being a company is a kind of asset. However, to conceal pre-operating expense under this head is unsound.

Interest incurred during construction is always a problem. There may be two or more sources of borrowed finance, typically a long-term debt and a short-term bank debt (the British system allows negative bank balances, i.e. overdrafts). Ex-ante prediction of these debts requires quarterly rather than yearly scheduling of the capital expenditure throughout the construction phase, and a detailed understanding of the method of calculating interest together with associated fees and charges. Many ex-ante studies assume the long-term finance will be enough to dispense with any short-term finance. This means that repayments follow a predetermined schedule, agreed in advance, so interest can be calculated from that, rather than from the fluctuating borrowing requirement to be computed from year to year from the balance sheets or cash flow statements.

Adding interest to the value of the fixed asset which has been financed by the debt is not uncommon. The test of whether the practice is sound is whether or not the asset value thus enhanced overstates the true asset value in the balance sheet.

It should be understood that this capitalisation of interest aims to avoid a loss in the income statement; it does not aim to avoid actually paying the interest, which is a matter for the cash flow statement. To avoid actually paying interest during the construction period it is necessary for the lender to agree to defer it by adding it to the debt. By this means the interest is *funded*. Interest may be funded (added to debt) but not capitalised (added to fixed or notional assets); it may be capitalised but not funded; it may be both. Confusion often arises here because the word *capitalised* is often used when *funded* is meant. To make the matter quite precise, the accounting entries are shown in Figure 3.3.

Transaction 1 is required in any event. Transaction 2 is optional; it clears the interest expense and increases the fixed asset value instead. Transaction 3 recognises additional long-term debt (funding) if the interest is going to be deferred; it merely converts an amount which is currently due to XYZ Bank into one which is due over some years to XYZ Bank; no ledger entry is needed though a journal voucher is desirable for the records.

	Transaction	Debit	Credit
1	Accrue for interest	Interest expense	Lender's name
2	Capitalise interest	Fixed asset or notional asset	Interest expense
3a	Fund interest	Lender's name	Lender (debt)
3b	Otherwise pay interest	Lender's name	Cash or bank

Figure 3.3 Accounting treatment of construction interest

RESEARCH AND DEVELOPMENT

In a famous detective story, Sherlock Holmes drew attention to the barking of the dog in the night. But the dog had not barked, Dr Watson objected, puzzled. That was exactly the point, however.

It is sometimes necessary to draw attention to something which is *not* a feature of a project. This is to make the point that a decision has been made, under circumstances which merit consideration, to exclude the feature. This presentation can be achieved in a spreadsheet simply by inserting a line with words and a series of zeros and an appropriate footnote. The cost of education and training has already been cited as a neglected item which is often omitted and could well be treated in this way. The cost of the research and development function (R & D) is another. This is an item which rarely appears in LDC investment projects but should always be given consideration. It can be listed by name in those income statements where costs are expressed in functional categories.

In commercial or in-house R & D, development (D) is directed towards the improvement of existing products and processes. These may be improvements in quality, reductions in cost, or cosmetic changes to meet the short-term needs of competitive marketing. Manufacturers undertake development work of this kind to defend or improve their market share, or to prolong the life of a product: most manufactured products go through a life cycle whereby after the market has been fully saturated the product becomes obsolete and finally dies off. In the latter stages of the product cycle especially, development work can extend its life and offer some more years of profitable operation to the manufacturer concerned. This assumes, of course, that manufacturers do have differentiated products; without an 'angle' you cannot thrive, you cannot afford to undertake R & D, and if you did sacrifice to pay for R & D, the benefits would be taken up by your competitors too.

Research (R) is not concerned with minor improvements to existing products within the product range but rather with the introduction of new products and ultimately with an entirely new product range. Its benefits are therefore both more risky and longer delayed than those of development (D).

In a manufacturing project with a life of fifteen or twenty years it is hardly credible that the product to be made at the beginning should still be marketable without change towards the end. Obsolescence has always been faster than that. The process of production moreover, as well as the product itself, can be expected to change. Typically in LDCs equipment is imported, its use is mastered, its limitations tested out, and its design parameters understood; then it is modified and adapted to local conditions and to the characteristics of local raw materials, and eventually improved upon. Admittedly the ability to do this varies greatly from place to place; India and Pakistan have been widely praised for their abilities in this direction. This is of course development (D).

It is not without cost, in labour and materials and other expenses such as outside laboratory work. These costs are often met informally, that is, without accounting. This can be achieved by including salaries for senior engineers in sufficient numbers for them to have time for development work without any specifically development people being shown on the payroll. Small parts can be made up in the factory workshop or garage, booked as maintenance materials. Fees for outside work are kept low and can be booked inaccurately as consumables, or as administrative expenses. In some cases the costs are accumulated until some point is reached where the development results in a change of process or of product; this will coincide with a modification or extension of the equipment in use, so the accumulated development expense can be transferred to the fixed asset account and capitalised. It seems a pity that accounting should be disabled so as not to record this creditable and necessary activity, but there is often an unwillingness to take responsibility for expenditure which is fruitless, as may be the case when experiments have negative results.

If development (D) is risky, research (R) is even more so. The development of the next generation of products through in-house talent involves speculation both in the relevant fields of technology and in marketing, since the research results of competitors over the next several years cannot be known either. Yet if an enterprise does not conduct R & D, its products will become obsolete, and it will continue to be dependent on the technology of others, occupying a subordinate position and paying royalties for ever. This dependency on the technology of more advanced economies is an irritant in LDCs, and it is generally recognised that R & D work in the LDCs themselves is necessary to escape from it.

To some extent the responsibility for anti-dependency R & D is undertaken by LDC government agencies rather than by the individual enterprises. Where this is so, R & D will not appear as such in an enterprise spreadsheet; it is a tiny part of the 'tax' line. Particularly in the production of staple agricultural commodities which are not differentiable, centralised R & D is the general rule. Unfortunately centralised R & D is not generally very successful; government departments are usually starved of funds, sometimes mis-managed, and handicapped by the attempt to deploy generalists to address specialised development tasks. Recognising this, a serious investment proposal will contain an element of cost provision for in-house development if not also research. Such a provision might range from less than 1 per cent of revenue in a market gardening project to 15 per cent in a micro-electronics enterprise.

In ex-ante planning, all such costs should be expensed, that is, treated as period cost, reducing profits in the years when the cost will be incurred. In ex-post accounting by contrast, there will be a known set of R & D projects, and it is legitimate to acquire fixed assets (such as laboratory equipment) with specific purposes in mind, serving several projects over several years. Such assets can be capitalised, subject to the principle of prudence.

Chapter 4

The balance sheets

According to Edwards (1989: 138), balance sheets ceased to be the principal statements used to assess the progress and prospects of an enterprise and were supplanted by income statements during the inter-war years. The usefulness of balance sheets until quite recently was diminished by hidden reserves, used to understate and so conceal the value of assets. These were extensively used, even by businesses of strategic national importance such as banks, shipping lines, and insurance companies. In the UK the legal right to disinform shareholders in this way ended only in 1990 when the last major bank abandoned the practice. There are still, however, temptations to overstate assets, using fictitious assets to inflate one's balance sheet. There is a delicious example of this in the satirical humour of Griffiths (1986: 24). This is the balance sheet of the fictitious conglomerate, Arthur Daley Enterprises, which has its office in Liechtenstein. Summarised, and with an error of arithmetic removed, it is as shown in Table 4.1.

Table 4.1 Balance sheet of Daley Enterprises as of 31 December 1979

		£
Net fixed assets and goodwill		427,700
Net current assets		−99,904
Net assets utilised		327,796
Represented by:		
Share capital: authorised		100
fully paid		2
Capital reserve	407,927	
Accumulated loss	−80,133	
Retained earnings		327,794
Capital employed		327,796

Here the fixed assets amount to only £3,600 but the miscreant Daley has valued his leasehold tenancy at £424,100, and has signed a certificate to that effect, declining the advice of his accountant who valued it at £23,500. This remarkable but intangible asset is not available in cash, of course, and so cannot be taken out by way of dividend; the promise which it holds for the future is therefore a capital reserve rather than a revenue reserve. As to the working capital, otherwise known as net current assets, these are negative, because although Daley has a substantial asset value in the form of trade stock (for which he has signed another certificate), he has even more debts which he owes to sundry creditors, and a large bank overdraft.

THE BASIC STRUCTURE OF A BALANCE SHEET

The Daley balance sheet is correctly structured. This is, in summarised form, the way we put together ex-ante balance sheets. We start with a statement of the value of the assets of the enterprise at the end of each year throughout the project life, and show how it will be financed, i.e. from what sources of funds these assets will have been paid for.

The assets which the project will require are called Net Assets Utilised. *Net* means *minus* or *after subtracting* something. In the case of fixed assets, net means after subtracting provisions for depreciation, whereby the value is progressively written down over the life of the assets. For example, a vehicle which originally cost £10,000 and is being written off to nothing over ten years will put £1,000 a year as a cost into the annual income statements, and £1,000 a year cumulative into successive balance sheets as a provision for depreciation. After three years the provision for depreciation will have reached £3,000, so the vehicle will show in the balance sheet at £7,000 net. This is called the Net Book Value.

In the case of net current assets (working capital), *net* means after deducting current liabilities from current assets. Current assets are not, like fixed assets, intended to serve a purpose over more than one year, but are available for early use. The principal current liabilities are cash – in cashiers' hands or in bank accounts, stocks (inventories) of various kinds, and debtors – customers who have not yet got round to paying for their purchases. We expect both stocks and debtors to be turned into cash within the year by normal turnover. The principal current assets are creditors – suppliers who have not yet been paid for their supplies, short-term debts such as bank overdrafts, and possibly the tax authorities. During the year following the date of the balance sheet we would expect all these current liabilities to be paid off. In normal circumstances, the current assets will be available to the cashiers during that same period, and all will be well if the current assets comfortably exceed the current liabilities. A healthy business normally carries a clear surplus of current assets; this surplus is needed for comfortable turnover without the danger and distress of running out of cash. We call this *working capital*. Daley Enterprises shows negative working capital because the current liabilities (including its bank overdraft) are unusually large, and the creditors are probably rather pressing since Mr Daley needs to employ a minder. Negative net current assets would not normally be projected in ex-ante spreadsheets, though there are a few legitimate exceptions in certain retail projects where trade credit is readily available and customers pay cash.

To finance these various assets there is a combination of the owner's funds and borrowed funds. The owner may be one person (in most countries, there must be at least two members of a company with its capital divided into shares), or a partnership, such as a husband and wife team, or shareholders in a company; such shareholders may include other companies. In some companies all the shares belong to the Government. The Government may or may not have paid money for its shares; some nationalised undertakings have struggled on sadly for years without any money invested in them by the owner. Some enterprises operate as Government departments and their funds are an inseparable part of Government funds; they are not business entities at all and do not have any balance sheet. Some co-operatives adopt the legal form of a partnership, others that of a company. Other projects are undertaken by groupings which have no clear legal framework at all; semi-military and criminal businesses are often of this kind.

So some investments are not financed by share capital. When we have to make a spreadsheet which will serve in such various situations we have to use a generic term like *sponsors' capital*.

In the great majority of cases, sponsors cannot or will not put enough capital into a project to finance it by themselves; even though accumulated profits can be kept in the project (retained earnings) to add to the sponsors' capital. Sponsors seek to borrow the remainder of the necessary finance; spreadsheet balance sheets can be used to calculate how much borrowing will be required. We are talking here about long-term borrowing, by which we really mean medium-term and long-term borrowings. These are those debts which, when appearing in a balance sheet, will still be outstanding in the balance sheet of the following year. In other words the period of the loan is agreed to exceed one more year. Loans for any shorter period are classified as current liabilities and have already been dealt with in calculating the net assets utilised.

Note that even a ten-year loan will include a current portion, when there is a repayment date approaching for one instalment. This is known as the current portion of long-term debt, and its reclassification as the maturity date approaches is a headache in writing computer spreadsheets.

TANGIBLE FIXED ASSETS

There is a stereotype of a project which begins as a suggestion by a machinery salesman. 'This is what you need', says he brandishing a catalogue, 'and we can adjust the price to suit, so there will be a good little drink in it for you.'

Negotiations follow and in due course the catalogue item, Grinding Machine De Luxe Model Four with an output of four tons per hour nominal and a pro-forma invoice in three copies, translates itself into a project proposal at a price of $75,000, seeking bank finance. Even when the figure is so fully documented as it is in this case, the planner faces some difficulties with it. In most cases, the cost of the fixed assets is much less clear.

Before we look at the problems we will consider the general principles and aims.

Tangible fixed assets are physically identifiable items which will be the property of the enterprise, acquired for the purpose of use in the project rather than for re-sale, with the expectation that the project will benefit from their use over a period exceeding one year. *Intent* is part of this definition. All expenditure on the acquisition, production or installation of fixed assets, and all fixed assets provided by shareholders by way of capital contributions, and all fixed assets donated as gifts (ICA 1987: 41), should be capitalised and included in the balance sheets every year until they are disposed of and cease to be the property of the enterprise.

The primary objective of an auditor looking at the figure in a balance sheet will be to check that *all* fixed assets are included, that they do physically exist, that they are the property of the enterprise, and that they are valued and classified correctly and consistently from year to year (Thornton Baker 1983: 237); this ex-post examination may be taken as an accurate guide to the conduct of a truthful ex-ante analyst.

Almost all fixed assets have useful economic lives of finite duration – 'depreciable lives'. Their life comes to an end because of (a) physical deterioration with passage of time, or (b) technical and commercial obsolescence, or (c) expiry of a fixed-term lease without which the asset cannot be used, or (d) depletion by extraction and exhaustion, as in the case of a mine or quarry.

Virtually the only kind of asset which has an infinite life is freehold land not subject to depletion. With that exception, depreciation should be calculated and allocated to the ex-ante income statement of each accounting period of the life, so as to charge a fair proportion of the total cost of the asset to each period. Except for land and depleting assets, we mostly use the straight-line method, otherwise known as the equal-instalment method, apportioning an equal expense to every year. Depreciation is a paper entry, not involving any payment of money. The ex-post book-keeping entries each year are: debit the depreciation account, which is an expense in the income statement and hits the profit every time; credit the provisions for depreciation account, which stays in the balance sheet and mounts up year by year.

At the year-end after acquisition, a fixed asset will appear in the balance sheet at the value known as original cost or historic cost. This is the amount spent in acquiring the asset, or the estimated value if received as a gift, or the agreed value if contributed as capital in kind. The amount received will normally be documented ex-post by invoices and other auditable items, even if the analyst believes these items to be inflated by fraud and theft. The original cost, once established, does not change, and the item may be carried in successive balance sheets at this figure until the end of its life; that arrangement, which is very common in LDCs except in South and Central America, is a long-established convention called historic cost accounting. From this original cost we deduct the provisions for depreciation, a rising figure in successive years, so that the fixed asset value net of depreciation declines over the life. This latter figure is known as the net book value (NBV) or depreciated value.

In economies which suffer from inflation, declining net book values may seem so unrealistic that the historic cost accounting convention has to be abandoned, and rules are introduced – or *ad hoc* adjustments are permitted – which allow fixed assets to be revalued, though the depreciation expenses and provisions have to be increased too. At the end of their lives the assets do ultimately fall back in net book value. But we shall return to the problems of inflation accounting as a separate matter. For the moment we assume no inflation.

Depreciation should be calculated so as to reduce to zero the value of the asset at the end of its useful economic life, unless it is intended to be disposed of at an earlier date, in which case an estimate of the residual value must be made. A simple example is shown in Table 4.2.

As the NBV declines, so the total net assets utilised in the balance sheet declines, since the former is a major component of the latter. As a further consequence, the capital employed declines also over successive years; this diminishing requirement for finance allows loans to be paid off, or dividends to be paid out. That does not mean, of course, that there is a direct and simple relationship between the equal instalments of fixed asset depreciation and the possibly equal instalments of debt repayments.

Table 4.2 Example of depreciation calculations

Year:	1	2	3	4	5 ...
Depreciation calculation: Original cost 1200 Depreciable life 10 years Residual value at end of period 200 Annual depreciation, straight-line (1200–200)/10 = 100					
Income statement effect	100	100	100	100	100
Balance sheet effects: Original cost	1200	1200	1200	1200	1200
Less: provisions for depreciation	–100	–200	–300	–400	–500
Net Book Value	1100	1000	900	800	700

Depreciable lives are normally assigned to individual assets when large and specific, such as second-hand ships or custom-built process plant. Otherwise lives are assigned to classes of assets, such as plant and machinery, small tools, furniture, fixtures and fittings, motor vehicles, animal-drawn vehicles, etc. In a few countries, the tax authorities fix the asset lives for all classes, and the accountants are required to use the same values for depreciation purposes as the writing-down allowances that are used in calculating tax liabilities. In nearly all LDCs, however, the lives for depreciation are separate from the tax lives, which means that whatever depreciation may be calculated as an expense will be disregarded by the tax authorities. That being so, each enterprise may make its own estimate of the useful economic life of an asset or class of assets, subject only to constraints of professional ethics if any. 'It is essential', says the British Accounting Standards Committee, 'that asset lives are estimated on a realistic basis.' The life chosen for depreciation in the income statements must be consistent with the provisions in the balance sheets. A realistic life chosen under historic cost accounting must be the same as a realistic life chosen under any other convention reflecting inflation (ICA 1987: 218).

The set of depreciable lives, in order to remain realistic, should be reviewed from time to time in the light of experience. Despite the accounting principle of consistency, we must recognise that assets used by poorly-trained operators in LDCs and especially in dusty, tropical conditions are likely to have shorter lives than identical assets used elsewhere. To obey the accounting principle of prudence, the maxim must be: When in doubt, go for the shorter option.

The fixed assets as they take shape in the mind of the project sponsor during the project identification phase may not be listed in asset classes; they are more likely to represent *procurement packages*, bundles of expenditures associated with various suppliers. The financial analyst therefore has to reclassify them. For the main categories, it is as well to avoid unusual categories, even though the project may present unusual features. The thinking here is that (a) the accounting categories used ex-ante are likely to be adopted ex-post, and (b) the assets of this project may be only one of a series of investments undertaken by the enterprise over time. If the enterprise already exists, the additional fixed assets may well be fitted into the categories already established in its balance sheets.

In view of the tendency to capitalise all possible items of pre-operating expenditures, a mixture of legitimate and illegitimate intended expenditures will present themselves to the analyst to be placed in one or another class of tangible fixed assets with the appropriate life. All such proposed capital-isations should be subjected to the tests that (a) these items actually will add to the income stream which is expected to flow from the beneficial use of the fixed assets during the operating phase, and (b) the treatment is consistent from asset to asset and from project to project. Any ex-post audit will have the primary objective of verifying these, and the main evidence looked for in respect of (a) will be the proposal itself along with the analyst's contemporary

Figure 4.1 Fixed asset add-ons

Proposed expenditure	Suggested fixed asset class
Access roads	Buildings
Ash/sludge pits	Buildings
Bicycle sheds	Buildings
Bund walls	Plant and equipment
Car parks	Buildings
Effluent retaining tanks	Plant and equipment
Electricity feeders	Plant and equipment
Fire fighting equipment	Furniture, fixtures and fittings
First aid equipment	Furniture, fixtures and fittings
Flagpoles	Furniture, fixtures and fittings
Foundations for plant	Plant and equipment
Fuel tanks	Plant and equipment
Gatehouse	Buildings
Generator controls	Plant and equipment
Installation of plant	Plant and equipment
Main gate	Buildings
Office furniture	Furniture, fixtures and fittings
Operator training	Plant and equipment
Perimeter fencing	Buildings
Pipe gantries	Plant and equipment
Rest rooms (male, female)	Buildings
Sewerage	Buildings
Space for religious worship	Buildings
Stand-by generators	Plant and equipment
Switchgear	Plant and equipment
Testing/commissioning materials	Plant and equipment
Turning circles	Buildings
Utility ducting (factory)	Plant and equipment
Utility ducting (offices)	Buildings
Warehouse racking	Furniture, fixtures and fittings
Water header tank	Plant and equipment
Water intake controls	Plant and equipment
Weighbridge	Plant and equipment
Yard lighting	Furniture, fixtures and fittings

notes. Subject to these tests, the classification suggested for some common items is shown in Figure 4.1.

Putting an item in a class entails assigning it the depreciable life which is used for that class; if that life is inappropriate, another class should be considered. Included in this figure are a number of items which are commonly omitted altogether by inadvertence, leading to ex-post overspending when the omission is discovered. Figure 4.1 therefore doubles as a check-list, to which readers can add from their own experiences.

REPLACEMENTS

Since fixed assets have different lives, the following will be true:

1 The life of the entire project is considered to be that of the principal asset.
2 Some assets will have a residual value after the project ends.
3 Some assets will terminate before the project ends and will probably have to be replaced, perhaps repeatedly, so long as the principal asset continues to function. Examples of relatively short-lived assets are vehicles, which it may be wise to dispose of after five years or even earlier. Heavy trucks are often planned to be disposed off after three years which is approximately the time at which a new gearbox might be needed.

Suppose a project will have its construction phase in a single year, which by convention we call Year 0, followed by an operating phase of twenty years, which is the life of the major item of machinery, in the plant and equipment category. Some motor cars are required; these will have an original cost of 22,000 and a residual value of 2,000 (we are assuming no inflation) after a depreciable life of four years. The annual depreciation of the cars will therefore be 5,000. Clearly the replacements have to be slotted into the ex-ante balance sheets on a four-year cycle.

The initial fleet of cars is bought in Year 0 along with everything else. The convention is to capitalise all the fixed assets as at the last day of Year 0, but with no depreciation during Year 0. For the main machinery, this is followed by twenty instalments of depreciation so that the balance sheet as at the end of Year 20 shows provisions for depreciation equal to the original cost and NBV is therefore nil. What about the cars? If we buy them in Year 0 and thereafter at four-yearly intervals, the first set will be in use during Years 1, 2, 3 and 4 and will be ready for disposal at the beginning of Year 5. Meanwhile the first replacement will on the fourth anniversary of the original purchase, towards the end of Year 4. Subsequent replacements will arrive in Years 8, 12, 16 and 20.

This raises two difficulties. First, on the last day of Year 4 the balance sheet will show two sets of cars, the original set just ready for disposal and the replacement set just ready for service. The time series of successive balance sheets will show a four-yearly blip in its fixed assets at original cost; this will disturb the financing patterns and various ratios, and will not be understood. It is in fact wrong. In dealing with the depreciable life of a class of assets we do not mean to decide upon the precise disposal date of any individual asset; we are thinking of the most probable disposal date for the class. It may indeed be prudent, operationally, not to let any car go until its replacement has arrived, but it is most unlikely that this will happen to all of them at once. To remove this anomaly, two courses of action are open to the analyst: either defer all replacements, or bring forward all disposals. Deferment of replacements would mean that they would no longer appear on the fourth anniversaries of the original set; after appearing in Year 0 with no depreciation, the next set of cars would show up in Year 5 with a full year's depreciation. No set of cars other than the first would ever appear in a balance sheet at its full NBV. This too produces blips and disturbances. We are therefore compelled to bring forward the disposals. What this means is that, although the cars are in service for a full four years, they cease to be the property of the enterprise at the last moment of the fourth year, and drop out of the balance sheet.

Whether in fact we have to pay for the replacements before being paid for the disposals depends on credit arrangements and whether the old cars are traded in against the new ones. There may indeed be a financing blip when old and new must be financed simultaneously, but since this is unlikely to hit the year-end for one pair of cars, and extremely unlikely for the whole fleet, it is better not to plan for that. Therefore, we normally assume that the cash proceeds of the disposal appear in the year of the disposal, and we do *not* need to carry them over as sundry debtors. This is a case where the accounting principle of prudence can be applied, not by assuming an extremely pessimistic coincidence of timings, but by providing a reasonable amount of stand-by credit in the form of bank facilities, probably unused. It contrasts with the recommended treatment of the disposal of the main machinery at the end of its twenty-year operating life, which it would be imprudent to assume will produce any cash from buyers (scrap merchants, auctioneers or whatever) until the twenty-first year.

The second problem is that of the final set of replacements, which on the regular fourth anniversary will arrive during the twentieth year of the project, ready to go into service just as the project ends. This may seem unrealistic. To solve this problem we have to return to the decision which preferably should be made early in the analysis as to how and why the project is deemed to terminate – whether at midnight without pain or by winding up and liquidation over a period of time in the hands of lawyers and auctioneers.

If the activity stemming from the investment under consideration will be of indefinite duration, so that the termination of this project at the end of the life of the principal fixed asset is an arbitrary arithmetical cut-off rather than a realistic hypothesis, it makes sense to visualise the project in its final condition as a *going concern* ready to continue further. Such a going concern could quite well have just purchased new cars ready for service. This is, in fact, the justification for not bothering with auction fees and other costs of liquidation in the final cash flow statement. Such treatment is common with agricultural   projects.

By contrast, for industrial projects, because the duration of the benefits is finite, and because each investment project comes up for judgement on its own, with no commitment as to subsequent projects, so the convention is to visualise some sort of managed halt at the end of the operating period, followed by an orderly liquidation of assets and liabilities. In virtually every case the last year of operation is a full year, unaffected by the impending managed halt, a full year with no progressive run-down. That may mean that replacement fixed assets should be added during that final year, but not at the last moment. If a replacement falls due near the end of the final operating year, the logical corollary is not to introduce that final replacement at all.

Where the project life is not an exact multiple of the replacement period of minor assets, there could well be some one-year-old or two-years-old assets at the end. These are assumed to be disposed of at their NBV values, with cash proceeds timed according to what is conceived to be the nature of the termination.

Projects where an authentic liquidation is envisaged with a liquidation phase after the operating period are numerous. These include cases where the boundary created by the project life – twenty operating years, in our example – is an uncertain, arbitrary and artificial one. The difficulty in being precise as to the timing of the termination should not alter your decision about the nature and treatment of the termination.

INTANGIBLE FIXED ASSETS

Intangible assets have no physical existence and cannot be verified by stock-taking. The justification for capitalising and amortising them instead of expensing them when the cost is incurred is that they will provide a flow of benefits over more than one year. This implies that they are robust and unlikely to suffer a cancellation of the expected benefits because of changing commercial circumstances. In the precarious economic and military circumstances of some LDCs, such capitalisations are rarely justifiable.

Examples of intangible assets are as follows:

1 Purchased goodwill – the price paid for buying another business, minus the values of its individual assets (net of liabilities) which are treated specifically. This is considered a justifiable expense because of its future income stream. In the case of a holding company, goodwill can arise in the consolidation of the group accounts. However, *inherent* goodwill, which attempts to inflate the balance sheet unilaterally by putting a subjective value on future earning potential, should be avoided (notwithstanding the example to the contrary in Arthur Daley's accounts).
2 Deferred development expenditure – the accumulated costs of development work (other than fixed assets) which is technically related to specific development objectives likely to produce an income stream over some future years, on a prudent view.
3 Patents, copyrights and trade marks, the use of which is likely to produce an income stream over some future years, on a prudent view. These may include sums paid for concessions and licences which give one the right to use the patents etc. of others, where such right extends over a period of

years, or sums spent on developing and registering one's own patents etc. Note that initial registration is often followed by quite heavy annual fees to lawyers for maintaining and defending one's registrations, particularly on a world-wide basis, so it cannot be expected that all the legal cost of protecting new developments can be capitalised.

The cost of such assets must be reasonable. The life of the amortisation should be a prudent assessment of the life of the benefits. Both cost and life should be treated with due regard for consistency. This means that it is not legitimate to treat an item as expense if the project 'can afford it' in the year concerned but as a fixed asset otherwise.

Chapter 5

Balance sheets: current assets and liabilities

Here we are dealing with minor items, in the sense that (a) current assets are usually smaller in value than fixed assets at original cost, (b) current liabilities are usually smaller than long-term liabilities when borrowing is at its peak, and (c) working capital being current assets minus current liabilities is smaller still and might even be negative. However, minor items can give the analyst major problems of estimation, and the persistent under-estimation of working capital – and therefore of the long-term money required to finance it – is a serious cause of project failure and probably more serious than under-estimation of fixed asset requirements.

COMPONENTS

Current assets consist typically of the following:

- Cash. This includes 'cash in hand' which is notes and coins in the possession of cashiers or petty cashiers, in cash registers, safes, and in transit between branches; it also includes 'cash at bank' which has been deposited in banks but is withdrawable on demand. In ex-ante work these two are not distinguishable and we treat them as one (we disdain the Arthur Daley approach, 'Demand cash from them, but always give them a cheque'). A few specialised projects also require funds which are close substitutes for cash, e.g. foreign money, travellers' cheques, gold, etc.
- Short-term investments. These might include Treasury Bills, and money placed in time deposits with banks, where a temporary surplus of cash can profitably be made to yield interest. However, because ex-ante work is normally done in whole years, and the precision required to forecast short-term investible surpluses is lacking, this category is conventionally ignored – except for projects in the banking and finance sector itself, where short-term investments are of vital importance in meeting the legal requirements of prudential legislation.
- Debtors (or in the USA, accounts receivable, or receivables). If some or all of the project output is sold to customers who are allowed time to pay,

these customers are debtors. Giving credit to customers is a commercial decision and must be consistent with the overall marketing strategy of the investment proposal. In preparing the ex-ante balance sheet at the end of each year, debtors can be calculated from the average time allowed, known as the *average credit period for debtors*, multiplied by the value of sales on credit during the credit period immediately before. Note that debtors include both deliberately allowed debts and overdue debts; thus the average credit period is longer than the policy-allowed credit period. In accordance with the accounting principle of prudence, it is also usual to foresee that some debtors will never pay. The way to make this provision is to reduce the value of debtors in each balance sheet by an appropriate percentage depending on the characteristics of the type of customer in the market concerned. The expense of creating this *provision for bad and doubtful debts* in the balance sheet must be shown as a loss item in the income statement and as a reduction of receipts in the cash flow statement, to avoid inconsistency. Note that *bad debts written off* is a slightly different concept requiring identification of specific debtors by name, ex-post. These write-offs may exceed the provisions and cause further losses, if the provisions are inadequate, but this is not applicable in ex-ante work, where it would be absurd to make provisions and at the same time suppose them to be wrong; so we assume that write-offs are equal to provisions, and the latter have to be re-created each time. Debtors can then be shown net of provisions for bad and doubtful debts.

- Stocks (or in the USA, inventories) are expressed at cost, without profit, since profit is not deemed to arise until sale occurs (on this point accounting practice rests on some controversial philosophical assumptions which we need not discuss here). Cost means historical cost, what it actually will cost to purchase or to make the goods in question. Since there are various accounting methods in use for measuring the cost of stock, all acceptable but giving different answers, the ex-ante analyst will have to decide which method to use. In LDCs, the first in first out (FIFO) method is far more common than either the last in first out (LIFO) or the average cost method (AVCO), and for work in progress or finished goods stock it is common to include only direct costs with no absorption of overheads in stock values. In general, ex-post stocks are valued judgementally with a view to tax avoidance; this produces inconsistent treatments, but in ex-ante work, all year-ends should be treated alike. On the other hand, inconsistency as between classes of stock (raw materials, fuels and consumables, possibly office and janitorial supplies, work in progress or in process, and finished goods) is permissible where reasons can be adduced.

- Prepayments and deposits. An example of a prepayment very commonly found is the telephone rental. Telephones are normally paid for on the basis of a quarterly rental in advance (plus specific usage in arrear). Unless the date of the advance payment happens to fall immediately after the end of the financial year, each year-end balance sheet should include as a current asset that part of the most recent quarterly instalment which pays for a rental period in the following year. Similarly with other utilities such as telex, electricity and water, and annual vehicle licences. Although these items can be quite sizable, they are impossible to predict unless you know (a) the usual arrangements of the utility undertakings and vehicle licensing authorities, (b) the date of the financial year, and (c) the start date of the rental agreements or vehicle licences. When project timing is not tied down, these items can be ignored, or a nominal sum inserted. On the other hand, where customs or other government regulations require deposits or downpayments for access to necessary supplies regardless of timing, these ought to be calculated more carefully. Note that downpayments and progress payments for the purchase of fixed assets are to be treated as fixed assets (capital work in progress) rather than as current assets.

Current liabilities normally consist of the following:

- Trade creditors (or in the USA, accounts payable, or trade payables) are suppliers who have supplied goods or services in the normal course of trade but have not yet been paid. It may be expected that some of the major items of raw materials used will be bought on credit, and an *average credit period for suppliers* can be assumed. Items of expense, such as utilities, as well as materials, may be involved. Note that the volume of trade credit depends on the average credit period and on the value of the relevant amounts *purchased* (not consumed, nor embodied in cost of sales) during the most recent credit period.
- Other creditors, i.e. non-trade creditors, include suppliers of fixed assets on credit not yet paid; employees entitled to holidays with pay not yet taken; shareholders for whom a dividend has been set aside but not yet mailed; and Government, when there has been a year of profit-making on which tax is due but has not yet been paid ('current taxation').
- Short-term debt which may be owing to banks or other financial institutions. Bank overdrafts, which are demand deposits temporarily drawn down so their balances are negative, may continue over several years but the bank has the right to terminate them at any time, so they are technically short-term. This arrangement is characteristic of banking systems influenced by British practice. Elsewhere, short-term borrowing is recorded in accounts opened separately from the usual customer accounts.
- The current portion of long-term debt is that part of a long- or medium-term debt which, at the date of any particular balance sheet, will fall due for payment before the date of the next balance sheet a year later. This may comprise one or more instalments depending on whether they are payable annually or at shorter intervals. This amount is entered in the current liabilities section of the balance sheet and deducted from the long-term liabilities section at the same time. It has the effect of reducing

the net current assets (working capital) and therefore affects certain ratios. Without this adjustment, those ratios would not be comparable with similar ratios elsewhere, and in particular the ratio of current assets to current liabilities would be overstated contrary to the principle of prudence.

- Prepayments and deposits received. This is the converse of prepayments and deposits paid. It is of particular interest to utility undertakings. It sometimes occurs in LDCs that difficulties of supply create a sellers' market in ordinary goods to such an extent that distributors and major customers can be made to give payments in advance, but this is rarely or never the intended commercial strategy at the ex-ante stage.

ESTIMATION OF STOCKS

Investment proposals to create goods for sale, as opposed to services, will require careful attention to stock levels (inventories). It is usually best to work backwards from finished goods stock to raw material stock, passing through work in progress (partly finished product) and then looking at consumables separately.

The finished goods stock is the cost of that volume of product which, at the end of a year, is ready for sale but not yet sold. It is rare that customers snatch your product straight off the production line; even if supply cannot keep pace with demand, there are likely to be some goods in the dispatch bay being batched up for transportation, or in a showroom for future customers to examine. Very often, there is also a quantity of stock simply waiting to be sold, and the ready availability of stock which might be wanted in a hurry is itself an important advantage from the customer's point of view, which a rival supplier might not offer.

However, too large a stock is pointless and wasteful; interest expense is incurred in financing the stock and in financing its storage facilities; insurance and watchkeeping costs are also involved. The optimum amount of stock to hold is therefore a matter of striking the right balance. Sales personnel are likely to press for large stocks to be kept; finance managers may prefer small stocks; while production and personnel managers may have a preference for keeping the level of production constant in the face of fluctuations in demand, which implies sharply fluctuating stocks. Commercial policy on this point is therefore to be decided by *general* management. It is difficult for the ex-ante analyst to generate the kind of discussion which would produce a balanced decision, before the project management is brought into existence. A common sense approach, remembering the principle of prudence – which in this case means tending towards *large* stocks – is required, having regard to the nature of customer demand, the keeping qualities of the product, and the pricing policy. It is important also to check that the maximum (as opposed to year-end) stock-holding is compatible with the provision of storage facilities under the heading of fixed assets. This does *not* mean that the former should always be adjusted to the latter.

Having decided upon the desired level of finished goods stock at the end of a normal operating year, it is next necessary to decide over how many years of production stocks will be built up to that level. The following possibilities exist and a choice must be made:

- The 'sell-out point' occurs exactly at the end of Year 1. Thereafter, output is limited by production (demand is limited by supply) and will be constant from year to year. In that case, only Year 1 is available for producing the initial stock. It is necessary to check that production capacity in Year 1 is adequate.
- Sell-out occurs before the end of Year 1. In that case the initial stockbuild must take place in a matter of months. Again it is necessary to check whether this is consistent with production capacity.
- Sell-out occurs during Year 2 or later. In that case the volume of sales taking place at around the end of Year 1 will be less than the full volume achieved later, and it is necessary to consider whether the stock of finished goods which it is desirable to hold at that time should also be less than that which will be held later. In other words, if finished goods stock is determined as so many weeks' sales, and sales are still rising, it will take more than one year-end before the stocks reach their final level. During more than one year, therefore, production must suffice for both stockbuild and sales.

Having thereby determined the annual volumes of production, a calculation may be made for the value of unfinished goods (work in progress or in process) at the end of each year. With certain foodstuffs, e.g. ice-cream, it may be a wise policy not to start any batch which will result in unfinished product being left overnight. By contrast, with non-perishables made in large batches, such as ball bearings, the value of work in progress at any time might vary from almost nothing to almost the full value of a finished batch. In such a case, it is reasonable to assume that on the last day of the financial year, *half* the value of a finished batch will be lying in bins on the workshop floor. In chemical manufacture, where the work in process may be solid, liquid, or gaseous, its volume and therefore its value will depend on the volume of the storage tanks and pipes and on the pressures; this in turn will depend on the process calculations, and sometimes on the hazards of storing dangerous intermediate products, which should never be stored in larger quantities than permitted by safety considerations.

The volume of production of both finished and unfinished goods each year provides a means of calculating the quantity of raw materials consumed – here we rely on the technical coefficients or standard usages relating inputs to outputs. This would be in a spreadsheet at the front-end of the sequence of spreadsheets, supporting the income statement. Having so determined the consumption of the main (or direct) raw materials, we can take a decision on the desirable stock levels of the latter.

In highly organised, wealthy economies one can plan ahead carefully and order new supplies of raw materials to arrive just before they are needed. They may not have far to come, since in such economies there are likely to be many suitable suppliers. This allows stock to be kept low. Such stocks are known as 'just-in-time stocks' and a similar policy may be applied to work in process and to finished goods stock. However, in LDCs, raw materials may have to be imported, and this will require possibly joining a queue for import licences or for foreign exchange. Applications for these may be refused at first, and delayed for months or even years. The time for inward transportation, including finding a ship taking the right route, customs clearance, and inland forwarding may also be unpredictable. Transport routes may be fired upon or be washed away by tropical rain. Naturally, any break in the availability of raw materials will bring production to a halt, as soon as stocks of raw materials have been used up. It is therefore normal to plan for several weeks' stocks to be held, especially in non-liberalised economies and in remote locations.

ESTIMATION OF CASH REQUIREMENT

When speaking of cash required, we have in mind those working balances of cash without which cashiers and petty cashiers cannot operate comfortably in the offices and retail outlets of an enterprise. Such cash fluctuates from minute to minute, but should never fall to zero, which would impede transactions and damage business confidence. In practice, cashiers are usually given initial sums (imprests) which they can spend; when takings exceed the fixed levels, the surplus is banked; when holdings fall short of the imprests, cashiers are required to explain and justify the outgoings and are then permitted to draw a reimbursement. The actual cash in working balances at any moment may be higher or lower than the total of the imprests, but will constantly tend back towards that total by virtue of these repeated settlements. It would seem sensible for the analyst to fix the required cash at that total, if only it were known, but in practice it is fixed by trial and error.

The convention which is mostly followed to estimate the required cash ex-ante is to work out how much will be the monthly expenditure in cash (this is operating cost minus depreciation and other provisions), subtract the monthly cash receipts from sales, and add an adjustment to be on the safe side. This adjustment for prudence may be to ignore the cash receipts entirely, so that cashiers can keep going for one month no matter what. In some situations (where receipts are reasonably continuous) one month may be too conservative. In other situations (where seasonal payments to suspicious small-holders are payable and must be seen to be payable) it may be too small.

Data-rich situations provide greater levels of sophistication. The 'required cash' is not strictly the *average* of the hourly fluctuations in working cash holdings which may be anticipated; that would be too small. It certainly is not the *worst* position which might arise; that would be zero. Nor is it the *best* position, i.e. the highest level which would be needed prior to the most serious fall (to zero); that would be too conservative, since it takes no account at all of management's ability to mitigate the problem. In principle it is the mean level plus some multiple of the *standard deviation*, where a large multiple would be needed if management was helpless to mitigate, and a small multiple if remedial action will be prompt and effective. Data on the standard deviation are almost certain to be lacking.

An example using standard deviation was quoted recently by Kelly Conatser (1991: 23). The technique originated in some US universities who raided the long-suffering Greek alphabet to name it the Lambda Index. Conatser gives details of a spreadsheet model of a hotel, experiencing seasonal variations in demand, and the figures are given monthly. The available cash at the end of any month is the cash at the beginning, plus the cash flow during the month, plus any unused short-term borrowing facility. This fluctuates from month to month, and for any given month you can calculate the cumulative degree of fluctuation (standard deviation) from the beginning of the year up to that point. The available cash divided by the standard deviation is the Lambda Index for the month. An index of 15 or more is considered really safe; below 2 is in serious trouble. The technique is proposed to be used (alongside others) by a cautious credit controller providing trade credit to the hotel and obtaining ex-post data for prior months from the hotel management.

Before transferring this more sophisticated technique to ex-ante LDC situations one must beware. First, most LDC spreadsheets are not monthly but annual. After the first few years all years are the same (apart from inflation) and there is no standard deviation visible. Second, if monthly or quarterly figures are to be used instead, to reflect *directly* the seasonal pattern which is certainly very important, data from an existing hotel chain are probably needed. It is this very lack of existing business which is at the heart of the data problem in LDCs. Of course, if there is no objection to multi-national investment, one of the big hotel chains can conduct its own financial analysis. Third, given proper cash management, what is important is not the *planned* variation from month to month but the possibility of actual cash movements deviating from the plan. The Lambda Index when used for ex-ante planning in effect uses the former as a close approximation to the latter, and to me there seems no valid basis to believe this.

These three caveats do rather rule out the sophisticated methods of forecasting required cash and so justify the crude adjustments recommended above.

It is important not to confuse this cash required with the surplus cash, or extra cash, which a successful commercial project will generate, because its outputs realise more money than its inputs cost, and which eventually the owners can appropriate. Surplus cash is good news; required cash is bad news.

TREATMENT OF SURPLUS CASH

With a commercial project, the 'net cash flow' whereby the project produces a stream of cash which is surplus to its own requirements and can be given out to its owners is not merely important: it is the whole purpose of the exercise. We shall see its pre-eminent position in cash flow statements later. First let us see how it affects balance sheets, and how it appears in the closely related income statements including the appropriation accounts.

We will assume a limited liability company with ordinary shareholders, which has undertaken a successful commercial project. After an initial period of build-up to the sell-out point, a net profit after tax is made. There is no bank overdraft or other short-term borrowing. The directors, appointed by the shareholders, meet together before the Annual General Meeting and decide how much dividend, if any, is to be proposed. This proposed dividend, if the motion is accepted as it virtually always is, will be mailed out in the form of cheques shortly after the Annual General Meeting has voted – some six weeks after the end of the financial year in which the profit was earned. For this purpose there must be sufficient cash in the bank at the time the proposal is formulated to meet the cheques, and this cash must be set aside. In ex-ante work, a common formula used is that dividend will be 100 per cent of the amount of profit after tax, or the existing amount of cash at the year-end minus the required cash, whichever is less.

In some cases analysts substitute 80 per cent or 75 per cent of the profit instead of 100 per cent, thus presuming that the directors will want to keep some retained earnings in the company; this is a more realistic assumption. Retained earnings kept in reserve in this way are usually intended to be spent later, to buy new fixed assets or to replace old fixed assets. In principle, the analyst can foresee the need for replacing old fixed assets and to regulate the dividend flow accordingly, but in practice, reserves are more likely to be devoted to new assets which are essentially new projects. These are unforeseeable at the start of the project currently under review, even though they may be undertaken within the same business area and constitute a logical growth pattern.

We are speaking here of an analyst guessing, or assuming, what dividend policy will be chosen by a Board of Directors, probably not yet appointed, when they face up to some genuine options. The reserves in question are *distributable* reserves, and can be paid out later instead of being spent on their original purpose, if the directors change their minds. They are legally the property of the shareholders even if not distributed.

In short, the analyst is compelled to choose between a dividend policy which pays out 100 per cent of the profits (subject to the year-end cash constraint) and some smaller, arbitrary but more realistic percentage. If the former course is chosen, no surplus cash will accumulate in the balance sheet. If the latter, it will, and we have a presentation problem with our financial statements. In the cash flow statement, it matters little, since both dividends and surplus cash are regarded as accruing to shareholders.

The presentation problem in the balance sheet arises from the fact that, although some retention of profit is realistic, its retention in the form of *uninvested cash* is not. As already mentioned, it is most likely to be spent on the fixed assets of other projects, which we cannot identify and even if we could ought not to appear in the balance sheets of this project now. Until that expenditure occurs, it may be invested in short-term securities, which can earn interest, unlike 'idle cash'. Again, any such interest is outside the scope of our present project. We are left with a notional quantity of cash in our ex-ante project balance sheets, which has no counterpart in ex-post reality. It will never be seen in real balance sheets and there is no rubric or heading under which it conventionally appears. Hence the presentation problem.

Rather than adding this surplus cash to the required cash line among the current assets, it is better to consider it as a separate line:

- Cash (required) ... R
- Cash (surplus) ... <u>S</u>

- Cash (total) ... T

BALANCING THE BALANCE SHEET WITH SURPLUS CASH

Suppose the profit after tax in the year 1995 is 100, and the dividend policy is to pay out 75 per cent. This leaves 25 per cent to pay out for retained earnings. In the capital section of the balance sheet, shareholders' funds rise by 25 per cent from their 1994 figure. It will then be found that the capital employed, including shareholders' funds, is more than enough to finance the net assets utilised including only *required* cash. The imbalance will be 25 per cent, of course. We must now insert the surplus cash somewhere to achieve the balance. One possibility is to insert it immediately below required cash, as shown above; this seems a neat solution, but unfortunately the surplus cash then enters into working capital (which over the years then inflates like a balloon for no good reason) and into net assets utilised which seems wrong since this notional idle cash is clearly not utilised in this project at all. A better alternative is to introduce the surplus cash as a separate asset category altogether:

- Net assets utilised ... X
- Surplus cash ... <u>Y</u>

- Total ... Z
- Represented by:
    capital employed ... Z

This has the merit of clarity. A third alternative would be to show surplus cash as a deduction from capital employed, in effect to net it out from both the assets and liability sides of the balance sheet; that would produce the same result as the assumption of a 100 per cent dividend payout, or rather, it would make the additional assumption that all retained earnings were spent on the purposes for which they were reserved:

- Net assets utilised ... $\underline{\underline{X}}$
- Represented by:
   shareholders' funds
   and long-term debt   Z

less:

- Cash reserves $\underline{Y}$

- Capital employed $\underline{\underline{X}}$

This procedure seems to make up in elegance what it lacks in intelligibility. It cannot be said that there exists any established universal convention on this point, and the analyst should check whether there is any established practice locally.

CASH POSITION MUST NOT BE NEGATIVE

In all three methods we then have to check that the surplus cash is positive; if not, the dividend must be reduced or cancelled. That is to say, whatever dividend is declared at the end of any year must not exceed the surplus cash (before dividend) shown in the balance sheet at the end of that year. As we shall see, there is an equivalent condition imposed on the cash flow statement, and it may be easier to determine the dividend by working out the cash flows and filling in the balance sheets later.

We have assumed that there is no bank overdraft or current debt of similar kind. If there is, it may be sensible to pay off that debt in preference to distributing a dividend. There are many projects where cash flow problems in the early years require the borrowing of funds which, because of heavy surpluses in later years, it is undesirable to take in as long-term debt or equity. Such borrowings typically carry fairly heavy interest rates, because of the risks involved, and as soon as cash becomes available to pay them off, this should be done. Analysts therefore often modify their dividend policy formula so that no dividend is paid until all short-term borrowings have been cleared.

An alternative approach is to make an assumption, not as to the policy of the short-term borrower, but as to what the short-term lender may insist on. We could assume, for instance, that at the end of each financial year the lender will insist that at least 50 per cent (say) of the otherwise surplus funds (if any) will be applied to reduction of debt. A variant of this, easier to calculate, is that if at any year-end surplus funds have been amassed, then at least 50 per cent of them will be applied to debt reduction in the following year. Either way, the debt reduction is achieved by reducing dividend, increasing shareholders' funds, and balancing this by an increase in working capital. Since short-term debt is a current liability, its reduction is an increase in working capital.

We are assuming here too that the long-term debt has fixed repayment dates, so there is no question of adjusting dividend with a view to reducing long-term debt. If that too were discretionary, we would have to make up a complex formula or algorithm which would give *priorities* to maintaining adequate cash, short-term debt reduction, long-term debt reduction, and a percentage of whatever was left being distributed as dividend, probably in that order.

It sometimes happens that the repayment dates of the long-term debt are not yet known to the analyst; the total loan period, and the initial grace period, are perhaps still negotiable. The financial analyst may be called upon to propose what terms would be reasonable and should be sought by negotiation. If the analyst seeks to make the spreadsheet itself calculate the loan parameters, so that loan repayment depends on dividend instead of the reverse, care must be taken not to produce a circular argument, the resolution of which would be impossibly complex. It is more convenient to have the loan parameters as inputs of data rather than as outputs of results, but to experiment with different values of them. In doing this, care should be taken to arrange a loan which will be suitable under inflationary conditions, even though the base case or first pass of the spreadsheet may be in fixed prices.

CIRCULARITIES

Facts do not always suit the analyst's convenience, however. Given the general logic that profits are used to pay off debts, and some formula must be put into spreadsheet calculations whereby the available profits (among other things) determine the levels of debts, it is a very inconvenient fact that debts in their turn determine profits, in that a higher level of debt means the payment of more interest expense, which in turn (after tax relief if any) means less net profit.

The chain of causation is as follows:

1 Reduction of debt as prioritised.
2 Revised debt figures.
3 Interest and
    3a tax.
4 Net profit
    4a of which a percentage is distributed.
5 Retained earnings adding to shareholders' funds.
6 Capital employed exceeds net assets utilised.
1 Reduction of debt as prioritised.

In order to break this circular argument we have to disconnect Step 3 from Step 2. This is a matter of timing. Assuming that the ex-ante balance sheets are being worked out on a yearly basis, debt is expressed as the balance owing at the end of each year. Interest is expressed in the income statement as the amount accrued (or paid) on the balances throughout the year on a daily basis. In effect we have 365 daily balances of debt, of which only two are known, that at the very end of the year and that at the very beginning (i.e. at the close of the previous year). Two is a small sample of 365, though better than one! If we take the mean of the two as representative, and calculate the interest on that basis, then the year-end debt does enter into the calculation of the year's interest, Step 3 follows from Step 2, and we have a circularity. If you are using a computer spreadsheet, the computer may beep, or show a small warning symbol on the screen (usually CIRC, C, ! or @).

Algebraically what we have here is a set of simultaneous equations. Most spreadsheets are not programmed to solve simultaneous equations, though a few are, such as MasterPlanner. This is not a satisfactory situation. You can work your way round and round the loop several times by 'editing' each number in turn, but so long as the warning symbol remains, you cannot be sure that anything on the screen is correct. The symbol could conceal some other circularity as well.

It is rather easier without a computer; you work round and round with a 2B pencil and a good eraser, always erring on the prudent side by rounding up the interest, until you have a hole in the paper, or until the numbers are fully self-consistent, within a reasonable margin of error. In the case of interest, this margin can be quite broad, because of the nature of the beast, when we are trying to use two observations as a representative sample of 365.

One way to cut the Gordian knot is to base the interest calculation solely on the balance outstanding from the previous year. This reduces the size of the sample from two to one. When interest is declining, the use of the earlier figure rather than the mean of the two gives a higher figure for interest which errs on the prudent side. This method of estimation is used, among others, by World Bank computer models. Naturally it gives a more accurate result if quarterly rather than yearly projections are made, and in commercial work this is probably the best scheme of all.

Chapter 6

Cash flow

In this chapter we discuss how to predict ex-ante the cash flow, or its close relative the funds flow, which will result from a proposed investment. It is necessary first to discuss some theoretical aspects of cash flow. Regrettably, the theory has its origins in the context of ex-post accounting, that is to say, in the derivation of cash flow statements from data contained in existing books of account rather than from data about the external environment in which the project will operate. The existing books of account reflect past transactions, each account being used to summarise transactions of a certain nature or with certain external parties. These accounts are likely to be held in *books*: a general ledger and a cash book, the latter covering cash and bank transactions. At each year-end these are summarised into an income statement (including an appropriation account) and a balance sheet.

From these last two documents, with the help of a few supplementary details from the ledger and the cash book, a cash flow statement can be drawn up. It does not involve any new transactions or any new entries to existing accounts; it is an extension of the classic double-entry system, which terminated with the balance sheet.

DERIVATION OF CASH FLOW FROM SUCCESSIVE BALANCE SHEETS

Table 6.1 illustrates how the balance sheets at two successive year-ends can be used to deduce what cash movements must have occurred during the year. Without supplementary information from the income statement of the year in question and from more detailed sources, the results are crude.

Two things are noteworthy here: (1) the third column balances, because it is derived from the differences between the first two columns which themselves balance; (2) cash movements have been denoted as positive (+) when cash is gained in exchange for an asset lost, and as negative (−) when cash goes out, as when an asset is purchased (or a liability discharged).

The results in the third column, though arithmetically unchallengeable, are not very enlightening. If we re-arrange the third column so that cash balances

Table 6.1 Crude ex-post derivation of cash flow

	Successive balance sheets		Deduced cash
	end-1985	end-1986	flow during 1986
Fixed assets:			
net (NBV)	600	500	+ 100
Current assets:			
Cash	50	160	−110
Stocks etc.	250	270	−20
Less:			
Current liabilities	−165	−175	+ 10
NET ASSETS UTILISED	735	755	−20
Represented by:			
Share capital	400	450	+ 50
Retained earnings	135	155	+ 20
Sub-total, shareholders' funds	535	605	+ 70
Long-term debt	200	150	−50
CAPITAL EMPLOYED	735	755	+ 20

Table 6.2 Restatement of crude cash flow

	Deduced cash flow during 1986
Cash movement	−110
Caused by changes in:	
Fixed assets:	
net (NBV)	+100
Current assets:	
Stocks etc.	−20
Less:	
Current liabilities	+ 10
Share capital	+ 50
Retained earnings	+ 20
Long-term debt	−50
	+110

against everything else as in Table 6.2 we arrive at a presentation where the basic concept is that the net movement in cash is explained as having been caused by the net inflows and outflows produced by all the other transactions.

In Table 6.2 we can see already that the cash balance has risen principally because of the fall in value of fixed assets. This fall in value is due to depreciation, and also perhaps to disposals of fixed assets, offset by the purchase of new assets, if any. We cannot see here exactly how much was

Table 6.3 Sources and uses of cash (ex-post)

	Deduced cash flow during 1986	
Cash at start	50	
Cash at close	160	
Cash movement		−110
Caused by:		
Net profit		+ 100
Fixed assets:		
Depreciation	+ 70	
Disposals	+ 50	
Purchases	−20	
net (NBV)		+ 100
Reduction in		
current liabilities		+ 10
Share capital		+ 50
TOTAL SOURCES		+ 260
Fall in stocks etc.		−20
Dividends		−80
Long-term debt		−50
TOTAL USES		−150

attributable to each of these three causes, since the movement (−100) is simply in the net book value, which combines these three items. However, the depreciation expense can be found in the income statement, and the other two can be found in the general ledger, which helps to fill out the picture.

Similarly, the cash inflow of +20 shown as a rise of retained earnings is a combination of net profit (inflow) and proposed dividends (outflow); these details can be found in the appropriation account. Likewise the item 'Stocks etc.' may conceal a rise in one class of stock, a fall in another, a rise in debtors, and perhaps a fall in prepayments: supplementary information is required to separate these, if the results are worthwhile. Sometimes a small combined figure may be the net of dramatic and important individual figures, in which case detailed presentation is clearly worthwhile.

In Table 6.3, some additional detail has been included, so the results are not so crude, and the table has been further restructured so that all the causes of inflow (sources of cash) are listed above the causes of outflow (uses of cash).

In this example, the net profit was 100 but the net cash flow was 110. It is common among inexperienced business people to suppose that profit is the same as net cash flow. Net profit, of course, is the surplus of revenues over costs and taxes, while net cash flow is the surplus of money coming in over money going out. Revenue does not necessarily bring money in *at the time*, since sales may be on credit, while costs do not necessarily expend cash at the time, since purchases may be on credit, or may procure stock which is not used up during the period and remains as an asset at the end.

Hence the net profit in any year differs from the net cash flow in the same year. Over the entire life of the project, if timing could be disregarded, the two would indeed be identical. But timing cannot be disregarded; that is why we have an income statement to show the profit over each year as well as a cash flow statement (or similar) to show the cash flow over every year. The former is required by law in the ex-post accounts, mainly for taxation, but the latter is at least as important in appraisal work so that we will have a time-series of cash flows for discounting and thereby arrive at various measures of project worth.

In ex-ante work we are not limited to deriving figures from pairs of successive balance sheets; we have access to all the project data and assumptions from which the projected balance sheets themselves are also derived. We can therefore make cash flow statements in much greater detail than is shown in Table 6.3. We must split net profit into profit before tax, and tax. Profit before tax must be split into revenue, costs and interest. Revenue can be split into cash sales and sales on credit, where appropriate and costs, taken together with stockbuild, can be split into purchases for cash and purchases on credit. The current assets (simply 'Stocks etc.' in Table 6.3) must be subdivided to show stocks, debtors and perhaps prepayments separately; likewise current liabilities should be divided to show trade creditors separately.

With these details, we can rearrange the structure of the statement, according to the particular format we wish to produce. These alternative formats are all essentially rearrangements of the cash flow statement and follow the logic which has been traced in the tables above. The possibility of different formats, and the need for the analyst to choose among them, arises for the following reasons:

- If sales are all on credit and amount to 500, and trade debtors rise by 10, the cash flow of receipts from sales is 490 during the period. We may either show the 490 as a single source of cash, or we may wish to show 500 as a source and 10 as a use of cash. This depends on whether the trade debtors are grouped with the sales or in working capital along with other debtors and creditors. The former puts the stress on cash collections and does not highlight sales as such; the latter highlights sales but also highlights working capital as a generic concept. A similar pair of choices is available on the costs side.
- Items may be grouped according to (a) whether they are (in most years) sources or uses of cash, or (b) whether they are trading items (cash exchanged for goods or services) or financial items, or (c) whether they arise from routine operations or from special decisions.

- The isolation of cash from all the other transactions which purport to explain the increase or decrease in cash may not be appropriate. If the category 'cash' is widened to include near-cash assets such as travellers' cheques, gold and foreign currency, and perhaps bank deposits where notice of withdrawal of up to three months is required, these are 'liquid funds'. In British accounting practice and convention, rules for ex-post disclosure call for a statement of sources and applications of funds, meaning liquid funds. Such a statement shows the change in liquid funds, balanced against (and purportedly explained by) the changes in everything else. Alternatively, the 'funds' can be widened further to include the entire working capital; this is the current US practice. Here, the net increase or decrease in working capital is regarded as being explained by everything else.
- The analyst should remember that whatever ex-ante forecasts are made, the ex-post results will be compared against them, or should be, later in the project cycle. It is therefore advantageous to select a format which corresponds to that required, by law or by convention, for ex-post disclosure in the country concerned.

There are three main varieties of cash flow statement: the cash flow statement proper, in which cash is narrowly defined; the statement of sources and uses (or applications) of funds, in which funds include cash but other items also, with UK and US variants; and the analytical cash flow statement, which is specially designed for ex-ante studies.

THE CASH FLOW STATEMENT

The cash flow statement in the correct, traditional sense of the term lists all the sources of cash coming in and all the purposes of expenditure for cash going out. The balance between these inflows and outflows is the net cash flow for each time period, and the cumulative total of the net flows from the beginning of the project up to the end of any year should be equal to the final amount of cash as shown in the balance sheet at that date.

That is the kind of statement used in short-term cash flow planning by businesses which are in financial distress, and is often used for medium- and long-term financial planning by healthy businesses incorporating a series of 'projects' or major and minor investments in their corporate planning. An example is given in Table 6.4.

This layout shows what one might call 'raw' cash flows, in the sense that they are in categories such as would present themselves to a cashier directly handling them. Such categories might well be used for emergency cash flow planning under conditions of financial distress, relating closely to the commercial decisions of an enterprise in that condition. However, this layout is also quite valid for planning when not in financial distress.

Notice that 'Increase in stocks' is not shown as a cash outflow. Instead,

Table 6.4 Cash flow of ABC Ltd for the year ending 31 December 1990

	Inflow	Outflow	Net Flow
Receipts from revenue:			
Cash sales	40000		
From trade debtors,			
following sales on credit	52000		
Payments for cost of goods and			
services used in operations:			
Cash purchases		30000	
To trade creditors, following			
purchases on credit		20000	
To other creditors		13000	
Interest payments		6000	
Sub-total: cash flow from operations	92000	69000	23000
Distribution of profits:			
Dividend payments		5000	
Tax payments		3000	
Payments for purchase of fixed assets		28000	
Receipts from disposal of fixed assets	16000		
Cash receipts from new share issues	7000		
Cash receipts from new borrowings	4000		
Loan repayments		10000	
Total cash flows	119000	115000	4000
Cash at start of year		2000	
Cash at end of year		6000	
Net cash movement			4000

'Purchases' includes materials bought whether for stockbuild or for consumption. That is because a cashier when asked to write a cheque for supplies is looking at a purchase order without knowing whether the supplies will cause a net rise in stock levels over the period. If this format is used in ex-ante work, the reconciliation of purchases with stocks must appear in a separate spreadsheet, such as is sometimes entitled 'Purchases Budget'.

The grouping of the items in Table 6.4, which shows only one of the available formats, is to be understood as follows:

- Cash flow resulting from operations by management and staff (known variously as internally generated cash flow, operating cash flow, or cash flow on revenue account). 23000
- Cash flow not within jurisdiction of internal management (known usually as external cash flow): dividends, taxes, and items on capital account.
  −19000
- Net increase in cash. 4000

THE STATEMENT OF SOURCES AND APPLICATIONS OF FUNDS

The funds statement, as we call it for short, is just like the cash flow statement except that the category 'cash' is broadened. The objective here is to avoid running out of funds rather than to avoid running out of cash, since the component items of funds are largely interchangeable. Whether current assets are sufficiently liquid to be regarded as part of the funds varies from country to country (Lee 1974). In the UK, accounting prudence has prevailed; stocks and debtors are regarded with suspicion; only 'liquid funds' are usually counted as funds, and in LDC conditions where stocks and debtors can be extremely slow-moving this is clearly sensible. Since near-cash items do not arise in ex-ante work in the majority of LDC investment projects (other than new banks), a statement of liquid funds is indistinguishable from a statement of cash flow. However, in the USA, tradition has extended the concept of 'funds' to the whole of working capital, i.e. all current assets including liquid funds, minus all current liabilities (Lee 1975: 179). In an apparent attempt to harmonise the British and American conventions, the Accounting Standards Committee in the UK has endorsed a hybrid format called a statement of sources and uses of funds which is actually a statement of movements in working capital, but which includes net liquid funds shown separately (ICA 1987: 209).

This moves away from what has been mentioned as more sensible in ex-ante LDC work and so is not recommended in general. An example of this type is given in Table 6.5. It is based on the same data as Table 6.4 to allow comparison.

Here the format is designed to meet the mandatory requirements of the UK ex-post standard, in which working capital (US 'funds') is balanced against everything else, but with the movement in net liquid funds (UK 'funds') disclosed as a separate component within it. Whereas Table 6.4 emphasised the 4000 increase in cash, Table 6.5 emphasises an 11000 increase in net current assets. The explanation of the 11000 is given in terms of operational cash flow (28000) and external cash flow (–17000), a distinction which has stewardship (responsibility) connotations and is of great antiquity.

Table 6.5 is much better than Table 6.4 in the degree of detail it reveals about the liquidity and therefore the creditworthiness of the enterprise, features which are of especial concern with private sector projects taken ex-post. It has the further merit that the top line – net profit for the year – can be copied directly from the income statement; the changes in assets and liabilities which make up most of its other figures can be taken from the changes from one annual balance sheet to the next. Alternatively they can be derived from a 'working capital schedule' in the absence of proper balance sheets, which may be more convenient in ex-ante calculations of a less sophisticated   nature.

Table 6.5 Sources and uses of funds of ABC Ltd for the year ending
31 December 1990

	Sources	Uses	Net
Net profit before interest and tax	31000		
Add: depreciation	6000		
Less: interest payments		6000	
tax payments		3000	
Cash flow from operations	37000	9000	28000
Payments for purchase			
of fixed assets		28000	
Receipts from disposal			
of fixed assets	15000		
Cash receipts for new share issues	7000		
Dividend payments		5000	
New borrowings	4000		
Loan repayments		10000	
–	26000	43000	–17000
			11000
Movement in working capital			
Increase/(decrease) in stocks		2000	
Increase/(decrease) in debtors		6000	
Less: decrease/(increase) in			
trade creditors	(1000)		
Net liquid funds at start of year	2000		
Net liquid funds at end of year	6000		
Net movement in liquid funds		4000	
	(1000)	12000	11000

THE ANALYTICAL CASH FLOW STATEMENT

The analytical cash flow statement (ACF), developed at the University of
Bradford for use in LDC investment appraisal, is exclusively intended for
ex-ante work. It is not a funds flow statement in the US style but concentrates
on 'cash', which includes, without distinction, cash in hand, cash at bank, cash
substitutes such as travellers' cheques, gold and foreign currency if relevant,
but not short-term investments. It does, however, distinguish between
cashiers' working balances of cash required for the smooth operation of the
project ('required cash') and that cash which is the surplus or net yield of the
project and which may be retained in the enterprise, distributed as dividends
to shareholders, or taken out wholly or partly as drawings by partners or sole
proprietors ('surplus cash').

Table 6.6 ACF section 1: project components inputs and outputs, categorised by nature[1]

*Revenues and costs at ~~market~~/shadow prices**

Currency: Rs.Mn. ~~constant~~/current**

Year:	0	1	2	3	4
Sales					
Product A		983	1938	2977	3960
Product B		983	2116	3566	5232
Cost of sales					
Material A		−393	−828	−1366	−1959
Material B		−393	−828	−1366	−1959
Other volume-related costs					
for Product A		−153	−296	−493	−699
for Product B		−153	−296	−493	−699
Labour costs					
Unskilled	−10	−70	−91	−109	−120
Semi-skilled	−10	−140	−182	−218	−240
Skilled	−10	−140	−182	−218	−240
Expatriate	−20	−31	−47	−65	−81
Other costs					
Pre-operating expense	−20				
Operating period		−327	−502	−690	−835
SUB-TOTAL:					
OPERATING PROFIT	−70	167	802	1525	2358
(agreeing with profit before provisions, interest and tax in the income statement)					
Stocks (changes in)					
Material A	−29	−16	−23	−25	−20
Material B	−29	−16	−23	−25	−20
Product A		−44	0	0	0
Product B		−44	0	0	0
Debtors (changes in)					
Product A		−113	−110	−120	−113
Product B		−113	−131	−167	−192
Creditors (changes in)					
Material A	2	24	23	31	34
Material B	2	24	23	31	34
SUB-TOTAL:					
OPERATING CASH FLOW	−124	−131	562	1251	2080
(agreeing with operating cash flow in statement of sources and uses of funds)					

continued . . .

Year:	0	1	2	3	4
Fixed assets					
Land	–50	0	0	0	0
Buildings	–551	0	0	0	0
Furniture, fixtures and fittings	–142	0	0	0	0
Plant and equipment	–676	0	0	0	0
Installation	–36	0	0	0	0
Motor vehicles	–65	0	0	0	0
TOTAL RESOURCE FLOW (agreeing with internally generated funds in statement of sources and applications of funds)	–1644	–131	562	1251	2080

Note: * Delete what is not applicable
1 The numbers in this table have been calculated with decimal places which are not printed here. Consequently they do not appear to add up to exactly the totals shown. Similar decimal rounding errors will be found throughout the tables in Chapters 6 and 11 and in Appendix 1.

The ACF statement lists all sources of cash and uses of cash, but it treats these in two groups, viz. those transactions where cash changes hands in exchange for real resources (goods or services rendered) and all other transactions (e.g. borrowing, lending, taxing, interest, disposition of surplus cash). Thus the net cash flow is analysed into a *real resource cash flow* and a *financial cash flow*. Since the financial cash flow includes the disposition of any surplus cash, these two sub-flows must be equal (though of opposite sign). Finally, the financial cash flows are analysed into transactions with investors, lenders, Government, and other financially interested parties.

This ACF format is recommended for project work. Tables 6.4 and 6.5 were included because they represent the most common current method and so provide you with a link between what has been done in the past and what might be done if improvements are introduced.

The ACF is often best prepared in three separate parts. The first part lists all the *real resource* transactions in the detail which is likely to be required by economic analysts as data for their shadow-pricing exercise. In many cases the resource inputs and outputs will have been calculated from front-end physical computations relying on technical coefficients. The second part summarises these resource flows; this part may be omitted in a very simple project in which there are very few different inputs and outputs. The third part shows the financial flows.

In these and the following tables only the first five years of an investment project are displayed. The project is to have two output products and two input raw materials; two stocks of raw materials and two of finished products. For simplicity no stocks of work in progress are shown (see Table 6.6).

The second section of the ACF contains a summary of the first. Such a

Table 6.7 ACF section 2: project 'real' cash flows at market/~~shadow~~ prices*

		Currency: Rs.Mn. constant/current*			
Year:	0	1	2	3	4
REAL RESOURCE FLOWS (minus indicates input)					
Operating profit	–70	167	802	1525	2358
Additional working capital (changes):					
Stocks	–58	–120	–46	–49	–41
Debtors	0	–227	–241	–287	–306
Less: creditors	3	49	46	62	68
Operating cash flow	–124	–131	562	1251	2080
Additional fixed assets	–1520	0	0	0	0
Disposal of fixed assets	0	0	0	0	
Total resource flows	–1644	–131	562	1251	2080

* Delete what is not applicable

summary adds no new information but is more manageable and is more convenient for comparing one project with another. It leads directly to the final section, which shows the financial transfers, i.e. all those cash flows which are not given in exchange for goods or services (see Table 6.8).

It is unfortunate that in some literature the resources shown here are confusingly referred to as cash flows. When discounted, these are better called 'discounted resource flows' (whether shadow prices are used or not).

WRITING THE CASH FLOW FIRST

If one reviews the different formats exhibited in Tables 6.1 to 6.8, it will become clear that although some of them were presented as being derived from pairs of successive balance sheets, and the arithmetical validity rests upon that concept, they could all be derived directly from basic project data in the absence of balance sheets. They do, however, require the prior completion of income statements, without which neither tax payments nor interest payments can be known.

If you attempt to project the cash flows before constructing either income statements or balance sheets, you can do the first two parts only of the ACF (real resources, see Tables 6.6 and 6.7). Interest can be introduced by assuming away short-term debt and by taking the parameters of long-term debt as exogenous, i.e. determined as an assumption without checking whether they lead to an acceptable series of balance sheets or not. Tax in any event cannot be determined, so the financial part of the ACF (Section 3, Table 6.8) cannot be completed, nor can any of the other formats be completed so as to achieve a balance.

Table 6.8 ACF section 3: project financial cash flows at contract/~~shadow~~ prices

	Currency: Rs.Mn. constant/current*				
Year:	0	1	2	3	4
FINANCIAL TRANSFERS (minus indicates payment out)					
Sponsor cash flow					
New share/~~personal~~*					
capital	654	395	0	0	0
~~Plus: capital contributions in kind~~*					
Dividends/drawing					
rights* accruing	0	0	−236	−236	−1190
	654	395	−236	−236	−236
Debt service					
Debt rise/(fall)	1000	0	0	0	−105
Interest (paid)	0	−100	−100	−100	−100
Realised exchange					
gains /(losses)	0	−50	−119	−191	−504
	1000	−150	−219	−291	−709
Government and Central Bank					
Subsidies/(taxes) paid[a]	0	0	0	0	−73
Required cash (rise)/fall[b]	−10	−114	−84	−106	−107
	−10	−114	−84	−106	−181
Disposable Surplus[c]					
~~(if known)~~*	0	0	−23	−618	−954
Total financial transfers					
to balance	1644	131	−562	−1251	−2080

Notes: * Delete what is not applicable

[a] This table analyses only transactions which pass through the accounting books of the enterprise undertaking the project. It does not include Government taxes on incomes earned. Nor does it include Government expenditure on supporting infrastructure, technical education and so forth needed by the project. Items not included are generically known as externalities and should be taken up in further analyses such as the economic analysis.

[b] Required cash, i.e. necessary working balances of cash, are regarded as an interest-free loan to the bank of issue. On a discounted basis this accrues to Government as though it were a tax.

[c] In some countries the cost of equity capital can be estimated by reference to a developed capital market, and can be regarded as the minimum yield necessary to attract equity capital for the project having due regard to its risks. If the internal rate of return (IRR) of the return to equity exceeds this, the excess is a disposable surplus yield. It is often assumed that this accrues to the equity investors, but this may not be so since it depends on the cultural and legal circumstances of the country. Some may go to managers, to provident funds, to workers' share schemes, to bonuses, to charities, or to environmental improvements.

When financial analysis is performed purely as a step on the road to economic analysis of the kind which is concerned only with real resources, defined as goods and services, we only need to complete the real resource part of the ACF (Table 6.6). It should be pointed out, however, that this procedure is open to criticisms:

- An economic analysis which ignores the taxation flow is a very limited economic analysis.
- Further, the absence of financial flows prohibits any consideration of whether the proposal is financeable.
- Finally, the absence of *balances* in an arithmetically valid framework is poor practice because it disables certain validity checks which the science of accountancy has evolved to detect errors and omissions.

In the earliest stages of project identification, such refinements as debtors and creditors are ignored and consideration of the entire method of financing may be premature. In such situations, a simple cash flow statement tends to be written, and this is handed on for further refinement in later stages such as a pre-feasibility study or a formal expenditure authorisation request. At some later stage in this sequence the analyst must introduce a valid arithmetical framework. This means: sever the direct connexion by which project data are entered directly into cash flows; prepare proper income statements; then either construct ACF followed by balance sheets, or balance sheets followed by ACFs.

Chapter 7

Discounting

Discounting is a technique which appears to be *hard*, that is, firmly based on an incontrovertible scientific foundation, in this case mathematical, when in fact it is *soft*. The reasons and sentiments which cause people to discount the future are culture-related and are not universal. Yet it seems that all cultures do have their reasons for disregarding future costs and benefits, and especially those of the very distant future, relative to those of the immediate present, and so for behaving in a manner which quite possibly leads to the ultimate destruction of earth. There may be an anthropological explanation for this, which we can simulate by a mathematical model called discounting, without quite knowing what we are doing.

The fluidity of the theory is encapsulated in the Rubáiyát of Omar Khayyám:

"How sweet is mortal Sovranty!" – think some:
Others – "How blest the Paradise to come!"
Ah, take the Cash in hand and waive the Rest;
Oh, the brave Music of a *distant* Drum!

(Fitzgerald 1909: xii. 1–4)

Hard or soft as it may be underneath, the mathematical model is extremely convenient. It allows us to condense a series of sums of money at different dates into a single sum of money at a single date. By this means all the monetary benefits and costs of an investment project can be condensed into a single figure, the *net present value*. This statistic offers a means of choosing between alternative proposals. Let us look at the arithmetic and then come back to the underlying anthropology.

COMPOUND INTEREST SEEN IN REVERSE

We need to assume three things. First, that money falls in value over time even if there is no inflation. Second, even though there is no inflation, £1 today is more valuable to us than £1 next year, perhaps for one of the following reasons or any others (this is where cultural differences come in):

- £1 invested today in an interest-bearing account will grow to a larger sum next year.
- £1 invested today in a commercial investment will derive profits and so grow to a larger sum next year.
- We want to spend the £1 and prefer not to defer the satisfactions we expect to receive thereby.
- We are in extreme need of £1 now.
- Next year we may be dead and miss out on the benefit of the money.

So £1 now is worth more a year from now, for instance £1.10. Notice that this is not due to inflation. If there is inflation, which lowers the value of the pound in itself, the difference will be even greater; but that is a red herring. The second assumption is that we have some way to quantify the future value which we have simply taken to be £1.10. The third assumption is that the increase in the figure over one year, in this case quantified at 10 per cent, will be the same again in every other year, i.e. 10 per cent per annum.

These three assumptions bring us to the position illustrated in Table 7.1. This kind of table is often called a compound interest table, because it shows the rate at which £1 will grow if invested in a bank at 10 per cent interest per annum with the interest re-invested each year. The algebra is very simple:

$$A = P\,(1+r)^{\,t} \qquad \dots \quad \dots \quad \dots \quad \dots \quad \dots \qquad (7.1)$$

where A = amount to which the investment grows
P = principal invested, in this example £1
r = interest rate, in this case 10%
t = time in years.

If £1 now is the equivalent of £1.100 a year from now, it follows that one pound a year from now is the equivalent of £1/1.1 now, which is £0.909 approximately. This latter figure is the *present value* of a future sum:

$$PV = A\,/\,(1+r)^{\,t} \qquad \dots \quad \dots \quad \dots \quad \dots \quad \dots \qquad (7.2)$$

where PV = the present value
A = the amount of the future sum being evaluated
r = the rate of discount, as it is called (here 10%)
t = time in years.

The figures shown in Table 7.2 are the reciprocals of those in Table 7.1. This shows that discounting is the converse of compounding. Nevertheless one should not be misled into thinking that the banking terms 'investment', 'principal' and so forth used to discuss compound interest necessarily relate to discounting. As has been pointed out above, banking and investment take place in a cultural background which provides only one of some possible reasons for discounting future money. The *arithmetic* of discounting is the same as that of compound interest (save that reciprocals are used), but the *motivation* may be quite different.

Table 7.1 Equivalence table: future values

The following sums of money are all equivalent in value to £1 today if one year is worth 10 per cent

Now	£1.000
One year from now	£1.100
Two years from now	£1.210
Three years from now	£1.331
Four years from now	£1.464
. . .	
Forty years from now	£45.260
. . .	
to infinity	

Table 7.2 Equivalence table: present values

£1 at any of these future dates is equivalent in value to the following sum today if one year is worth 10 per cent

Now	£1.000
One year from now	£0.909
Two years from now	£0.826
Three years from now	£0.751
Four years from now	£0.683
. . .	
Forty years from now	£0.023
. . .	
to infinity	

NET PRESENT VALUE

Table 7.3 provides a simple example of how sums of money at different dates can be condensed to a single value at today's date. Here we continue to assume that dates are one year apart and the rate of discount is 10 per cent. Cash flows are derived from the cash flow statement of a simple project, set out year by year, and then *discounted* to arrive at discounted cash flows, that is, present values (PVs). The discounting is achieved by multiplying the 'raw' cash flows by multipliers taken from a table such as Table 7.2. The PVs are then aggregated, bringing the inflows and outflows together to a *net present value*.

Here we can see that, although the net cash flow of four years at 300 per year exceeds the initial cash investment of 1000, the net present value (NPV) is negative. This is because, in this project as in virtually every other, the cash benefits tend to arise later than the cash outlays, and are therefore discounted more heavily. With a negative NPV this project is unattractive. If the rate of discount were zero, or negative, this project would show a positive NPV.

Table 7.3 Example of discounted cash flow

Year:	0	1	2	3	4
SOURCES AND USES OF CASH					
Uses:					
Initial investment	−1000				
Operating costs etc.		−500	−500	−500	−500
Sources:					
Revenues		800	800	800	800
Net cash flow	−1000	300	300	300	300

Discount factors (multipliers) calculated at 10 per cent per annum

	1.0000	0.9091	0.8264	0.7513	0.6830
DISCOUNTED CASH FLOW					
Uses:					
Initial investment	−1000				
Operating costs etc.		−455	−413	−376	−342
Sources:					
Revenues		727	661	601	546
Net cash flow	−1000	273	248	225	205

PRESENT VALUES:	
Initial investment	−1000
Operating costs etc.	−1585
Sources:	
Revenues	2536
NET PRESENT VALUE:	−49

APPLICATION OF DCF TECHNIQUE TO VARIOUS PROJECT ELEMENTS

Bearing in mind that there are various formats for cash flow statements and funds flow statements, each with many rows of figures in them, the reader may ask which row of which statement is 'the' cash flow which is to be discounted.

For discounting, the analytical cash flow (ACF) is recommended. In the ACF we have flows of resources for which cash flows are exchanged. These resource flows are summarised, and the total resource flow year by year is balanced against total finance flows year by year. The finance flows are analysed according to the person or party involved: equity investors etc. The ACF when presented in three sections states the resources, the summarised resources, and the summarised financial transfers.

When we want to evaluate the investment proposal *regardless of its financing pattern*, we can apply discounting to the total resource flows. If we want to investigate whether the proposal is attractive to an equity investor, we turn to the last section of the ACF statement in which the flow of funds from and to the equity investor are stated, and calculate the discounted equity cash flow. If we want to look at the fiscal impact, we discount the Government cash flow shown in the ACF. And if we want to negotiate financing, we propose a financing pattern, work out the ACF, discount the financial flows of the various parties, and compare their NPVs, hoping that the other parties will not be doing this and will not notice how much bigger than theirs is our NPV under this proposal.

PARTS OF YEARS

There is no magic about a *year* which makes money grow or shrink when the progress of the earth round the sun brings it back to its position of a year before. If we discount the future, we should logically do so for months or weeks as well as for years.

If the rate of interest is 10 per cent per annum, the compound rate for two years is not 20 but 21 per cent:

$$(1 + 10/100) \times (1 + 10/100) - 1 = 21/100$$

The multiplier for each year is 1.10 or 1+10/100, and 11× 11 is 121. The multiplier is squared to give 1.21 and we then deduct the original amount leaving 0.21 or 21/100 which is the growth.

Similarly with discounting. If the rate of discount is 10 per cent, the multiplier for each year is 0.909 and squaring this for two years we get 0.826 which is the discount factor for two years at 10 per cent. Whether the period is a year or some other length of time, if the rate of discount per period is 10 per cent, and hence the multiplier is 0.909 per period, we have to *square* this – not double it – to get the factor for two periods.

Hence the discount factor for one year is the square of the factor for six months. If the factor for one year is 0.909 we take the *square root* of this and find that 0.9535 is the appropriate factor for six months. The twelfth root, 0.9921, is the corresponding figure for a single month. For eighteen months we multiply the one-year figure by the six-month figure. In this way we can arrive at the discount factor for any given period at any given rate of discount.

In project analysis there are some cash flows that take place at year-ends and others that take place at other times, or evenly throughout a year. Many flows reflect revenues and operating costs; these come into this last category, normally. We do not bother to split them into quarters or months unless there are marked seasonal variations. When a flow arises evenly during a year, it is simpler to take its *average flow date* as being in six months through the year. Adopting the convention that today – the date to which sums are discounted to express their present value – is an exact number of years before the first day of the operating period, this brings the average flow date six months after the anniversary of today. For example:

Event:	Project begins	Construction phase	Operating phase	Revenue, Year 3
Date:	Today	Year – 1 and Year 0	Years 1 onwards	4.5 years from today

Using discount factors at 10 per cent per annum, the appropriate factor for the revenue in Year 3, which arises on average four years and six months from today would be found by multiplying 0.909 by itself four times and then by the square root of itself, giving 0.651 which is of course intermediate between the four-year and five-year factors.

The initial investment in capital goods, or more precisely in fixed assets, working capital, and preliminary expenses, cannot be assumed to fall either at the year-ends of the construction period or at mid-year dates. Payments for fixed assets tend to be large, lumpy flows at particular dates related to progress achieved in making, shipping, delivering, or commissioning the most important assets. Timings can be estimated from implementation plans, contracts, or plain common sense, according to whichever is available, if any.

Sadly, it has become so common in project appraisals to be lazy about these refinements and to work only in whole years, that any analyst who introduces square or fourth roots risks incomprehension. One of the reasons for this inaccuracy is that computer spreadsheet software such as Lotus provides short-cut methods of discounting over entire periods, e.g. the @NPV( ) and @IRR( ) functions in Lotus, whereas for part-periods a more laborious set of formulas is required. Nevertheless, for a commercial project in which pressure of competition makes it necessary to sharpen the pencils a little, the refinement of part-year calculation can make the difference between abandonment and success. No matter how rough and inaccurate the rest of the data may be, there is nothing to be gained by introducing further inaccuracies.

It has also become common to be careless about the definition of 'present' in the concept of 'net present value'. This is essentially that point in time at which numbers are tabled for discussion and a decision is made either to go for that NPV or to drop it. As a rule this decision will be made shortly before expenditure begins, that is to say, before the implementation phase. That is why the standard software functions such as @NPV( ) discount back to the period shortly before the first number in the range of flows. If you discount the numbers in columns C to Z you will get a present value at the time shown by column B. That is what most customers who buy Lotus want it to do. That date in Column B is Year 0 in the algebraical sense that the applicable discount factor at that date is $1/[(1+r)^0]$, i.e. one. It is not Year 0 in the planning sense that it is the date immediately before commercial operations begin, i.e. the end of the implementation phase. It is regrettable that these two senses are sometimes confused, so that the 'present' is taken to be the end of implementation instead of just before the start of implementation.

REPEATED PAYMENTS

When an investment proposal is studied in terms of constant prices, i.e. before looking at the impact of inflation, we often find that the figures are the same year after year – not for the fixed assets, of course, but for revenues and

Table 7.4 Annuity factors at 10 per cent per annum

Time	Discount factor	Annuity factor
1 year	0.9091	0.9091
2 years	0.8264	1.7355
3 years	0.7513	2.4868
4 years	0.6830	3.1698

operating costs after full operational volume has been reached. A series of equal annual sums is called an *annuity*.

It is convenient to compile a table of discount factors for such annuities as shown in Table 7.4. This gives us a single multiplier which can be used for the entire annuity, and removes the labour of calculating a multiplier for each sum separately. In Table 7.4., the factors in the third column are obtained by cumulating the factors in the middle column. For instance, the factor for a two-year annuity is obtained by adding the figure for Year 2 to the figure for Year 1.

Annuity tables are useful occasionally, when the figures really are the same every year. For instance, taking the numbers of Table 7.3, we have an annuity of four cash flows each of £300 from Year 1 to Year 4 inclusive. The annuity factor from Table 7.4 is 3.1698 in such a case. Multiplying 300 by 3.1698 gives £951, the PV of the net yield. Adding this to the Year 0 flow of –1000 gives the NPV of –£49, the same answer as before but more elegantly derived.

Actually annuities crop up more often in simple cases chosen to illustrate points of principle than in real life. Nevertheless it does sometimes happen that several years do have the same cash flow. Suppose it happens in Years 7 to 11 only. We can still use the annuity method. The annuity factor for a full eleven years would be 6.495; subtract from this the annuity factor for the missing Years 1 to 6, which is 4.355, and we get the factor we need, which is 2.140. This kind of short cut is very useful when working with a calculator, but when working with a computer, it is a long cut.

Just as the discount factors are reciprocals of the compound interest table, so annuity factors are reciprocals of *capital recovery factors*, which are useful in calculating debt service annuities.

THE BENEFIT/COST RATIO

The NPV is only one indicator of the *net worth* or value of the project. Another is the benefit/cost (B/C) ratio. This is the PV of benefits divided by the PV of costs. This indicator is chiefly used in appraising real resource flows, leaving aside financial flows, as occurs in Section 2 of the ACF statement. In that context, the project benefits are its outputs of goods or services, measured by the revenues, and its inputs are its costs of goods and services including both investment – fixed assets and working capital – and operating costs.

Table 7.5 Example of B/C ratio

Year:	0	1	2	3	4
Cash flows (£) discounted at 10 per cent					
Benefits					
Revenues		727	661	601	546
Costs					
Initial investment	−1000				
Operating costs etc.		−455	−413	−376	−342
Present values					
Benefits	2536				
Costs	2585	(ignoring sign)			
B/C ratio:	2536/2585 = 0.98				

Taking the data of Table 7.3 as an example, this is illustrated in Table 7.5. You may remember, this was an unsatisfactory project with a NPV of –£49. If it were a little better, with a reduction in its initial investment of £49, the PV of its costs would be exactly equal to the PV of its benefits; it would then have an NPV of zero pounds and a B/C ratio of one.

The connection between NPV and B/C ratio is as follows:

NPV	B/C Ratio	Comment
< 0	< 1	unsatisfactory
0	1	marginal
> 0	> 1	satisfactory

These indicators are calculated at a particular discount rate. We have been using 10 per cent without any discussion as yet of the derivation of this rate of discount. A project can be satisfactory at one rate and unsatisfactory at a higher rate. Therefore, the results of these indicators should never be quoted without stating what rate was used.

The rationale for using the B/C ratio is that the divisor represents all costs, that is to say all inputs; although the early-year inputs are given greater consideration than the later inputs by the process of discounting, capital costs as such are given no more weight than operating costs. This makes sense from the point of view of an investor who is asked to provide X amount of cash in Year Y, because the nature of the expenditure does not affect the burden of finding the cash. Likewise in economic analysis, the burden of injecting real resources into a project is not affected by whether the expenditure is booked into a capital or a revenue account.

A problem in using the B/C ratio is that you sometimes get situations where a reduction of income may be regarded as a reduction of benefit in the numerator or as an additional cost in the denominator, and these give different results. Usually it is clear which is appropriate, but there are borderline cases. For example, opening a new factory may temporarily depress the sales and thus the contribution to profits of an existing factory. Personally I would class this as a cost, but some might call it a reduction in benefit. In irrigation schemes, the damming of a river should increase agricultural incomes downstream, but will reduce incomes in the flooded zone. Again, I personally would class the latter as an extra cost, but Finney (1990), drawing on his experience in Pakistan and Turkey, regards it as borderline.

Finney advocates the use of another indicator which was popular in the sixties, the *net benefit/investment ratio*, abbreviated NB/K taking the old symbol K for capital (economists can spell, but use C for consumption) or investment. In normal use, the denominator K is the project cost, consisting of initial fixed assets (but not replacements) and initial working capital, but Finney adds the funding of cash deficits in the early years. If these items are spread over more than one year they are reduced to a present value by discounting at a stated rate. They all require to be financed, and because finance is scarce in LDCs, Finney argues that it is sensible to use this measure. The numerator is the discounted present value of all the other resource flows: operating revenues and costs after early-year losses have ended, replacement fixed assets, and disposals. The Finney treatment of early-year losses means that K is the total cash flow during the years when total resource flows generate a negative cash flow, and NB is the subsequent cash flow (discounted of course).

INTERNAL RATE OF RETURN (IRR)

If the rate is varied, the NPV and B/C ratios will vary. That rate at which NPV is zero and B/C ratio is one is called the internal rate of return (IRR). The IRR can be positive or negative.

Again taking the data of Tables 7.3 and 7.4 as an example, here we have a project which if discounted at 10 per cent produces an unsatisfactory result. A lower rate of discount will have a less severe effect on the later years when the benefits arise. We therefore need to find a rate below 10 per cent. You might expect that, as the B/C ratio at 10 per cent was so close to unity, the IRR would be very close below ten. In this particular project there are only four operating years, so discounting does not have so severe effect on benefits as you might suppose. In fact, we have to come down to 7.71 per cent before the project shows an NPV of zero and a B/C ratio of unity (see Table 7.6).

The following methods are available to ascertain the IRR:

- Trial and error. If you are working with a computer you can change the discount rate up and down until you hit a rate which gives you zero NPV. Without a computer, this is too slow to be practicable, and even with a computer, it may be very slow if you have a complicated spreadsheet and a slow machine.
- Interpolation or extrapolation. If you calculate the NPV at two different discount rates, you can calculate the IRR approximately. It is important

that both test rates should be close to the true IRR. This means (a) the first attempt should be a good guess, (b) the second rate should be well judged having regard to the result of the first. If the first attempt gives a negative NPV, the second attempt with a lower discount rate should hopefully give a positive NPV, or *vice versa*. We can then interpolate the IRR between our two guessed rates. If both attempts produce NPVs with the same sign, we have to extrapolate. In either case, the arithmetic used (see Table 7.7) gives only an approximate result because it assumes a linear relationship between discount rate and NPV. The actual relationship is non-linear but approximates to linear providing the two rates are close together. It is best if the two rates are not more than 2 per cent apart and produce NPVs of opposite signs. To achieve this, you must either guess the rates with good judgement, or try again.

- Direct calculation by computer. Most spreadsheet software contains a mechanism whereby the discount rate is varied automatically until it produces an NPV of zero or very close to zero. This appears to be a direct calculation because it happens very fast, but is actually done by the trial and error method ('iteration') starting from a first guess, which the user must provide. Some programs are better than others in the way they respond to negative IRRs, very high IRRs, all-positive cash flows, and other abnormal situations and so the results of this direct calculation should always be treated with reserve, and preferably checked by making the spreadsheet apply discount factors as shown in Table 7.6.

The method of estimating IRR from two trials is as follows. Again we will use the data from the previous example. At 10 per cent we had a negative NPV at –£49, so our second attempt should be at a lower NPV. Knowing that the two rates should be not more than 2 per cent apart for accuracy, my second attempt was at 8 per cent. This produced the figures shown in Table 7.7 but unfortunately the NPV is still negative. This result is very close to zero NPV

Table 7.6 Discounting at the internal rate of return

Year:	0	1	2	3	4
Cash flows (£) discounted at 7.71 per cent					
Benefits					
Revenues		743	690	640	594
Costs					
Initial investment	–1000				
Operating costs etc.		–464	–431	–400	–372
Present values					
Benefits	2667				
Costs	–2667				
NPV	0				
B/C ratio:	2667/2667 = 1.00 (ignoring sign)				

Table 7.7 Second pass at 8 per cent

Year:	0	1	2	3	4
Cash flows (£) discounted at 8.0 per cent					
Benefits					
Revenues		741	686	635	588
Costs					
Initial investment	−1000				
Operating costs etc.		−463	−429	−397	−368
Present values					
Benefits	2650				
Costs	−2656				
NPV	−6				

Table 7.8 Final pass at 6 per cent

Year:	0	1	2	3	4
Cash flows (£) discounted at 6.0 per cent					
Benefits					
Revenues		755	712	672	634
Costs					
Initial Investment	−1000				
Operating costs etc.		−472	−445	−420	−396
Present values					
Benefits	2773				
Costs	−2733				
NPV	+ 40				

so I know that if I go down by a further 2 per cent I will get to a positive NPV. This is shown in Table 7.8.

So 8 per cent gives −6 and 6 per cent gives +40. Clearly the IRR lies between 6 and 8 per cent, closer to 6 than to 8. We can now forget the 10 per cent altogether; we call 8 per cent our first trial, and 6 per cent our second trial. The arithmetic now continues as follows:

$$IRR = R_1 + (R_2 - R_1).N_2/(N_2 - N_1) \text{ per cent} \dots \quad \dots \quad (7.3)$$

where

R_1 is the rate of discount in the first trial, here 6
R_2 is the rate of discount in the second trial, here 8
N_1 is the NPV from the first trial, here − 6
N_2 is the NPV from the second trial, here +40.

Formula 7.3 thus gives 6 + (8 − 6). 40 / [40 − (−6)] which is

6 + 2. 40/46 = 7.74 per cent.

Note that it is not quite the same as the 7.71 per cent proven above; this is because of the non-linearity error. But as it is the convention to quote IRRs to one decimal place, 7.74 is near enough to 7.71 to be satisfactory.

If we did not want to bother to make the trial at 6 per cent, we might observe that the 8 per cent trial produced an NPV which was very close to zero, and reason that we could extrapolate from the 10 and 8 per cent trials to hit something just below 8 with reasonable accuracy. Extrapolating with formula (3) produces:

$$8 + (10 - 8) \cdot -6 / [-6 - (-49)] \text{ which is}$$
$$8 + 2 \cdot -6 / 43 = 7.72 \text{ per cent.}$$

This too is close enough to the truth to be satisfactory.

MEANING OF IRR

The IRR can be calculated from the total of all resource flows, as has been shown above, or from financial flows affecting specific parties. Using Section 3 of an ACF statement, you can for instance see all the cash transactions by the equity investors: first investing in the project, then receiving dividends or drawings out of it. The IRR of such a stream measures the profitability of the project from the equity investors' point of view, and so may be compared with the IRRs of other projects in which they could alternatively place their funds, or with the rate of interest which they could get by placing their money in a bank, or indeed with the rate of interest they pay if they themselves borrow the money to put in a project.

The IRR of the financial flows involving parties who lend to the project, notably the institution providing the long-term finance, is called the *effective rate of interest* (Harvey 1983: 7) and is to be distinguished from the apparent or nominal rate of interest expressed in the loan agreement.

The terms economic internal rate of return (EIRR), financial internal rate of return (FIRR) and internal rate of return to equity (IRRE) are sometimes encountered. The EIRR is calculated from those cash flows representing flows of real resources, as shown in Sections 1 and 2 of the ACF statement, after applying shadow (notional) prices to those resources in place of actual prices. The FIRR is calculated without shadow pricing, and may either refer to the total of resource flows (which is always equal to the total of financial flows, as seen from the balancing of Sections 2 and 3 of the ACF statement), or occasionally is used to mean the IRR of the equity flow. The latter usage is confusing and it is preferable to speak of the IRRE where the equity flow is intended.

We therefore have an array of indicators all based on discounting:

• Total project resource flows or financial flows:

FIRR
NPV
B/C ratio
NB/K ratio
EIRR (shadow-priced)
NPV (shadow-priced)
B/C ratio (shadow-priced)
• Equity flows:
IRRE
NPV of equity stream
• Debt and debt-service flows:
ERI

The NPVs depend upon the discount rate chosen. How it should be chosen will be discussed below. They also depend on the starting date of the project in relation to the date of 'present' values. The IRRs, by contrast, are unaffected by these considerations.

Table 7.9 shows how the ACF of a project has been used to find out the FIRRs and FNPVs of the three financial parties involved: equity investors, lenders and Government. In this particular case, Government did not put any money into the project (its spending on infrastructure is not seen in the financial analysis and would be picked up separately in the economic analysis) so its cash flow was all one way. Under these circumstances no IRR can be calculated; hence the emphasis on NPV instead.

DIVISION OF CASH FLOW STREAM INTO TWO OR MORE PHASES

Discounting is always applied to a finite stream of inflows and outflows with a beginning and an end. For an investment project, this begins after the go-ahead decision, runs through the implementation and operating phases and perhaps a liquidation phase at the end. These phases cannot be considered to have *separate* costs and benefits; they must be appraised as a whole.

It sometimes happens, however, that there is a net outflow in one or more years of the operating phase as well as the implementation phase. The usual reason for this is that some important fixed asset has to be replaced; different classes of asset have different depreciable lives, and whilst the project as a whole may be considered to continue over the life of the principal asset, this may require repeated replacements of other assets, not necessarily insignificant in value. The cost of these replacements can sometimes exceed the operating yield so as to bring the whole cash flow into the red when it happens.

The analyst should consider whether it would be sensible to consider terminating the project immediately before a major replacement instead of continuing to the end of the project. This can be achieved by regarding the continuation as a second project in its own right. The effect of this is to divide

Table 7.9 Analytical cash flow with summary

ANALYTICAL CASH FLOW
Part Two

Rs.Mn. in constant terms

	Year:	0	1	2	3	4	5	6	7	8	9	10	11	12	13	14	15	16	17	18	19	20	21
Real resource flows (minus indicates input)																							
Operating profit		-90	30	630	1030	1030	1030	1030	1030	1030	1030	1030	1030	1030	1030	1030	1030	1030	1030	1030	1030	1030	
Additional working capital (changes):																							
Stocks		-68	-200	0	0	0	0	0	0	0	0	0	0	0	0	0	0	0	0	0	0	0	268
Debtors		0	-185	-162	-115	0	0	0	0	0	0	0	0	0	0	0	0	0	0	0	0	0	462
Less: creditors		4	54	29	29	0	0	0	0	0	0	0	0	0	0	0	0	0	0	0	0	0	-115
Operating cash flow		-154	-301	497	944	1030	1030	1030	1030	1030	1030	1030	1030	1030	1030	1030	1030	1030	1030	1030	1030	1030	614
Additional fixed assets		-2000	0	0	0	0	-270	0	0	0	0	-1308	0	0	0	0	-270	0	0	0	0	0	0
Disposal of fixed asset		0	0	0	0	0	26	0	0	0	0	26	0	0	0	0	26	0	0	0	0	26	100
Total resource flows		-2154	-301	497	944	1030	786	1030	1030	1030	1030	-252	1030	1030	1030	1030	786	1030	1030	1030	1030	1056	714

ACF Part Three

Financial transfers (minus indicates payment out)

Equity flow

New share capital	1166	509	0	0	0	0	0	0	0	885	0	0	0	0	0	0	0	0	0	0	0
Dividends paid	0	0	-359	-805	-825	-616	-512	-539	-535	-531	-130	-1111	-721	-721	-477	-794	-721	-721	-721	-747	-565
	1166	509	-359	-805	-825	-616	-512	-539	-535	-531	756	-1111	-721	-721	-477	-794	-721	-721	-721	-747	-565

Long term debt service

Debt rise/(fall)	1000	0	0	-105	-128	-116	-140	-154	-170	-187	0	0	0	0	0	0	0	0	0	0	0
Interest (paid)	0	-100	-100	-100	-89	-78	-65	-51	-36	-19	0	0	0	0	0	0	0	0	0	0	0
Realised exchange gains/(losses)	0	0	0	0	0	0	0	0	0	0	0	0	0	0	0	0	0	0	0	0	0
	1000	-100	-100	-205	-205	-205	-205	-205	-205	-205	0	0	0	0	0	0	0	0	0	0	0

Government and Central Bank

Subsidies/(taxes) paid	0	0	0	0	-69	-209	-286	-290	-294	-298	81	-309	-309	-309	-236	-309	-309	-309	-309	-347	
Req'd cash (rise)/fall	-12	-109	-38	-38	0	0	0	0	0	0	0	0	0	0	0	0	0	0	0	198	
	-12	-109	-38	-38	-69	-209	-286	-290	-294	-298	81	-309	-309	-309	-236	-309	-309	-309	-309	-149	

Total financial transfers	2154	301	-497	-944	-1030	-786	-1030	-1030	-1030	-1030	252	-1030	-1030	-1030	-786	-1030	-1030	-1030	-1030	-1056	-714

Financial Analysis Summary

	Net Present Values			FIRR
	at 5%	10%	15%	%
	Rs.Mn. in constant terms			
Equity	5056	2586	1316	28%
Debt	285	0	-182	10%
Government	2307	1321	822	
Total project	7648	3907	1956	27%

the project into two phases, first and second, each with its own financial indicators. If the second phase looks unattractive, it may be supposed that management will decide not to continue; then the whole project should be appraised on the indicators of the first phase alone.

In general, replacement of fixed assets does not provide a strong incentive to discontinue. The cash needed to obtain the replacements is exchanged for a fixed asset of equal value. Subsequent earnings, including the residual value of the new asset, will justify the replacement just as they justified the initial fixed assets, providing that market circumstances have not deteriorated. A cash outflow is not to be confused with a loss.

In the rare event that phase two is marginally unattractive, but the project as a whole is more attractive with it than without it – not a mathematical impossibility – arrangements will need to be made to ensure that phase two is undertaken. This is called phase-binding, and may be achieved by contract or by built-in inducements.

MULTIPLE IRR SOLUTIONS

A second problem that arises when the stream of operating benefits is interrupted by one or more years of negative figures is that the analyst needs to check whether there may be more than one rate of discount which will produce a zero NPV. That is to say, the IRR is found by what may be regarded as a set of simultaneous equations with multiple roots (more than one correct solution). This is a possibility whenever there is more than one reversal of the direction of the cash flow. Consider Table 7.10. Here the reversal of flow suggests that the project may be divided into two phases with a danger of suspension after Year 1; Years 2 and 3 are unattractive. Assuming, however, that there is phase-binding and the project must run for four years or not at all, there are two rates at which the NPV is zero. The project may be regarded as having a rather poor IRR of 5.9 per cent or as having an exceptionally high IRR of 343 per cent. If the IRR is calculated by computer using the automatic iterative procedure, only one solution will be found. Which one it is depends

Table 7.10 Example of multiple solutions

	Year:	0	1	2	3
Cash flow		−200	+ 1100	−950	+ 10
Discount factors @ 5.9%		1.000	0.944	0.892	0.842
Discounted cash flow		−200	+ 1038.7	−847.1	+ 8.4
NPV (sum of flows)		0	hence IRR = 5.9%		
Discount factors @ 343%		1.000	0.226	0.051	0.012
Discounted cash flow		−200	+ 248.3	−48.4	+ 0.1
NPV (sum of flows)		0	hence IRR = 343%		

on the guess used as the starting point for the iteration, so it is very likely to be 5.9 per cent and not 343 per cent.

Such multiple solutions cause trouble by placing a question-mark over every one. The way to deal with them is to reject solutions which are extremely high or extremely low; cases which pass through this filter are fortunately rare.

The justification for rejecting very high IRRs – say, over 200 per cent – when there is a lower alternative is simply the accounting principle of prudence. The reason for rejecting very low IRRs is one of arithmetic. A discount rate of –100 per cent or below is impossible. If the rate is –100 per cent, the compound interest factors for all years fall to zero, and their reciprocals, the discount factors, become one divided by zero, which is an error. At even lower rates, the discount factor in Year 1 becomes negative, in Year 2 positive and alternating thereafter, which quite clearly produces a meaningless DCF result. Therefore, we reject any IRR variant lying above +200 per cent or at –100 per cent or below.

THE HURDLE RATE

The point of calculating the IRR, in any of its various contexts, must be to determine whether the investment proposal achieves a minimum acceptable IRR. Such a minimum is called a *hurdle* or *test* rate.

When we calculate the FIRR of total project resources we are looking at the return which the project will yield on total project finance. The provision of this finance is not free of charge: there may be interest and/or dividends to be paid, and even if the finance is an interest-free loan, there may be some other putative use for it which would have yielded a positive FIRR but which must be foregone. One way or the other, the cost of devoting finance to this particular project is known as the *cost of capital* (CoC).

In general a proposal ought not to be approved unless its FIRR is at least as great as the CoC. The enterprise which owns and operates the project must suffer the cost of capital, but receives the benefit of the FIRR; if the benefit is less than the cost, the equity within the enterprise will fall.

Indeed, many enterprises require a FIRR which is much higher than the CoC in order to avoid accepting too many projects for their management to handle. In principle this raised hurdle rate is equivalent to inserting high administrative expenses on the assumption of management overload. The latter procedure has the merit that it works through into profitability ratios as well as the discount indicators. The former procedure has the merit that a project with a very good FIRR will be accepted whether there is management overload or not.

When we calculate the FIRR for the equity holder (the IRRE) or for an individual financier, again the CoC sets a minimum. Investors must be induced to invest by expectations of either dividends or interest, or a mixture of both, which exceeds their individual cost of capital. The latter may reflect the terms on which they borrow, or the alternative FIRR which they forego by not placing their money elsewhere.

In a country which has well-developed financial markets, the cost of borrowing and the yield foregone by not lending elsewhere (assuming similar degrees of risk) will be not far apart in percentage terms. In a perfect market with no risks and no inflationary expectations they will be identical rates. Hence the nation-wide CoC in neo-classical economics is the rate of interest which elicits supply and demand for finance in equal quantities and thus clears the market. However, in real life, market imperfection is the name of the game, in financial markets as in other markets, and if we must proceed by successive approximations from a theoretical construct, monopoly would be a better starting point than perfect competition. In general every LDC investor will have to consider a relatively small range of lending options and an even smaller range of borrowing options available to him or her at the time.

Taking reported financial markets as a starting point, attempts have been made to estimate the national CoC in several countries. It is necessary to select one of the many rates of interest quoted, as being most representative. Such rates are naturally higher when inflation is expected to continue: the lender must be compensated for inflation which reduces the value of his or her capital. This expected inflation factor naturally varies from currency to currency, but it is necessary to try to estimate it if an investment appraisal is to be made in constant prices. The inflation factor should be taken out of the market rate so as to determine the CoC and then see whether or not the FIRR is above the CoC.

Next, a risk premium must be considered. It is not practical to find a quoted market rate which is similar in riskiness to a specific project. We therefore look at market rates to find a risk-free CoC. The rate of interest on short-term lending to Government (Treasury Bills) is usually the closest approximation. We then adjust this upward by a margin which reflects the project risk, and this gives a hurdle rate.

In corporate planning, an enterprise looks several years ahead and contemplates a number of investment proposals. The CoC in that case must be studied by forecasting the enterprise's complete balance sheets, looking at the mix of equity and borrowed funds, the CoC for each source of finance, and a weighted average which will be applicable to all projects. In such a context, the composite CoC may be reduced by tax relief. In most countries, interest expense (but not dividends) reduce the tax payable by enterprises. It is, of course, possible to compute tax relief on a specific project as well as on a corporate plan, but the tax background of the whole enterprise must be known in order to determine correctly the tax relief accruing to any single project.

NATIONAL COST OF CAPITAL

The hurdle rate of discount for an enterprise or for a single financier must depend on their circumstances, and if they are participants in a developed financial market, their CoC can be estimated using the concepts described above. For a whole country, however, which has the financial market within itself, the CoC cannot be understood as depending on market quotations but rather *vice versa*. There are four other concepts which may be helpful here.

First, the country may participate in financial markets elsewhere in the world. In LDCs this tends to be as borrower rather than as lender. Borrowing takes place at a spectrum of rates. The application of composite or weighted average rates as in corporate planning might be a useful technique, but no hurdle rates arrived at by that method have been published as yet.

Second, the IRR foregone by not investing elsewhere can be estimated by studying what returns are in fact being earned elsewhere in 'typical' projects, an obscure and unsatisfactory concept. This is sometimes attempted using shadow prices. The rate thus estimated is called the marginal productivity of capital, a neo-classical expression which confuses physical and monetary capital.

Third, the rate of discount may be seen as essentially a rate of exchange between present goods and future goods (Keynes 1936: 93). This has nothing to do with finance, investment or profit but rather with our attitude *as consumers* towards resources at different dates. It is argued that in all economies, even those without money and perhaps even in a Robinson Crusoe economy without exchange, resources today are preferred to resources tomorrow. Alfred Marshall in 1895 characterised this as a 'defect in the telescopic faculty' of human beings. To quantify this is difficult since subjective preference is a feeling or emotion which is not scientifically measurable in any units. Nevertheless the *social rate of discount* is defined as the percentage decline in the 'value' of a marginal unit of consumption between this period and the next in the special case where the decline is constant over several years, as judged by national planners (Sen in UNIDO 1972: 30). There is a tendency to slip into the neo-classical paradigm here too, by reverting to the utility theory of the 1920s in which subjective preference was deemed to be expressible in units if not actually measurable. Marglin (UNIDO 1972: 155) refers to the social rate of discount as the 'declining marginal utility of consumption' as though the utility of consumable resources declines over time as a result of an increasing availability of resources just as, at one particular time, the utility of a unit of resources is greater for a poor person than for a rich person. Most economists today refer to the social rate of discount or *consumption rate of interest* (CRI) as being based on consumer time preference without resolving the underlying problem of value-theory (Ray 1984: 15).

Fourth, if we agree that consumers exhibit this preference universally, even in static non-market economies, we must look for a very fundamental explanation in anthropology and even in human biology. Recent anthropological studies of *altruism* in human (and animal) behaviour have drawn attention to the *genotype*, which is a set of genes, rather than the individual as being the ultimate beneficiary of all consumption – a concept popularised as the 'selfish gene'.

Suppose we consider time preference from the point of view of an individual, who of course is a carrier of the genotype, and who acts as though programmed to serve the genotype. He or she will have children each of which will carry only half of his or her genes, half the genotype. He/she must regard £100 of resources available for his/her own consumption and survival as being twice as valuable as £100 of resources available at a later date for his/her children. Thus, £100 in the first generation is worth £200 for the second generation, £400 for the third generation, and so forth. If the generations are 25 years apart, say, this gives a genetic discount rate of about 3 per cent per year.

Of course, people are not programmed, and their behaviours vary. Suppose we introduce cultural and psychological variation as a 'love of children' factor ranging from zero to two. Zero represents a total disregard of children and later descendants, a complete state of individual selfishness or current-generation selfishness and will produce a discount rate of infinity. One represents the genetic discount rate as described above. Two represents doubled love of children, i.e. loving children as oneself; this is the opposite extreme and produces a discount rate of zero. As the reader can verify, this produces the results shown in Table 7.11 where the rates vary from zero up to about 13 per cent per annum. Of course, these rates are not boosted by risk or inflation premiums. What is interesting is that the central zone of results is not inconsistent with observed real rates of interest on bonds.

Nobody of course conducts any transactions with these biological motives consciously in view. As with any anthropological or biological mechanism, what happens is that whatever individuals may decide, those cultural elements and systems which do not work satisfactorily as communities die out. Behaviour which fails to provide for descendants as well as providing for the survival of the current generation, striking a near-optimal balance between these two, is clearly threatening to the survival of any community. After all, in the long run resources are scarce. Therefore, all communities will be found to have cultures, institutions and other mechanisms which induce individuals to act in a biologically satisfactory way.

Table 7.11 Modified genetic discount rates

Generation gap (years)	Love of children factor							
	0.25	0.50	0.75	1.00	1.25	1.50	1.75	2.00
15	13%	9%	6%	5%	3%	2%	1%	0%
20	10%	7%	5%	3%	2%	1%	1%	0%
25	8%	5%	4%	3%	2%	1%	1%	0%
30	7%	5%	3%	2%	2%	1%	0%	0%
35	6%	4%	3%	2%	1%	1%	0%	0%

SOCIAL RATE OF DISCOUNT

A very interesting discussion of psychological and religious influences upon time preferences has come out of Sri Lanka (Gunatilleke 1989). 'The moral will to act with due regard for the future is derived eventually from the life paradigms which underlie a society's value system', he says. Gunatilleke points to the immediate self-centredness of children and adolescents in the West, and to the improved but belated concern for future decades on the part of parents and grandparents. Thus, the 'telescopic faculty' comes from individual psycho-sexual development. He also discusses relevant religious precepts and concepts, such as reincarnation. It may be significant that Gunatilleke, like Sen and Ray, draws experience from Asian cultures, in which the struggle for survival by families threatened by lack of food is a more pervasive influence than the ethos of participation in financial markets.

This variety of influences has already been summarised in the quotation from Omar Khayyám. There can be no doubt that any explanation of time preference which derives from the possibility of placing funds on an interest-bearing deposit is a culture-bound error.

Bearing in mind these origins of individual time preference, there must be great diversity within a nation, and the selection of a hurdle rate of discount to reflect the time preference of an entire country presents a difficult problem for Government economists. It is clearly not a matter which can be decided democratically by ballot box or referendum, yet it must have its basis within the preferences of the people.

Discussions of this problem in the 1960s stressed that nations, unlike individuals, are immortal and need not suffer from the 'defect of the telescopic faculty'; their Governments could and should, therefore, depart from the will of the people which in a period of famine might be for a very high CRI, and take the longer view which would permit trees to be planted and dams to be built. Sen (UNIDO 1972: 164) suggested that economists should deduce the hurdle rate from the yes-no decisions on projects made by Government ministers in the recent past, which overcomes the problem of democracy nicely, but unfortunately this presupposes a record of consistent, single-minded decision-making based wholly on the internal rates of return of project proposals. Sen's suggestion has never been put into successful operation. Hansen (UNIDO 1978: 51), acknowledging the serious difficulty of determining a CRI empirically, suggests two alternatives which, despite their obvious weaknesses, have been widely adopted:

1 Use the 'opportunity cost of capital as a crude first estimate of the CRI'. In effect this means observing rates of interest in financial markets, taking the preferences of financial borrowers and lenders as representative of the people as a whole. The yield on risk-free or first-class bonds, adjusted downwards for the built-in anticipated inflation rate would be a good indicator here. At the time of writing, in the UK, inflation for the next year

is anticipated to run at around 10 per cent, and Government bonds redeemable a year from now are selling at a discount of just under 15 per cent, implying a real rate of discount of 4.2 per cent.

2 Let the planners set a rate which they judge will be high enough to rule out of consideration some projects, so that the available capital will then suffice for the remaining projects. This is called *capital rationing*. It is of course difficult to know how much capital will come forward in an arbitrarily defined period of time (say three months) and how much investment will be demanded by project proposals coming forward in the same period (excluding proposals considered unsatisfactory on other grounds). This can only be estimated by a series of periodic reviews, looking to past periods for a shrewd assessment of the supply of capital in the immediate future, while building up a queue of project proposals from which the cream can be taken off at the appropriate level by setting a rate which equates supply and demand for that period. The deliberate delaying of projects for competitive review in this way is naturally very damaging in many cases. For the first such period, when no prior history is available for guidance, Hansen suggests that 'in practice the planners would not go far wrong as a tentative first step to try a discount rate of ten percent.'

For some years after Hansen's remarks were published, 10 per cent became the standard first – and last – step in most LDCs, but more recently the World Bank economists have urged 15 per cent as a more reasonable level to achieve capital rationing in Sub-Saharan Africa. This reflects the perception that many projects have proved disappointing, and a higher hurdle would have been beneficial. Other economists believe that the disappointments show that the project data or assumptions were unsound rather than the social rate of discount, and a 15 per cent rate would rule out many very desirable projects including the replanting of depleted hardwood forests. The Government of Tanzania has taken a sceptical view of all this and has required projects to be discounted at 5, 10 and 15 per cent, without adopting any official hurdle rate.

The cost of capital in an entire nation state is much harder to determine than in a private enterprise. We may all be sceptical that the official rate is fixed with accuracy or in a representative manner. However, governments do have a responsibility, to find a method of setting a minimum acceptable rate of return on the capital which a society of disparate individuals entrusts to them, and if we are sceptical, we need not be cynical.

Chapter 8

Debt

The analysis of debt falls into three parts: first the *terms and conditions* of debt, and especially the constraints and limitations which govern the borrowers' access to the pot of gold which we call the capital market; second, the arithmetic of calculating how much the debtor has to pay to the creditor and when, which we call *debt scheduling*; and third the analysis of whether this deal is a good deal, from the viewpoint of each party concerned, which is the *analysis proper*.

CLASSIFICATION: TERM AND SECURITY

Debt is classified according to the period of time over which repayment may or must be made. If the creditor is entitled to insist on repayment one year or less after the date of the borrowing, that is *short-term debt*. In LDCs, much of this is seasonal credit for farmers. However, we also classify as short-term those borrowings which are intended to run for two or three years or even indefinitely subject to the lender's right to call them in at short notice. This includes in particular *overdrafts* which are ordinary demand-deposit accounts overdrawn by permission so as to produce negative balances. Over one year and up to five years is medium term, and over five years is long term, but to avoid the clutter of having three categories, we often refer to *long-term debt* as meaning anything over one year.

Debt is sometimes also classified according to the rights which the creditor has if the debtor defaults on a payment. Some lending is unsecured, which means that the lender joins with other unsecured creditors in seeking to be reimbursed out of the proceeds of whatever is left over from the mess. Some lending is secured, which means that a certain asset or list of assets is named in the contract between borrower and lender, to be *security* for the loan; and in the event of default, the secured creditor can then *foreclose*, that is, take possession of the security, sell it, and from the cash proceeds may keep whatever sum is due, returning the remainder to the debtor to be fought over by less privileged creditors. Any asset which is listed as a security in this way is described as a *pledged* or *mortgaged* asset. Sometimes the security consists of the very asset or assets which are financed by the loan; that is to say, the intention of the parties is to use the proceeds of the loan to purchase assets which will then be pledged as security against default. But this is not always the case. Sometimes other assets are also listed; these are known as *collateral securities*. Quite frequently the assets which are to be purchased are not regarded by the lender as sufficiently secure for the debt; this is particularly the case when the LDC legal framework does not provide a cheap and reliable means of taking possession and selling off secured assets. Then collateral will be looked for. However, if the loan is to provide only a small fraction of the cost of the purchased assets, the balance to be financed by a generous contribution from equity, and if the assets in question command a ready second-hand market in the location where they will be, and if the law supports foreclosure, it is sometimes possible to confine the pledge to the assets which are to be purchased.

In everyday usage, the terms security, collateral security, and collateral, may be used interchangeably.

Borrowing to finance working capital presents a special problem because current assets are transitory. Cash is converted into stock, stock when worked upon becomes work in progress and ultimately finished goods. Goods sold to a customer on credit become *debtors* in the books of account (accounts receivable) and when the debtors pay their bills they turn into cash again. This is the nature of current assets. Now you see them, now you don't. Accordingly, when it is agreed that current assets shall be pledged as security, no attempt is made to list them, but the borrower takes a *general lien* on whatever current assets may happen to exist at the time of foreclosure following default. Such liens are particularly common in short-term debt agreements, because very often short-term borrowing is perceived as an appropriate way to finance working capital, but they are also found as collateral in long-term debts.

When one borrower borrows from two or more lenders, their rights as regards security may clash. If they are secured on separate securities, there should be no clash; however, this is rarely the case. Rather, the creditors will have a hierarchy of rights; one will be subordinated to another. Sometimes they have equal rights, known as security *pari passu*, over certain assets or over all assets. Each borrowing agreement will stipulate that the lender's consent is required for any new agreements which would have an adverse impact on the existing security.

Where foreclosure is problematical owing to defects in legislation or in judicial process, the lender of one thousand rupees may be compelled to ask for security amounting to two or three thousand rupees, including some subordinated or *pari passu* rights, reckoning that on a calculation of probability about one thousand might be extracted from the process.

A healthy business in a healthy economic and social environment, if it is not trying to grow at an overweening rate, will as a rule have sufficient equity to hold down its borrowing requirement well below the level of the assets to be financed. If the total debt is well below the total asset value, each debt can be separately secured on an appropriate asset or group of assets. That means that each debt is adequately secured, no *pari passu* or subordinated rights are required, and because the security is so safe a relatively low rate of interest (and related charges) will be paid. Unfortunately this is rarely the case in LDCs where indigenous equity is scarce. Collateral security is often a can of tangled worms. In developed economies the worms are less tangled. Equity can still be scarce, of course, because of the highly developed greed factor which stimulates overweening asset growth, but the presence of a reasonably predictable system of commercial law means that creditors are not always induced to take far more collateral than their loans are worth.

In the negotiations which occur between a would-be borrower, suffering from the humiliation of owning little or no equity and forced therefore to request heavy borrowings, the lender does not necessarily always have the whip hand. In strict commercial terms they evidently do, but there are often non-commercial pressures at work, since bank officials also have to find personal survival strategies, and banks are therefore not immune to covert pressures of various kinds.

One might suppose that *international* borrowing, such as official borrowing from the International Monetary Fund (IMF), would be strictly commercial and therefore the negotiations for IMF credits, World Bank loans and the like would be very one-sided, with the poorer LDCs in financial distress negotiating under duress. However, a study by Stiles (1991) on IMF negotiations shows that this is not the case. Turkey, Argentina and India were assertive and successful while Jamaica and Zaire were passive and poor negotiators. Stiles describes these negotiations in terms of a technocratic model, a political model, and a more subtle bargaining-game model, but none applies everywhere. There seems to be considerable variety in the professional abilities of bargainers on both sides of the table, just as there is in commercial price bargaining. No doubt this is true of other international agencies also.

SHORT-TERM DEBT ARITHMETIC

With short-term debt there is usually a fee payable when the debt is agreed upon. Charges payable at the outset in this way are known as *up-front charges*. They vary from bank to bank. In addition there is the *interest charge* which is usually calculated on a daily basis and payable monthly, or every three months or every six months. The reason why interest is calculated on a daily basis is that the amount owing may fluctuate from day to day.

Some short-term loans have an agreed schedule of repayments with dates running up to a year ahead, while others merely have a vague agreement that the loan will be paid off at the end of the crop marketing season, or in a year or two, unless abnormal circumstances arise. In the case of an overdraft, even if there are fixed dates for sums to be drawn out and fixed dates for sums to be paid into the account, the balance will fluctuate unpredictably because that same account is also used for ordinary day-to-day transactions.

When we say that interest is calculated on a daily basis, we do not mean that every day a calculation is made and the amount which has accrued is debited to the debtor. We mean that, whenever interest is calculated, it is done by going back over the account, and working out the interest according to the balance owing at the end of each day. For this purpose, if there have been no transactions on an account for several days and the balance is therefore constant for that period, it is treated as a block of days; the daily interest charge is multiplied by the number of days in the block.

A bank normally takes the interest which is due to it by debiting a customer's current account. If the lending is by overdrawing that same account, we find that principal and interest are both shown on the same account. If there are no payments of either principal or interest by the customer, the amount owing will grow at compound interest. However, such a situation would be considered unsatisfactory by a banker, and therefore one would not expect it to be incorporated in the ex-ante design of a project. Interest is in general expected to be paid as it falls due, not added to the debt; there are some exceptions to this rule, but certainly major European development finance agencies would expect that equity contributions by sponsors should suffice to pay interest on both long-term and short-term debt as it falls due to bankers.

Short-term lenders make known the dates when interest will be calculated, but do not usually send any invoice or other notification of the sum calculated, and the debtor may remain unaware of what has been debited to the account until for some unrelated reason a statement of account is received and reconciled. The sending of statements of account at regular intervals is not to be depended upon in LDCs as it is elsewhere. Given that the daily basis of calculation is error-prone if done by hand, and incomprehensible if done by computer, it can come as a nasty shock to the borrower. Sometimes there is a 'little drinkie' in it for the bank officer.

LONG-TERM DEBT ARITHMETIC

The points to watch for when calculating long-term interest are the start date; the period of grace, if any; the method or system of repayment; and special charges, such as a commitment fee. Little drinkies are not calculable ex-ante.

The start date is a complex matter. If a project is to go through a one-year period of construction, and expenditure on fixed assets is to be financed by long-term borrowing during that year, when does the loan start? Assuming that it is all arranged and ready on the first day of the year, it is likely that there will be a series of *disbursements* through the year so that the amount outstanding rises progressively, and the amount remaining available falls progressively. We call this *drawdown*. Assuming furthermore that the timing was correctly forecasted, the closing date for drawdown will coincide with the end of the period of loan-related expenditure; this may be a little before or after the end of the construction phase. The *tenor* or life of the loan then begins; in project work we assume that this starts on the first day of the operating phase.

There may be then a period of grace before the period of repayments begins. The grace period is typically a whole number of years, e.g. two years. During the grace period, the borrower is excused from making payments of principal, but so far as interest is concerned, it may be payable during the grace period, or it may be added to the principal; exceptionally, it may be completely excused, as though it did not arise. This depends on the terms and conditions of the loan agreement. Sometimes one finds that each drawdown is followed by its own grace period and its own repayment period, as though it were a separate loan.

Payments of principal and interest then begin, or such is the expressed intention. Sometimes principal is payable annually and interest quarterly; sometimes both principal and interest are payable every six months, simultaneously, and other arrangements are found. Ideally the schedule of maturity dates should be tailored to the needs of the borrower, i.e. to the cash flow of the project, but one generally finds that lenders have standard arrangements and are unwilling to depart from these. The two most common arrangements are the declining-balance system and the equal-instalment system. These will be briefly described.

The declining-balance system held the field until the middle of the twentieth century and is still prevalent in UK and Commonwealth banking. The principal is divided into a number of equal parts and paid off one part at a time. Thus a five-year repayment period with six-monthly instalments will require one-twelfth of the principal to be repaid every six months, the first beginning six months after the end of the drawdown (or of the grace period) and the last on the fifth anniversary of that date. The balance owing therefore declines step-wise. Interest is calculated on a daily (or monthly) basis having regard to the amount of principal outstanding, so as the principal is progressively repaid, the interest payments progressively diminish. This is a simple arrangement. Provided the rate of interest is fixed, and the principal and start date are known, it is a simple matter to calculate the *debt service schedule*. In ex-ante work, we arrange for a loan facility somewhat larger than we calculate will be needed, in case there is an overspending on capital costs, and we work out the debt service schedule on the assumption that it will be fully used, conforming to the accounting principle of prudence. As to the closure date for drawdown, which is the start date of the grace period or of the repayment period as the case may be, we normally assume that we can negotiate an arrangement whereby that date coincides with the end of the construction period and the beginning of the operating period. In complex projects which cannot be divided into periods in this way, we have to decide in more detail what assets are to be procured with the help of this particular loan, and at what date the last disbursement will occur.

Table 8.1 Debt service schedule, declining-balance method

Scheduling for long- and medium-term debt	Currency:				Thousands of Dinars	
	Principal:				1000 originally	
	Interest rate p.a.:				10.00%	
	Paid (1) or added (0) during grace period				0	
	Months in Yr 0 (0–12):				6	
	Grace period (years):				1	
	Total period (years):				5	
	Repayment period (years):				4	
	Instalments:				annual	

Year:	0	1	2	3	4	5
Balance at start of year	1000	1050	1155	866	578	289
Repayment of principal	0	0	289	289	289	289
Balance remaining	1050	1155	866	578	289	0
Interest Paid	0	0	116	87	58	29
Added	50	105	0	0	0	0
Total payment	0	0	404	375	347	318

Table 8.1 shows a debt service schedule on the declining-balance system, with a life of five years comprising one year of grace and four years of repayments. The drawdown takes place during Year 0. This is likely to be made up of several drawings as payments are made under the various procurement contracts spread over Year 0. If the data can be obtained, a month-by-month schedule of drawings can be made in order to predict the interest which will arise during Year 0; in this case the analyst has based the calculation on the simplifying assumption of a single drawdown right in the middle of the year. During the grace period, interest is to be *funded*, that is, added to the loan.

Note the 50 interest during Year 0, which is 10 per cent of the principal for half a year; and note how there are four actual payments to be made, of diminishing amounts, although the four payments of principal are equal. The amount drawn is 1000, but as interest is added to this figure, the principal rises to 1155. This is paid off in four annual instalments of 289. True, 4 × 289 is 1156. It does work out exactly, but the small change is not shown on the schedule, in ex-ante work.

Table 8.2 shows the same calculations but under the equal-instalment method, sometimes called the American method or World Bank method. Here the four actual payments are to be equal. Each payment includes some

Table 8.2 Debt service schedule, equal-instalment method (details as in Table 8.1)

Year:	0	1	2	3	4	5
Balance at start of year	1000	1050	1155	906	632	331
Repayment of principal	0	0	249	274	301	331
Balance remaining	1050	1155	906	632	331	0
Interest Paid	0	0	116	91	63	33
Added	50	105	0	0	0	0
Total payment	0	0	364	364	364	364

principal and some interest, though these may be combined in a single cheque. As the principal is paid off in each instalment, the interest payment due on the next instalment falls, but the total payment is kept up, so the principal repayment rises.

Note that the interest added during Year 0 is the same as before. The grace period is the same as before. It is only during the period of repayment that the schedule is different: there are now four equal instalments, each of 364. Within this total of 364, the interest element falls from 116 to 33. It falls because the principal on which interest is calculated has fallen, just as it does in the declining-balance method. But this leaves a larger element for repayment of principal (*redemption*) so we see that element rising from 249 to 331.

From a borrower's point of view the latter method is usually better in that it avoids heavier repayments at an early date, which are characteristic of the declining-balance method, and which may occur at an early stage in the operating life of the project when cash flows have not yet built up to their full potential.

The trick with the equal-instalment method is to calculate the amount of the instalment, in this case 364. It must be exactly that amount which will repay the last of the principal on the last day, together with interest at the appropriate rate on whatever principal is outstanding from the penultimate instalment. Computer spreadsheets usually have a built-in function which calculates this payment for you. In Lotus 1–2–3, for instance, you find out the payment by using the function @PMT (*principal, interest rate, number of instalments*). If you have no computer, you need to consult *capital recovery factors* in a book of discount tables. If you have no discount tables, the capital recovery factor is the reciprocal of the annuity factor, which is the cumulative total of the series of discount factors for the various instalments; each discount factor is the reciprocal of the compound interest factor.

For instance, taking a 10 per cent rate of interest, £1000 invested for one year becomes £1,100 and for two years (at compound interest) becomes £1,210. The compound interest factors are 1.1 and 1.21. Discount factors are the reciprocals of these: 1/1.1 is 0.909, and 1/1.21 is 0.826 rounding to three decimal places. If there are to be two instalments, we cumulate the 0.909 and the 0.826 by adding them; 1.736 is the annuity factor. The reciprocal of this is 0.576, and that is the capital recovery factor for two years at 10 per cent. If 1000 dinars has been borrowed and is to be repaid with interest at 10 per cent by two equal annual instalments, each instalment must be 576 dinars. We multiply the principal by the capital recovery factor: 1000 × 0.576 is 576, and that is how we calculate the value of each of the regular instalments. The first of these instalments will contain 100 of interest and 476 redemption of principal; the second will contain 52 of interest and 524 of principal.

This arithmetic is based on a known number of instalments, which should not be confused with the number of years; instalments may well be every six months or every three months. In cases where the amount to be borrowed is not known precisely (although there will be a maximum), the loan agreement usually specifies the capital recovery factor, as an amount per thousand of principal, which must be paid at each instalment.

In addition to interest, there are other charges involved usually, with long-term debt. These include the following:

1 Negotiation fee. A front-end charge which is a percentage of the full amount of the permitted loan. This is usually payable when the borrower accepts a formal offer by the lender. The acceptance of this offer brings into existence a contract, except in some old-fashioned banking systems where vital details such as collateral are left to be settled later, notwithstanding that the negotiation fee is not to be delayed.
2 Legal fees. In some cases the lenders' lawyers' fees are payable up-front in addition to the negotiation fee. If the lender is not the only lender but the leader of a syndicate of lenders, lawyers' fees can be massive.
3 Commitment fee. This is payable during the period in which drawdown is permitted, being a percentage of the outstanding balance which has not been drawn. It is supposed to compensate the lender for having to hold sums at the borrower's disposal, which in fact are not needed until later and so do not produce interest.

INTEREST DURING CONSTRUCTION

During a period of grace, interest may be payable while payments of principal are excused; alternatively interest may be excused, or may be postponed by adding it to the principal sum so that it is repaid over several years. The latter is more common, when the lender is a development finance institution (DFI); commercial banks do not normally offer grace periods at all.

DFIs commonly expect the equity investors to subscribe enough equity capital to pay interest as it is incurred, from the start of the loan. Suppose they do so; the accounting double-entries will be as follows:

1 DEBIT commercial bank; CREDIT share capital.
2 DEBIT interest expense; CREDIT commercial bank.

The above pairs of entries show (1) shareholders sending in cheques in exchange for shares; these cheques are lodged in a commercial bank; then (2) the enterprise issues cheques in favour of the DFI to pay the interest due. At the year-end, the income statement (profit and loss account) is drawn up including interest expense showing the loss incurred.

Now suppose the DFI agrees that interest may be *funded*, that is, added to the loan. Shareholders and commercial bankers are not involved. The single pair of entries is:

DEBIT interest expense; CREDIT DFI loan.

Still the expense appears as a loss item in the income statement for the year. This is likely to be during the construction period, or in the earliest years of the operating period, so that revenues are not likely to be arising in significant amounts. Consequently, any interest expense which is recognised in the accounts during this sensitive period will result in a net loss on the bottom line. This may be embarrassing if it is not foreseen and understood. To avoid this, LDC businesses like to pretend that interest does not arise at this time, and they often debit an asset account, avoiding accounts such as interest expense which flow through into the income statement. The aim is to imply that a lasting asset has been created.

Four asset accounts present themselves as candidates for this dubious practice. The first is the account holding the cost of the fixed assets which are financed by the loan, e.g. equipment. The resulting increase in the value of the fixed assets in the books of account is not, of course, genuine, and this 'capitalisation' is not good accounting practice. Even more dubious is to add to the book value of the assets which are *mortgaged* as collateral security for the loan. The third is the account called 'preliminary expenses', which strictly speaking should hold expenses such as legal fees which are incurred when forming a company and yet are permitted to be regarded as the legitimate business expenses of that company and may be amortised over an arbitrary period of years. To include interest among preliminary expenses without separately disclosing it is certainly dubious. A variant of this is to have an asset account called 'pre-operating expenses'. This too may be amortised, though as the name suggests it ought to be expensed, not capitalised. Again, the interest element certainly ought to be disclosed.

If these expedients are adopted the accounting entries are:

DEBIT asset account; CREDIT DFI loan.

and the impact on the income statements is postponed. This is contrary to the accounting principle of prudence which militates against the postponement of recognition of expense. It is defended on the ground that it conforms to the 'matching principle' which puts the expenses in the years in which the supposed lasting benefits will be reaped. It is also defended on less convincing grounds: that DFIs do not object to it, and that in any case the cash flow statements are not affected, so it does not really matter. In any event, mature businesses which have sufficient revenues from existing operations not to worry about interest during the construction of new projects do not do it, by and large, in LDCs or elsewhere. This seems to be a symptom of under-development.

EXPORT CREDITS

A special kind of medium- or long-term debt is the export credit, which may be subdivided into supplier credits and buyer credits. In essence, both are loans to buy imported goods, and to some extent imported services, at a rate of interest which is subsidised by the Government of the exporting country in order to strengthen the latter's balance of payments. This is not a form of aid to LDCs and the subsidy is not likely to be greater if the merchandise is consigned to an LDC buyer than if it is consigned elsewhere, just so long as it is exported.

In the case of *supplier credit* the buyer is an organisation, usually a company in an LDC, and the seller is an exporting organisation, usually a manufacturing company or a firm of consulting engineers. The latter is located in a country in which the government has set up supplier credit regulations, e.g. western Europe, North America, Japan, or occasionally elsewhere. The merchandise is sold on credit, usually with a downpayment and perhaps some progress payment but with a substantial portion of the selling price spread over a period of years. This 'credit portion' is usually 80 or 85 per cent of the selling price, sometimes more, and the credit period is often five years but sometimes longer, counting from the date of completion of delivery. The debt for the credit portion is acknowledged by the signing of bills of exchange (sometimes promissory notes). These bills are signed by the buyer, returned to the seller, and then sold at a discount to a commercial bank. It is therefore this bank which actually finances the scheme.

Should the buyer fail to pay a bill on its maturity date, or should the buyer's banking system fail to give the buyer the necessary convertible currency to permit payment of the bill, the bank will register the default and go through ordinary legal channels to try to collect. When these legal remedies have failed, the bank is entitled to collect from its insurers. The insurers are a special Government department or parastatal established for the very purpose of ensuring export credits. The insurance premium is paid by the exporter, and with foresight is built into the selling price. Likewise the bankers' discount is built into the selling price; for these reasons a 'credit price' is always higher than a cash price, and if it is known that the buyer is highly dependent on credit, a further profit margin may also be built into the credit price.

Under such a scheme, the banks have a risk-free investment, and offer a lower rate of interest than they would offer to the exporting company itself. The rate of interest is normally fixed by Government under the scheme.

The purpose is to support the balance of payments, and therefore Governments do not wish to encourage export contracts in which the credit portion is very high, nor the credit period very long. The Government insurers are therefore under instructions to refuse to insure contracts which exceed certain limits, or which are risky in any other ways, e.g. badly drafted contracts, unless there is evidence that another Government competing for the export trade has offered terms going beyond the limits. In recent years these limits have been more effectively standardised than formerly, and export credits are accordingly less attractive to LDCs than they used to be. In fact, many LDCs cannot get them at all, because once a country is in default, new insurance becomes first expensive and then impossible to obtain, and this has happened extensively as a consequence of huge LDC debts.

Buyer credits are basically similar but are arranged differently when larger sums of money are involved. Government to Government negotiations rather than company to company negotiations take place; a sum of money known as a *line of credit* is agreed upon, and a bank or syndicate of banks is nominated to offer the credit. It is announced that the importing Government, or a group of companies nominated by it, may borrow up to X amount from the lending bank provided the money is used to purchase merchandise of a certain character for a certain scheme or purpose. In fact, no money goes overseas; the exporting company gets its bills signed and sends them to the bank which buys them at a discount and keeps them until they mature. Again the specialised insurers provide insurance cover which is paid for by the exporter and of course built into the selling price. Again the contract is vetted by civil servants and subjected to limits.

In both types of export credit, the costs to the buyer are (a) interest, which is however often at a favourable rate, (b) export credit insurance, which is typically expensive for LDCs both because of their greater probability of default and because they want cover for larger credit portions and for longer credit periods, and (c) legal fees and stamp duties though these are not more onerous than with other forms of long-term borrowing.

EXCHANGE LOSSES

The list of costs above does not include losses on exchange, which are losses sustained by a borrower when the debt is contractually expressed in a foreign currency and when the value of that currency goes up in terms of the borrower's accounting currency. Such losses can arise both on short-term and on long-term borrowing, but of course the longer the term the greater the chance of an exchange rate movement occurring before the debt is fully paid off.

Naturally, exchange rates can move down as well as up, and so both losses and gains on exchange are possible. But LDC projects are almost always borrowers rather than lenders, and if they borrow abroad it is likely to be from a developed economy which can afford to be a lender. Many LDC economies have chronic economic difficulties, which among other things cause occasional devaluations of their currency. Knowing this, the foreign lenders prefer that their loans should be denominated in their own currencies, and limit very strictly the lending they are prepared to undertake in borrowers' currencies. The upshot is, that whenever one of these periodical devaluations occurs, LDC borrowers sustain losses.

Suppose a debt is expressed in US dollars. One thousand dollars are borrowed at a time when the official exchange rate is 80 rupees per dollar. The borrower's books will show a debt of 80,000 rupees. On the declining-balance system, there may be ten repayments due, each of one hundred dollars or 8,000 rupees, plus interest. After some time, the rate shifts to 90 rupees per dollar. Suppose the third instalment is just about to be paid. It will be necessary to pay the banking system 9,000 rupees in order to buy one hundred dollars which is the amount of principal to be remitted. When that happens, an exchange loss of 1,000 rupees is sustained. But what is worse, there are still six instalments to follow, and if the rate stays at 90, there will be further losses to come ultimately totalling 6,000 rupees.

The loss of 1,000 rupees actually sustained when a payment is made is called *realised exchange loss*. It must be shown in the income statement as a loss during the period in which it happens. If large, it will probably be given a rubric to itself; if small, it may be included under financial expenses or 'other items'.

The expected further loss of 6,000 rupees is called an *unrealised exchange loss*. This is something which can go up or down as the rate changes further, and so is not yet fixed. However, prudence requires that some recognition be given to the impending loss as soon as it is perceived. It must therefore be shown in the income statement during the period in which it is foreseen. Current UK best practice (ICA 1987: 257) requires that all monetary liabilities denominated in foreign currency should be shown (in the Balance Sheet at any given date) by translation using the rate of exchange ruling at that date, and the exchange gain or loss which arises whenever a translation rate changes should be reported as part of the profit or loss for the preceding period. It further requires that such gains or losses should be reported as ordinary, not as extraordinary items, unless the underlying transactions are themselves extraordinary.

However, what is best practice in the UK is not necessarily common practice in LDCs. We often see such losses debited directly to reserves in the balance sheets without any reporting in the income statement. Even more of a departure from the precepts of prudence and honest disclosure is the practice of showing the unrealised loss as a negative reserve as though it were some kind of intangible asset, thus suppressing the effect on shareholder reserves as well as the effect on profit.

Whereas, with a realised exchange loss actually paid to the bank, the double-entry system will record: Debit Income; Credit Bank. With an unrealised exchange loss, the entries will depend on which of the three systems just mentioned is adopted, viz:

1 Debit an income statement account (which will reduce retained earnings), credit loans (best practice).
2 Debit retained earnings directly, credit loans (by-passing the income statement).
3 Debit a reserve for unrealised exchange losses, credit loans (denying all concessions to the principle of prudence).

Just as all three systems are found in ex-post accounting, so all three are found in ex-ante projections, which goes to show how ex-ante analysis designed to recognise inflation and currency movement is still in its infancy. Where the enterprise already exists and has adopted a convention, the analyst may adhere to it for new projects, but otherwise, since ex-post conventions are often influenced by ex-ante studies, best practice should be introduced at the ex-ante stage.

So far as cash flow and funds flow statements are concerned, realised losses are cash flows and will appear as such, but unrealised losses are not, and will not appear until eventually they become realised. These points assume great importance if we are forecasting devaluations, which we may do alongside the forecasting of inflation, when we drop the assumption of constant prices.

OWNERS' CAPITAL AND THE LIMITS TO BORROWING

If only you could borrow enough to finance all of the assets utilised in a new project, however large, you could instantly go for economies of scale, produce high quality at low cost, become a dominant actor in the chosen market, become a price-leader and a Knight Grand Star of the Worshipful Order of Bulls. Given average managerial competence and a willingness to delegate, only your deplorable lack of single-mindedness would prevent you from owning eventually every business in the country if you lived long enough.

This is particularly applicable in export-oriented manufacturing projects, where the world market is virtually unlimited, and where modern technology requires a capital investment per worker of one to two hundred thousand pounds, ten or a hundred times more than in domestic small-scale industry.

The part played by limited finance in limiting the growth of an enterprise was clarified some time ago by Kalecki (1954: 91). In earlier literature there was a good deal of nonsense to the effect that (a) a firm is owned by an entrepreneur but financed by rentiers; (b) the entrepreneur's contribution is not one of finance, but of management, risk-bearing, creativity, etc. and therefore lack of entrepreneurial capital cannot be a problem; (c) each firm is conceived of as producing and selling one product in one market, and the demand for any commodity in any market is limited, so every firm has a commercial limit; and (d) since economies of scale lead to the failure of smaller businesses, and since small businesses are clearly visible all around us, there must be dis-economies of scale in excessively large production facilities.

Kalecki pointed out five basic facts:

- 'The access of a firm to the capital market, or in other words the amount of rentier capital it may hope to obtain, is determined to a large extent by the amount of its entrepreneurial capital. It would be impossible for a firm to borrow capital above a certain level determined by the amount of its entrepreneurial capital.' There is, in other words, a limit to the ratio of debt to equity. This ratio is usually called *gearing* or *leverage*, both terms deriving from mechanics.

- 'In addition, many firms will not use to the full the potentialities of the capital market because of the "increasing risk" involved in expansion.' Since borrowing involves a definite commitment to pay interest, and since cash flows are likely to be subject to unpredictable bad years, a high gearing will bite deeper into dividends in the event of a bad patch than a low gearing would, and in the event of a very severe cash flow problem carries a greater risk of total failure. This is clearly something that both owners and lenders would wish to avoid, by limiting the gearing.

- 'Indeed, some firms may even keep their investment at a level below that of the entrepreneurial capital, a part of which may be held in securities.' Borrowers, like lenders, do not like to risk all their eggs in one basket, and are likely not to place all their entrepreneurial capital in one single business or indeed in any business, but may keep a part in safer form, invested in gold or convertible securities. This reduces the base for the gearing. We must remember too that, in a country where there is a developed capital market, the owners should be perceived not merely as persons endowed with X of personal fortune, but as participants on a capital market in which they may be simultaneously borrowing and lending as well as buying and selling equity. In that event, their view of what is the best gearing ratio for a project of given degree of risk is likely to be closely tied to the average in the financial market for projects of similar risk. This leads into an elegant analysis called the Miller-Modigliani model (1961), but that is a branch of analysis suited only to very highly developed capital markets, not found in LDCs. In any case, knowing that a project is closely bound to the norms of the capital market is not very helpful in predicting market opinion on gearing limits either for this specific project, or for this firm, nor indeed for all projects or firms taken together. In LDC situations especially those involving powerful but shadowy financial families operating within weak tax-collection régimes the Kalecki model seems more realistic than the much more recent Miller-Modigliani model. Specifically, the latter requires that the proposed project and its inherent risks should be recognised by market analysts as falling into a class of business activities with which they are already familiar and to which they have assigned a risk factor ('Beta') based on a statistical analysis of past experience. Unfortunately no such market, no such recognition, no such class, and no such experience may exist in LDCs.

- 'A joint-stock company is not a "brotherhood of shareholders" but is managed by a controlling group of big shareholders while the rest of the shareholders do not differ from holders of bonds with a flexible interest rate.' This means that bondholders, who can monitor what is going on in a business with the privilege of inside information and direct access to the most senior executives, typically have at least as much influence on corporate matters as majority shareholders. The latter have powers to vote on a much wider range of topics in general meetings if they can find out what is going on but can always be outvoted. The position of a minority shareholder is therefore an uncomfortable one. Many investors are disinclined to hold more than 10 per cent but less than 50 per cent of equity, for this reason. This disinclination makes it more difficult to issue fresh shares to them and that is another factor which constrains the access to finance. It is another form of gearing, the ratio of outsiders' equity to insiders' equity. Entrepreneurial capital therefore means insiders' equity, and this is what is always limited.

- The controlling group 'if it is to continue to exercise control cannot sell an unlimited number of shares to the public. It is true that this difficulty may be partly overcome, for instance, by building up holding companies.' Here Kalecki points to the practice of retaining a 51 per cent voting control while owning only 26 per cent of the equity capital. This is achieved by owning 51 per cent of the shares of a holding company which in turn owns 51 per cent of the shares of the operating subsidiary. But this device has its limitations; lenders are likely to insist on having some representatives on both boards and to arrive at agreements on corporate policy by exchange of letters by-passing the formal structure of puppet board meetings.

It is assumed here that the controlling group of shareholders wishes very much to retain control of the enterprise. This is vital to our perception of the whole financial framework. This desire to retain control is not only for the sentimental reason that the parent wishes to remain close to the brain-child. Nor is it entirely based on the legitimate proposition that the investment can be best protected by ensuring that it remains in the charge of those persons who originated the business concepts on which the operating profitability is based. A third reason is the social prestige which accompanies directorships. We must also remember that *in the short term* there is often more money to be made by buying and selling shares, takeovers, mergers and break-ups, golden hellos and golden good-byes and generally speaking by the covert exercise of 'insider' power than there is from plodding on with the everyday operations of a business. If the original sponsors genuinely wish to establish a project for the benefits to be derived from its operation, they will have to abstain from 'short-termism' and destructive wheeler-dealing themselves and *retain control to prevent raids by others*. These are four powerful reasons for wishing to retain control and avoid relegation to the uncomfortable position of minority shareholder.

If the total equity is a limited multiple of the equity held by the major controlling shareholders, how is the medium- and long-term debt limited to a multiple of the equity? There are two simple reasons why it should be so limited.

The first stems from the inherent unpredictability of the entity's cash flow, that is to say, of the resource cash flow arising from the several investment projects undertaken by the organisation. Since interest is at a fixed rate while dividends are not, dividends act as a buffer between fluctuating cash flows and fixed debt service commitments. If gearing is too high, the debt service commitments are increased and the buffer is reduced. Thus the inherent riskiness of the project is geared up or magnified by the debt. All parties concerned will have a view on the inherent unpredictability of the project cash flow, and they may not share the same assessment of that, but they will all agree that there is a limit beyond which it would be unsafe to go; the equity must be something greater than zero per cent, and the debt something less than 100 per cent of the net assets utilised at any time.

The second reason is that the owners, not the lenders, have the legal right to manage the organisation and its projects, at least until things go so wrong that the creditors are entitled to appoint a receiver or an administrator. The lenders rely to a great extent on the honesty of the borrowers, i.e. that the business will be conducted in the manner described to them. They rely on the competence of the borrowers, who should know their business from the inside, rather better than non-specialist bankers can be expected to know it from the outside. Above all, they rely on the commitment, dedication and hard work of the directors, without which the enterprise is likely to fail with obvious implications for satisfactory servicing of the debt.

These conditions can best be obtained by insisting that the entrepreneurs invest a substantial amount of their own money. With an investment of their own to protect, they are likely to be strongly motivated, and are not likely to proceed without the needful competence. As for honesty, once the sponsors have put in some money and it has taken the tangible form of some buildings or other assets, that goes a long way towards demonstrating that they are serious about the project.

It is of course impolite for bankers to mention these fears openly, and it is sometimes very difficult for a bank director to stipulate a tighter gearing limit for one customer than for another without pointing out the very weaknesses in the proposal which would undermine it in the deliberations of the bank's own board. This is especially the case in public sector banking with political intervention in lending decisions. Consequently, it is common practice to publish gearing limits for certain broad classes of projects and to apply these uniformly.

The constraint that states that debt may not exceed X per cent of equity may be applied, in negotiations with bankers, to the year-end position at the end of Year 0, or to the date when the ratio will be at its highest. It is in either event a calculation based on the pro forma balance sheet at a single date. More precisely, it looks at the project as a whole and at its cash flows and determines which date is the critical date and applies itself to that. In most projects this will be immediately after maximum drawdown. If the ratio is satisfactory then, it will probably be more than satisfactory later; the average ratio over the entire project life is therefore unimportant.

An alternative measure is to look at the cash flow projections and calculate the debt service cover ratio. This is the cash flow stream available for servicing debt, divided by the stream required for servicing debt. When this concept is applied to long-term debt, the stream available for debt service (the numerator) is the resource cash flow minus the tax cash flow, or what amounts to the same thing, the streams going to dividends and retained earnings, plus short-term debt service which is treated as subordinate, plus the long-term debt service itself. A rule of thumb often used is that this ratio should be at least 1.8 or 1.7; where there is a history of defaults, this may be raised to 1.9 or 2.0. But clearly this ratio varies from year to year during the debt service period, and is not calculable during those many years of the project before and after the debt service period when there ought not to be any debt service. A good workable arrangement is one that sets a minimum figure both to the average during the debt service period and to the maximum or worst year. As with the gearing constraint, the worst year is likely to be at the start, when debt is at its highest and revenues at their lowest. If this gives an unsatisfactory ratio, the preferred solution is to extend the grace period into the revenue-earning years, and this should produce a satisfactory ratio. Once this has been done, the later years will probably be well above the minimum, so the average over the period does not really matter.

There are some cases where the average over many years does matter, whether a gearing ratio or a debt service cover ratio is being used as a limiter. Water schemes are typically long-lived projects with rather shaky revenue prospects, which means that they attract soft loans of ten, twelve, even fifteen or twenty years; throughout this period the cash flow is weak and may cause the ratio to oscillate around its minimum acceptable value. This will then be seen clearly by calculating its average over the period. Even then, this long-term average is of limited importance. The lending agency cannot monitor the average, until it is too late; they can and do monitor on a quarterly or yearly basis, and intervene to protest about the revenues when the cash flow drifts away from plan.

ANALYSIS BY AND FOR THE BORROWER

The use of analytical cash flow (ACF) techniques permits the analyst to calculate the present value of the financial cash flows for each of the financing parties to the deal, including the various lenders, and so to see whether these IRRs are all above their respective walk-away minima, who is getting the lion's share, and what might be negotiated from whom. However, so far as the total of all the financing transactions is concerned, this must always be arithmetically equal to the total of the resource flows, so its present value is determined by those. It therefore makes no sense to say, as one occasionally hears it said, that a project is feasible if the IRR of its resource flows is equal to or greater than the IRR of its finance. What is true is that, from the point of view of any one party, such as the equity investors, the project is attractive if the following apply:

1 The IRR of its resource flows is equal to or greater than the IRR of all the *other* financial parties.
2 The IRR of that one party's financial flows is equal to or greater than that which could be obtained by investing in some other project of similar size and risk.

But these approaches look at the project from the viewpoint of the financier. What of the finance, looked at from the viewpoint of the project? This is an issue which was raised first in Botswana by the civil servant and academic Charles Harvey, whose book (Harvey 1983) is still influential. It may seem odd that a project can be said to have a viewpoint, unless it be that of its owners, who are one of the financing parties, or that of its managers, who are answerable to the owners. But seen in the perspective of national economic development, a project is an investment opportunity which exists, and if the resource cash flow is favourable (there are debates about whether actual or shadow prices ought to be used in this calculation) it is in the national interest that favourable finance be found and applied to the project.

Does it matter in the national interest who the financiers are, how they share the burden of financing and how they share the yields? One might argue that Government, representing the national interest, need not concern itself with this, but should leave it to the workings of the financial 'market'. Let the sponsors find their own project funds, and if a project goes unfinanced it must be inherently unattractive. This laissez-faire approach is used, for instance, in western Europe, except for major projects of national importance like the Channel Tunnel or Airbus Industrie.

One might argue that financing should be left to the financial markets to the extent that these are experienced and capable. This supervisory approach is used, for instance, in semi-developed Turkey, where inward investment is almost invariably accepted without amendment by the State Planning

Organisation provided it is shown that the financing parties have properly considered the cash flows up to five years ahead and have consented to them.

In many LDCs, however, Government intervenes actively in the financing. The rationale is as follows:

1 Unlike western Europe and Turkey whose currencies are convertible, these countries have unconvertible currencies. The small demand which exists elsewhere to hold their currencies for transactions purposes has been amply filled. For them, foreign currency is a real resource; it is equivalent to goods and services. The management of the balance of payments requires husbanding of this resource. Some financing arrangements will have a better or worse effect on foreign exchange than others. The Government cannot therefore be indifferent to the choice of financing arrangement.
2 Government is continuously in negotiation with the IMF, World Bank and other international and bilateral agencies to arrange international borrowing for the years ahead. Much of this is on 'soft' terms. Many of the projects which are notified to Government will qualify for loans under these programmes. There must therefore be some organisational arrangement which will marry projects to loans and loans to projects.
3 Government is itself one of the financing parties. While it is true to say that the tax revenue from project to Government remains within the country and therefore has no net impact on the country, Government cannot be indifferent to its fiscal impact. By this I do not mean simply that tax revenue should be maximised, much as I sympathise with civil servant colleagues who, in these discussions, have told me 'Remember, we have to live too.' I mean that Government has to support these projects with expenditure on infrastructure of various kinds, and there must be some calculation which checks that the tax revenue from projects *on the average* attains a volume which will pay for that expenditure. This suggests that projects should be divided into classes and for each class Government should require a minimum take, not an easy calculation to introduce but surely better than simply maximising the tax or ignoring the fiscal impact altogether.

Harvey's approach is to examine each financing stream as though it were a separate proposal, which may or may not be tied to a specific project. We are concerned, of course, specifically with foreign currency borrowing. Each 'financing proposal' involves the receipt of a sum of currency, or more likely the import of some goods or services without payment by the LDC. Either way this is a benefit. After the end of the drawdown, and after a possible grace period, there will be a series of painful experiences in which convertible currency has to be found, to pay off the principal and to pay interest. We make a schedule of the amount and the dates, and apply discounting to arrive at the net present value and the internal rate of return.

This is just what we would do in Section 3 of an ACF statement except that Sections 1 and 2 are missing and we are only looking at that part of Section 3 which deals with an overseas borrowing package.

The IRR of borrowing, viewed in this way, is called the *effective rate of interest* (ERI); it may be expressed in constant-prices terms, in which case it is the *real* effective rate of interest.

The net present value of borrowing, when discounted at the Government's test rate of discount for economic evaluations, is the *grant element* in the loan. For example, a loan may have a nominal rate of interest of 10 per cent and an ERI of 11 per cent (due to front-end charges). If discounted at 10 per cent, it will have a negative present value to the lender but a positive present value to the borrower. Harvey considers it from the borrower's point of view. Say the PV at 10 per cent is 1000 rupees, but, the Government discount rate may be 15 per cent. Discounting the stream at 15 per cent, we get a much larger PV, say 10,000 rupees. This sum is the grant element. This loan is as attractive as a notional loan at a 15 per cent ERI combined with a grant of 10,000 rupees. In this way a soft loan can be perceived as a hard loan together with a grant element, and in present value terms the two can be disentangled, provided of course the Government knows what discount rate to use. In this situation the appropriate rate would be the going rate on hard loans.

This is a useful kind of analysis, and even where Government is not involved, provided there is some kind of institutional financing on soft terms, the grant element in it can be worked out in this way.

Harvey goes on to deal with *hidden costs*. These are as follows:

1 The extra procurement expenditure associated with *tied aid* whereby merchandise is not eligible for financing unless it is bought from a particular country or group of countries, whose exporters are inclined to take advantage of this fact to raise their prices.
2 The costs of delaying project implementation to give time for negotiations, and for delay in disbursement even after finance is contractually tied up.
3 Reduced benefits to be expected from the project because its choice of technology is distorted towards heavy use of imported capital equipment, which is more readily financed than locally produced equipment or indeed appropriate-technology equipment.
4 Bureaucratic costs (and benefits), by which Harvey means the tendency to give preference to projects which maintain the custom and practice and the momentum of institutions in the aid business. Agency bureaucrats may continue with annual allocations in a sector which is no longer beneficial, through institutional inertia, and this is a cost. On the other hand, an aid agency may continue to disburse aid in a country for some time after it has been signalled as politically undesirable, and this may be a benefit to the country.
5 Political costs, which are the concessions that have to be made in the realm

of international diplomacy in order to maintain cordial relations with donor countries.

The first three of these costs are damaging to the resource cash flow. This indicates a situation where it is not possible to assess a financial proposal in isolation from the project which is to be financed. And this brings us to the general question of the framework in which the resource cash flows and the financial cash flows are evaluated.

The framework may emerge from the following axioms:

1 Every project should be appraised on its resource cash flow alone, to see how it stands up regardless of its financing pattern, since the financing arrangements may change from time to time anyway, because of takeovers etc.
2 The financial cash flows if taken together will be equal to the resource cash flows, though of opposite sign (the flow equality principle), so there is no sense in seeking to appraise them in that way, if the resource cash flows have already been appraised: the answer will be the same.
3 A financial proposal is sometimes specific to a project and has no validity in the absence of that project. It should be appraised (a) as a whole, only to the extent that it has an impact on the resource cash flow because of hidden costs; (b) in its separate elements, to determine what is the yield to each party (beneficiary analysis); (c) in its separate elements, to ensure that the proposal does not violate any of the financial constraints imposed by the parties, such as an impossible gearing ratio, or an impossible overdraft requirement, bearing in mind that to go ahead ignoring these violations would create financial distress or insolvency and possibly the failure of the whole enterprise.
4 If a financial proposal is not specific to a project, but can be negotiated for a programme of projects not yet specified, it can be appraised in terms of its grant element and in terms of its effective rate of interest (ERI). The hidden political costs may also be assessed, though not quantified in money terms. The hidden costs of tying can also be assessed, though very roughly indeed, by adding an estimated percentage (to the nearest 5 per cent) to the cost of tied imports, and this can be added to the ERI. The costs of bias, negotiating delay, and programme inertia, which will have their impact on resource cash flows, cannot be estimated even roughly when the project details are not known, and like political costs can be assessed only in qualitative terms. Despite the unknowns in this kind of appraisal, it is still possible sometimes to reach a rational decision to accept a line of credit, to refuse it, or to put it in a ranking with other accepted lines of credit, which means that it is accepted in principle but you do not assign projects to it until better sources of finance have been exhausted. Of course, once a line of credit is accepted by contract, commitment fees become payable and it is a matter of which contracts should use it rather than whether it will be used at all.

Chapter 9

The best of all possible worlds

When an investment proposal has been modelled by a suite of spreadsheets, in which the front-end calculations deal with physical parameters and the subsequent calculations deal with the financial consequences, it becomes possible to adjust the physical parameters and see what difference this makes to the financial consequences. The best possible project design can often be found by a process of trial and error. Of course, what is best in terms of the financial net present value may not be best in terms of the national economic net present value. What is best in terms of the financial internal rate of return for the equity investors may not be the best design from the viewpoint of the long-term lenders. What is best for the customers may not be what is best for the employees. What seems best under constant prices may differ from what seems best if inflation is assumed.

In principle, these conflicts should be explored, negotiated and settled between the parties. In practice, physical parameters tend to be left to non-financial experts such as engineers, agriculturists and other natural scientists, who keep out of the financial areas, while the financial negotiations tend to be left to bankers and accountants who regard the scientific areas as 'technical'. There is often a lack of collaboration between the disciplines. The result is that the physical parameters are decided upon by the natural scientists using crude methods of approximation to some economic or financial optimum according to who pays them for their work. We might characterise this as a 'partial optimum', meaning that it is not impartial. Their conclusions are then usually taken over by the financial analysts as *project data*, and treated as though cast in concrete, or at least, as firm as any project data can ever be.

However, it is only fair to say that many engineers and agriculturists have sufficient knowledge of financial matters to be aware of the situation outside their own remit, and bring some important 'technical' options to the attention of the financial analysts by identifying more than one set of results for further consideration. These are usually presented as a Base Case, Option A, Option B, and so on. Where only one case is proposed, that may mean that there are no others remotely worth considering, but usually it means that the design put forward is the partial optimum, and the party who has guided the study has reasons to resist consideration of alternative possibilities. If other options are to be explored, the financial analyst and the economic analyst must be able to suspect what their nature might be, and be able to ask questions which will elicit the hidden data.

An attempt is sometimes made to avoid this problem, when the various interested parties jointly guide the experts, as is sometimes done by setting up a steering committee to deal with consultants, with terms of reference, preliminary report, interim report and final report. This committee work adds hugely to the overhead cost and to the time taken. No private sponsor would entertain the idea and it does not always succeed. Frequently, whether the range of options is left to the discretion of the consultants or is guided by a steering committee, we find that all the options presented have exactly the same choice of technology and require major imports of fixed assets and subsequent spare parts from a country which, by coincidence, is the country of the consultants. But you must be diplomatic. So then you need more consultants from some other country to give you their impartial advice on the 'highly technical' but 'possibly somewhat dated' work of the first consultants. This kind of nonsense bedevils publicly aided projects in LDCs, and places those investment proposals which can be decided unilaterally (small private sector investments) at a distinct advantage.

A few Asian LDCs, and some private sector company directors, require capital expenditure applications to incorporate a discussion of technological alternatives. This simple rule seems worthy of imitation elsewhere.

SOME TYPICAL OPTIONS

One of the most difficult choices concerns the determination of the *scale* of the project, that is, the volume of benefits (outputs) which its initial inputs (fixed assets, working capital, and labour/management structure) will be capable of delivering. Here we have to reconcile the volume which the beneficiaries or customers are likely to take with the volume which the project will be capable of supplying. The former – let us call it the demand – is a maximum figure, often limited by estimated market share; the latter – let us call it the supply – is a minimum figure, in the sense that we want to ensure that the proposed expenditure on initial assets will secure a supply of *at least* the volume on which we base our calculations of benefit.

The demand ceiling is not certain if it may be affected by price; pricing policy is itself a variable. Demand is to be understood in the context of an intended marketing strategy including a pricing strategy.

The supply capability may be uncertain if there are options of multiple shift working, though this is not generally feasible except in urban environments where it is already well established and family life has adapted to it. Passenger transport does not usually cater for two or three shift systems. However, the length of the single shift may vary from eight to twelve hours.

It is necessary to know the people and the place concerned before passing judgement on hours of work, and it is necessary to know the competitors before passing judgement on the pricing policy. The analyst may be able to make personal enquiries, or to commission specialists to do so, but will mostly have to be content with finding out that intelligent questions have been asked, and that a project design has been formulated which is consistent with the few known facts.

Given that a certain volume is to be produced, basically by a certain technique of production, there are at least five factors which can be traded off against each other in various combinations:

- Environmental impact.
- Product quality.
- Reliability of operation.
- Capital cost.
- Operating cost.

If we sometimes make the error of accepting the basic technique without examining radical alternatives, we almost invariably fail to consider all possible trade-offs among these five. With five factors there are ten possible trade-off pairs to be considered and adjudged.

In principle we ought to consider the basic technique and the scale of operations as not settled until their consequences have been assessed in full detail with the trade-offs optimised; in other words, the basic technique and the scale of operation should be put into the melting-pot along with the five other factors, making seven in all, with twenty-one possible trade-offs. Clearly we do not systematically look at all of these; absence of data (an acute problem in nearly all LDCs) and the limitations of the human brain make it impossible. We tend to make some key choices first – scale and basic technique – and then tinker with the consequences. This shows why there is nearly always scope for improvement in investment design, and it shows the importance of imagin-ation, experience, lateral thinking, and quantitative approach in designing the best possible projects.

The trade-off between capital cost and operating cost is relatively straightforward and is usually considered after the scale and basic technique have been chosen. It may be possible to reduce the cost of operating labour by installing additional instruments, so that one operator at the control panel can directly read certain meters without the need for an assistant to go and report, or can remotely control certain motors or valves without the need for an assistant to go to them. These are examples of reducing labour cost during the operating phase at the expense of additional fixed assets (perhaps imported materials) during the construction phase. Note that this kind of mechanisation – for that is what it is – may be perceived by economists as choosing a different technique, substituting capital for labour. However, we are referring to relatively minor shifts in the degree of mechanisation. There is no change in the *basic* technique of production here. These close variants on a basic theme are sometimes called *families of techniques* or *technologies*.

After establishing the cost of the additional instrumentation, and the annual cost savings of the reduced labour, the project can be appraised in terms of IRR and so on with and without this variant, to see whether it makes the investment better or worse. Alternatively, the variation can be looked at alone – treating the additional capital cost as that of a separate *incremental* project, and the annual cost savings as its benefit or output; this incremental project will have its own IRR which investors may compare with the minimum acceptable (hurdle) rate of return.

The appraisal of the variant as an incremental project is simpler and easier than the with/without study, which involves making a full set of spreadsheets with the variation, a second set without it, and a third set subtracting the second from the first. The real resource flows – as set out in Sections 1 and 2 of an analytical cash flow statement – will be the same, whichever way you do it, but the fuller study enables more financial questions to be answered. The full 'with' balance sheets permit consideration of the questions – Can finance be found for the project with the additional mechanisation? and How will it affect the financial ratios? – which would not be seen on the incremental balance sheets alone.

We turn now to a trade-off which is less often looked at: capital cost versus reliability of operation. We shall consider this in a manufacturing context, though there are other processes in which it should be investigated.

STATISTICAL OVER-DESIGN

Manufacturing, including agro-industrial and mineral-processing operations, involves the use of plant and machinery which is not running all the time. Even plant which is extremely difficult to switch off, such as that which produces solid-setting plastics by continuous process, has to be switched off at times for planned maintenance, and switches itself off at other times by unplanned breakdown. Ordinary plant is switched off frequently, usually at night, sometimes during meal breaks, often if there is an interruption in the supply of electric power or of raw materials, for maintenance and repair, and for re-setting when a range of products is required from the same equipment. The time when equipment is not up and running may be divided into intended and unintended interruptions of work. Time lost by failures during working hours when equipment is intended to be running, and by stoppages for maintenance which unfortunately cannot be delayed to non-working periods, is called unscheduled down-time, or simply down-time. A good list of causes of down-time in process plant can be found in Wells (1980: 66) together with a discussion of *availability analysis*.

A plant with a nominal capacity (having due regard for scheduled down-time) of ten tons per hour working an eight hour shift might be scheduled to produce 80 tons, but if unscheduled down-time averages 5 per cent the effective output is only 76 tons. Put the other way round, if our sales revenues assume 80 tons per shift, the plant must be designed for 84.2 tons, i.e. 80/0.95 tons per hour. This may seem to be over-sized, but it is not.

The term over-design does not imply mistaken design; nor in fact does it necessarily suggest design work at all, since over-design of a project can be achieved by selecting larger machines from a catalogue, all of which were fully designed already.

The pattern of stoppages has to be studied statistically in order to estimate the average down-time. Data can be obtained from previous operations, or from similar plants operating under similar conditions elsewhere; manu-facturers' guidelines may be poor guides to this, since they normally disregard power supply failures and other operating problems which are common in LDCs. Moreover, such guidelines usually indicate the average period before failure without showing the average duration of down-time.

The average period of running before an unwanted stoppage occurs is called the mean time to failure (MTTF) and for the purpose of forecasting can be defined as a probability function or frequency distribution having a mean and a standard deviation. Likewise the average down-time needed to restart the equipment and resume operations is a frequency distribution with a mean and a standard deviation. It is simplest to treat these as normal distributions, though if greater sophistication is wanted, exponential or Poisson distri-butions can be assumed; some discussion of this can be found in Wells (1980: 61–7).

The mean time between failures (MTBF) is the sum of the MTTF and the mean repair time; for instance, if the MTTF is 50 days and the mean repair time is ten days, the equipment will be expected to fail every 60 days (MTBF = 60). That works out at 6.08 failures per year since 365/60 = 6.08; and since each failure has a duration of ten days, the down-time is 60.8 days. The up-time is 365–60.8 or 304.2 days. The down-time percentage is 60.8/365 which is 16.7 per cent, and the up-time percentage is 83.3 per cent. If the desired output from the equipment is 1000 tons per week, the equipment must be designed to produce 1000/0.8335 which is 1200 tons per week, not 1167 as you might think. The working year is effectively shortened so that the design output goes up to 1000 × 365/304.2 tons.

That calculation takes account of the mean down-time, but it ignores the standard deviation. Suppose that in a year the MTTF is 50 days, as above, with standard deviation four days, and the mean repair time is ten days with standard deviation three days. This gives a MTBF of 60 days, as above, but with a standard deviation of five days, $\sqrt{(4^2+3^2)}$. We want to be very sure of producing the stipulated volume, because any shortfall will be disastrous for our customers and will attract large commercial penalties, let us suppose. Assuming that the MTBF frequency distribution is Normal, we can be 95 per cent sure that the MTBF will lie within two standard deviations of its mean, i.e. it will be 60 days plus or minus ten. Let us suppose that 95 per cent security represents the degree of security we need. The worst case apart from the 5 per cent-likely scenario we have chosen to disregard will be a MTBF of 50 days. That would represent 7.3 failures per year (365/50). On each such occasion we have to expect a down-time of ten days on average. This figure too is subject to variability, and has a standard deviation which we have supposed is three days. Note that the standard deviation of a sample is always higher than that of the full population from which it is drawn. If three days is the standard deviation of *all* repair times, that of a sample of seven occurrences would be 3.4 days, obtained by multiplying three by $n/(n-1)$ where n is the sample size. However, it is not likely that data are available for a large population of repair times; it is much more reasonable to suppose that reports are available for one year, so the figure of three days does not need to be adjusted.

We can be 95 per cent confident that the down-time would not exceed two standard deviations above the mean, that is, ten plus 6 or 16 days. The total annual down-time would be $7.3 \times 16 = 116.8$ days or 32 per cent of the year. To cope with this, we would have to specify a plant rated at 1471 tons rather than 1200 tons. Let us be clear: we want 1000 tons per week since that is the basis of our revenue calculations; plant specified to have a capacity of 1200 tons/week will *in an average year* deliver 1000 tons, but plant specified at 1471 tons/week will be 95 per cent sure to do so in any given year. Whether it is worth the candle to buy the larger plant depends on how much dearer it would be and how severe are the consequences of short delivery; it may be that a lower level of security, such as 92.5 per cent or 90 per cent, requiring fewer than two standard deviations from the safe side of the mean would offer a more satisfactory all-round compromise. This enlargement of plant design based on a probabilistic assessment of its performance is called *statistical over-design*. The following formulae summarise the above remarks:

MTBF	=	$MTTF + MTTR$	and
TBF_{SD}	=	$\sqrt{(TTF_{SD}^{2} + TTR_{SD}^{2})}$	and
F_Y	=	$365 / (MTBF + 2\,TBF_{SD})$	and
C_D	=	$C_N \times 365 / \{365 - [F_Y \times (MTTR + 2\,TTR_{SD})]\}$	
where MTBF	=	mean time between failures	
TBF_{SD}	=	time between failures (standard deviation)	
MTTR	=	mean time to repair	
TTR_{SD}	=	time to repair (standard deviation)	
MTTF	=	mean time to failure	
TTF_{SD}	=	time to failure (standard deviation)	
F_Y	=	failures per year	
C_D	=	design capacity required for 95 per cent confidence	
C_N	=	nominal capacity.	

However, in practice the data are seldom available to permit such a calculation to be performed. Nor can it safely be assumed that the probabilities follow Gauss's Normal distribution, on which the above calculations are based, or indeed any other recognised distribution. Instead, over-design is entered according to a concept of safety margin based on professional experience, adding between 10 and 50 per cent to the installed capacity according to the circumstances.

There is some danger that this unsupported over-specification might be suspected of having its origin in the dishonesty and greed of machinery salespersons or the corruption of buyers. Some such enlargement is, however, necessary whenever reliability and security of output are important. Over-design is a costly corollary of the difficult operating conditions found in LDCs and one of the factors which make it difficult for them to compete with their rivals in developed, stable economies.

IMPROVING THE RELIABILITY

In the arithmetical example given we saw how capacity of 1471 tons would be needed to be 95 per cent confident of delivering 1000 tons/week, a very substantial uplift, though it is unlikely that the capital cost would increase by quite so much. That example supposed stoppages lasting ten days after up-times of fifty days; many engineers would react with horror to such bad figures, but when power failures are frequent and foreign exchange with which to buy spare parts is not readily available, such results are not implausible.

We have been considering plant and machinery here as though it were one single machine with a characteristic pattern of failures and repair times. In reality, production processes commonly involve a series of operations each with its own pattern of down-time.

This is not quite the same in agriculture as it is in manufacturing or in agro-industry. In agriculture, for example, we may think of the nursing of seedlings as a process, followed by planting out, followed by growing which itself may involve several distinct operations, followed by harvesting – any of these can be interrupted by lack of care, by unseasonable weather, by warfare, or by lack of necessary inputs. Such interruptions, when there may be nothing to do but wait, are analogous to periods of repair time. When the interruption ends we can resume normal or near-normal operations, with a net reduction in the output for the year. Probably also the quality of output will be affected. But if the interruption has been severe, there will be death of the crop and/or farm animals and no output at all for the rest of that season. In the most severe and prolonged interruptions death of the producers themselves will ensue, or emigration; that is, however, true of industry as well as agriculture. We are not considering such cases here.

Clearly, whatever output is produced must come through all stages of the production process successfully, and is vulnerable to stoppages at every stage. If there are two processes to progress through, and one has an up-time of 95 per cent and the other has an up-time of 98 per cent, the combined up-time is

95 per cent × 98 per cent = 93.1 per cent. We express this by saying that *in serial processes the up-times are multiplicative*. Unfortunately 93.1 per cent is worse than either 95 per cent or 98 per cent. If we take a series of three, four or more processes in sequence the overall up-time becomes steadily worse.

On the other hand, if one process can be undertaken by either of two machines, each machine can act as a stand-by for the other, and overall availability is improved. The down-time for each machine makes no difference unless it happens to coincide with the down-time of the other. If one has a down-time of 5 per cent and the other a down-time of 2 per cent (for the sake of illustration these correspond to the up-times of the previous example) the combined down-time is 5 per cent × 2 per cent = 0.1 per cent, which is better than either of them separately. We can express this by saying that *in parallel processes the down-times are multiplicative*. The same formula works for three or more machines operating in parallel.

It follows from this that in general we can improve the reliability of production processes by installing multiple units operating in parallel and by avoiding single-train production especially where long sequences of processes are involved.

When we speak of the up-time or down-time of specific items within an overall configuration like this, we are assuming that they are in fact independent in their characteristics. A pair of machines in parallel can be back-ups for each other only to the extent that they are immune from failure by common cause. This will not be entirely the case if they depend on the same power supply, the same control panel, or the same instrument air compressor. Only the breakdowns inherent in the machines themselves are backed-up; this may be insignificant in relation to power failures, so stand-by generators are provided in a large number of LDC factories, hotels, banks and offices.

In agriculture which is very dependent on weather, division of a farm into separate fields will not improve matters since they will all suffer the same weather if it is unseasonable. Stand-by weather is unavailable, and large reservoirs of water are extremely expensive. Implements, tractors, stud animals such as good bulls, blacksmithing facilities, and veterinary services are, however, backed-up and this is common and normal practice in agricultural systems though not necessarily within individual agricultural projects. Pioneering agricultural projects which attempt to introduce new processes to a district suffer particularly from lack of back-up in these areas, and it may be a safe generalisation that the greater variability of climate associated with global warming will contra-indicate such lone pioneering projects.

Besides availability considerations, there are other features of process and equipment selection which have a bearing on reliability:

• Equipment in novel application, i.e. equipment which is to be used for a purpose other than that in which it has been tried and tested elsewhere, carries a degree of additional risk; not only the risk that it will fail utterly to perform its new purpose, but the risk that it will perform with more frequent failures and/or longer repair times than were experienced before. Within this category we must include agro-industrial processes in which the raw material is to be of a different quality, perhaps even biologically an improved quality.

- Equipment of unproven design may also disappoint with respect to down-time. Such equipment may be on offer cheaply, since all equipment is new at some stage, and manufacturers have to induce customers to buy it nevertheless. Sometimes it is hard to see that the design is new; there may be unannounced modifications, or new models within an old range, or new sizes which just stretch the performance of the old designs outside their limits. No catalogue of tried and tested equipment, however satisfactory, can remain so for long.

- Some equipment is traded which has been tried and tested and found unsatisfactory. The seller may simply conceal this past history, or may attribute the failures (genuinely or falsely) to operator failures rather than to design failures. Past experience may well be mixed and hard to characterise; despite doubts, it may be felt that it is premature to discontinue production.

- Much plant and equipment is designed to suit customers' requirements by scaling up or scaling down earlier designs which were found satisfactory. So long as the adjustment is minor and no critical limits are exceeded, this is an acceptable and normal kind of design method. However, if the new proposal calls for a scale which is substantially outside the manufacturer's previous experience (by say 15 per cent or more), scale-up or scale-down can be dangerous. A fundamental rethink might be needed to detect new problems, particularly with complex, state-of-the-art plant, but scaling by-passes this procedure. Therefore, substantial re-scaling can produce new problems in operation and disappointing up-time performance.

- Equipment which requires spare parts that are hard to obtain is naturally likely to have longer repair times than other equipment. One cannot expect to hold a comprehensive stock of stand-by spares corresponding to all parts which might conceivably be needed. Items which have to be imported, from countries where computerised spares systems are typically poor, from source organisations which are financially fragile and may go out of existence while their products outlive them, replacement parts for old and obsolescent designs (chosen perhaps precisely because they were well tried and tested elsewhere), items which contain complex or patented pieces and so cannot readily be imitated by a local workshop in an emergency – these carry additional risk.

- Equipment which is vital for the health and safety of operatives and indeed of the population living outside the site must be highly reliable, and consideration should be given to duplicating and triplicating such items.

Examples are safety valves, respirators, radiation monitors, and warning systems of various kinds. The locations of these should be considered to ensure that items would not be rendered unavailable *together with their back-ups* in case of accident.

The above remarks should not be taken to mean that equipment should always be so robust that down-time is minimised regardless of cost. Clearly there will be a premium on equipment supplied by firms which have a long record of product acceptance and of financial survival, and have an R & D strategy which is well-balanced and mature. Indeed, this is the very type of company which LDC manufacturers must seek to displace in world markets. Such suppliers, however, are aware of their merits and can command higher prices in general for their products. This permits buyers to strike a balance between price and reliability. Unfortunately the standard procedure of procurement by formal competitive bidding often sets a minimum level of reliability and goes for the lowest price above that level, so that buyers often cannot exercise a completely optimal choice.

STORAGE: AN ALTERNATIVE TO RELIABILITY

As an alternative to reliability in the productive processes themselves, the provision of extra storage should be considered. This is another way of achieving overall reliability, which is what matters.

Storage can be at the front-end (raw material storage), in between components of the sequence of processes (intermediate storage), or downstream (finished product storage). These should be considered separately and in conjunction. In each case there is a capital cost for the storage containers (additional fixed assets) and for their contents (additional working capital), plus additional operating cost for moving material into and out of storage as required and perhaps also for additional wastage due to deterioration of material within storage.

RAW MATERIAL STORAGE

Raw material storage is almost always necessary to some extent to smooth out lumpy deliveries. This is especially true of agro-industrial materials which may be concentrated into a month or two of the year in certain cases. The producers of the raw material may have no adequate storage facilities of their own and have no alternative but to deliver bulk quantities immediately after harvest time, whether the downstream processes are up and running or not.

The normal size chosen for storage of this kind is such that no deliveries are turned away in normal operating up-time. That is to say, during the delivery season, the agro-industrial process works flat out drawing material out of store. In the first half of the peak period, deliveries exceed drawings, and the quantity in store rises. After the peak has been reached, deliveries slacken off, production continues flat out, and the quantity in store falls. Thus the stored quantity has a maximum level and it is on this that the planned storage capacity is based. If there is any interruption of the production when the store is full, deliveries will be turned away; if at other times, the stored quantity will rise abnormally and if it reaches its limit again deliveries will have to be turned away. In some cases the effect of turning away deliveries is to miss material which would otherwise be at its best in terms of quality, and to take it back in later at a lower grade; in other cases the material will be wasted completely, and obviously this depends on the material, the period of the delay and on the manner in which the material is stored in its alternative off-site storage facilities, if there are any. Thus, any decision to provide additional storage capacity in these circumstances depends on a judgement of the wastage loss, and quality loss, and on the likely down-time of production processes at that very moment of the year when they are expected to be most critical and when the attention of management is likely to have been focussed especially on this problem. Such decisions are likely to be made on the basis of recent experience by incremental adjustments to existing storage; the sizing of raw material storage for brand-new factories is much more difficult, but should be based on experience elsewhere.

Where raw material supplies are not subject to seasonal peaks, an item to be considered is the quantity which will be purchased whenever supplies are re-ordered. The classic formula for calculating the optimum re-order quantity depends in part on the cost of storage and is therefore not a convenient starting point for determining the specification of the storage arrangements, but again we are concerned with reliability in the sense of security of supply: if supplies are sporadic with weekly peaks and troughs in availability we may want to hold a few weeks' stock, and if the peaks and troughs are sporadic on a monthly basis we may want to hold a few months' stock. If supplies must be trucked in specially over a long distance we shall probably find it uneconomic to buy less than a truck-load at a time. If the material is imported by sea, much will depend on the frequency with which ships call at the nearby port. In short, common sense must be the starting point, and the analyst will find it helpful to translate the purchasing budget into volumes and weights in order to visualise the logistical problem here.

INTERMEDIATE STORAGE

The purpose of placing storage facilities between successive processes is to improve the overall reliability of the total operation. When the upstream process has failed, the downstream process can continue taking its input from intermediate storage. Even if the storage is emptied before the upstream process is repaired, there will be some overall improvement. The benefit will be greatest if the storage is normally kept full and if repair times on the upstream process are short. In order that the storage should be normally full, there must be a statistical over-design of the upstream process, which will allow it to replenish the storage as well as to feed the downstream process, but if production is not round the clock, replenishment can be achieved by overtime working on the upstream process after the downstream process has finished its shift for the day.

It is also possible to obtain benefit from intermediate storage when there is a failure in the downstream process, in that it allows the upstream process to continue, producing into storage; this may be valuable when the upstream process is very unreliable, and it is deemed important not to disturb it during the valuable little up-time that it has. However, for this policy to work, the storage must be kept normally empty, and the downstream process must be over-designed to draw down (later) any stock which is built up. Therefore, this usage is incompatible with that described in the preceding paragraph. The former usage is superior, since the latter usage pre-supposes very unreliable upstream plant, which you would never suppose in the ex-ante stage. We must therefore conclude that intermediate storage is normally kept *full*, which has obvious implications for forecasting the working capital.

This means that the primary purpose of having storage between upstream and downstream processes is to mitigate the unreliability of the upstream process. The provision of such storage has both capital and operating costs but should never be automatically ruled out. There are no less than four possibilities to consider in the trade-off:

- Suffer the consequences of unreliability.
- Pay extra for more reliable plant (upstream).
- Pay extra for statistical over-design of plant both upstream and downstream.
- Pay for intermediate storage.

In principle the net benefit of intermediate storage should be investigated having regard to the failure patterns of the upstream and downstream processes; the costs of system failure; the costs of providing storage, holding material in storage, and moving material in and out of storage as compared with movement directly from process to process; and the cost of over-designing the upstream process. Some of these items are capital costs and others are operating costs or cost savings, so to bring them together we must also have regard to a ninth item, the appropriate discount rate.

In practice the uncertainties surrounding the pattern of failures and the mean time to repair, which as stated above often lead to crude rule of thumb over-design, apply also to the sizing of the intermediate storage. It too is judgemental, and the analyst should not expect strong theoretical support for the figure chosen. However, care should always be taken to challenge any storage configuration which involves the following:

- The improvement in downstream up-time would be insignificant.
- The quantity which can effectively be drawn out of store during a typical upstream failure is significantly less than that which is held in store (as when a vent is above the bottom of a tank).
- The time taken to draw material out of store would be too long to prevent interruption to the downstream process.
- The operating costs of storage (including pumping and similar material handling and including storage losses such as evaporation) would add significantly to overall operating costs.
- The part-processed material which it is proposed to store contains toxins or exhibits hazards other than those presented by either raw materials or finished products.

An example of this last point was furnished by the Bhopal disaster in India. Methyl isocyanate was stored as an intermediate product; according to Vic Marshall (1990), the Union Carbide facilities there provided for three tanks with capacities of forty tons each, while the safety limit applied in Europe at that time was for a maximum of one ton.

FINISHED PRODUCT STORAGE

It is to the advantage of both producer and customer that there should be some stock of finished goods. The producer obviously will need some loading facilities and a truck-load or two may be expected to be found there even in times of the most brisk demand; you cannot load a truck out of a completely empty warehouse. Beyond this minimal amount, however, it may well suit the producer to keep a finished goods stock as a buffer stock so that production can proceed smoothly despite fluctuations in customer offtake. Production managers like to have ample storage facilities for finished goods; so do personnel managers, for the same reason.

It is in the interest of the customer to know that goods are available from stock. This means that they are available quickly when needed, which is a qualitative improvement in the product package. In the case of intermediate products, availability from stock may remove or reduce the requirement for the customers to hold their own raw material stock. It also allows customers to inspect the goods, particularly important for such items as household goods which are customarily sold from display stocks and open to impulse buying. Naturally, what enhances the attraction to the customer is also in the interest of the seller. Therefore, sales managers also like to have ample stocks of finished goods.

The benefits in terms of smoothing out production figures, avoiding temporary hirings and firings, offering prompt supply and showroom facilities to enhance the sales, are all intangible. The finance manager who is concerned with the interest penalty of holding finished goods stock and with the cost of additional insurance may have to argue with the production, personnel and sales managers to reach a compromise. Ex-ante, it is extremely difficult for the analyst to judge what this compromise will be; yet again a common sense judgement has to be made.

This chosen figure is often expressed in terms of so many weeks' sales, or more precisely cost of sales since no profit is included in the valuation of unsold stocks. In furniture, which is usually slow-moving, you may need as much as four weeks in a factory project and twenty-six weeks for a distributor; for ice cream, a day may be too much. So there is no point in asking for any industrial average or LDC norm.

ARISTOTLE ON PARDONABLE IGNORANCE

Students often ask what quantities of storage, or other working capital, are normally provided in project estimates. I personally always refuse to give a straightforward answer to that question, and I see that I have stuck to my guns this time. This is not an exact science. One may rely on professional rules of thumb within fairly narrow ranges of project situations, but these too can be challenged and are hard to substantiate. If a bridge falls down you build the next one stronger; fair enough, only 'do not make mine the guinea-pig'.

This does not mean that one is a professional charlatan. There are theoretical structures available, and several such with their arithmetical procedures have been described above. But these depend on data which are, as a rule, not all available. At times the only professional axiom left on which to fall back is the accounting principle of prudence. You do your best and must rest on that. Ignorance of the trade-off principles is inexcusable, but ignorance of specific data may be excused. As Aristotle put it in his *Ethics III*:

> What makes an act involuntary is not ignorance in the choice (this is a cause of wickedness), nor ignorance of the universal (for this people are blamed), but *particular* ignorance, i.e. of the circumstances and objects of the action; for it is on these that pity and pardon depend, because a man who acts in ignorance of any such detail is an involuntary agent.

Chapter 10

Staging

Every investment proposal has its boundaries and limitations; no one expects investors to sign a blank cheque. If it is for 10,000 acres of oil palms and ten tons per hour of milling capacity, that is the end of it. However, looking down from the heights of Olympia, every investment can be seen to be an expansion of capacity in a sector, or subsector; it has forerunners and it has followers. It is one of a series of responses to growing needs or perceptions of need.

Needs grow steadily, but supply responses are discrete. There cannot be a *continuous* increase in oil-mill capacity. Enlargements therefore require a choice of scale and frequency.

This choice is constrained. There may be an option to choose between adding a new ten-ton plant every six years and adding a new five-ton plant every three years, but a one-eighth ton (kitchen-scale) plant every month would be uneconomic, and a pocket-sized oil-mill every day quite impossible. The same applies to railway routes, clinics, prisons and telephone exchanges.

In such a perspective, where the demand is perceived as growing, the choice lies between frequent small expansions of capacity and fewer larger expansions; in other words, a view is taken of the optimal time interval between successive expansions of the system. This view is obviously important in selecting the size of the investment which is currently under consideration.

Though important, it may not be the over-riding consideration. In the case of a new firm struggling with insufficient entrepreneurial capital, or in the case of a public investment struggling with the fiscal constraint – both of which are vicious and powerful dragons – the owners may look for the cheapest possible equipment consistent with getting a foot-hold in the business, a minimal presence in the activity, the smallest project that will give the management some credibility with the public and in its own eyes.

We must also remember that the size of a project is not unconnected with the size and organisational structure of the entity which runs it. Some businesses take pride and prestige from being large and doing large things. There are many small companies, however, which enjoy the flexibility and speed of management action which comes with being small, especially below the 100–200 employees barrier above which the methods of management become formalised and require new (bureaucratic) skills. We must also remember that a large project in a small community brings with it powers, privileges and responsibilities which may be perceived by the owners and putative managers as either welcome or unwelcome. These strategies of size are discussed by Argenti (1989: 308).

The analyst faced with a proposal of a certain size is therefore entitled to ask whether this size is the optimal size consistent with the expected rate of growth of demand and if not, whether it has been distorted by the prejudices of organisational culture for one of the reasons just mentioned.

INCREMENTAL CAPACITY AND THE RATE OF EXPANSION

The expansion of demand, in terms of volume, can be put into mathematical terms as a rising line or curve. Several formulae are available for curves, as well as the simple straight line which models linear growth. However, in practice, linear growth is the model which is most commonly selected, in order to make an assumption or a judgement with the virtue of prudence. Certainly in the medium term, a sales force comprising a fixed number of salespersons can only achieve a fixed maximum of new customer additions every month. In the longer term, the sales force can be expanded, but then new uncertainties appear. For these reasons, no prudent sales manager would undertake to achieve an exponential or other dramatic growth curve.

Assuming that growth is linear, the annual increase in capacity which would meet that demand must be the same size every year. If that linear demand is to be met by capacity expanding periodically by a series of investments of equal size, the size of each increment will depend on the time interval between investments. For instance, if the demand expands at the rate of 1,000 tons extra every year, new plant built at five-year intervals will have to be of 5,000–ton size, whereas plant built at ten-year intervals will have to be of 10,000 tons size, and so on. Choosing the interval of time implies choosing the size, and any choice of size implies a certain interval of time. This is what we call a strategy of *staging*. Every investment proposal contains or implies, usually without making it explicit, a staging strategy.

Since the expansion is step-wise while demand growth is linear, there will be periods when demand and supply are out of step. Either investment runs ahead, and in the extreme case each new facility will be severely under-utilised during the early years of its life, reaching full capacity just before its successor comes on stream, or investment runs behind, and demand is intermittently unsatisfied to a degree which in the extreme case reaches a volume equivalent to a whole new incremental facility just at the time when the next new facility is about to come on stream:

- The former strategy suffers from the cost of under-utilisation; costs are incurred which are less than fully matched by benefits, especially in the periods immediately after each new start.

- The latter strategy suffers the effects of short supply; either customers go without, or supplies are purchased from competitors, perhaps using foreign exchange. These effects are economically damaging in terms of resource use. There can also be commercial damage, in that the intermittent shortages cause a loss of customer satisfaction and customer goodwill.

Staging policy is therefore usually a compromise between these two undesirable results, with some degree of shortfall just before each increment of capacity, and some degree of under-utilisation just after it.

The smaller the increments and the closer the intervals between them, the less damage will be done, so the 'little and often' staging strategy may be perceived as a way to avoid the twin evils of short supply and under-utilisation. However, this too has a disadvantage in that it loses the 'economies of scale' which as a general rule favour large expansion projects. One 2,000–ton plant is usually cheaper than two 1,000–ton plants. This is a subject to which we should now turn our attention.

THE SCALE FACTOR

Consider a cubical tank, representing a component of a typical fixed asset. It has six steel faces making up the cube; each face is one metre square, so there are six square metres of sheet steel. The capacity of the tank is therefore one cubic metre. An alternative design on a bigger scale can be made from larger sheets, each two metres square (four square metres) requiring $24m^2$ of sheet steel. It measures two metres in each dimension, so its capacity is eight cubic metres. An eight-fold increase in capacity requires a four-fold increase in steel sheet (and therefore in cost). Comparing the bigger tank with the smaller tank, the increase in the scale of cost is less than the increase in the scale of capacity. We can express this by saying that the scale factor for cost is less than one, where the increase in cost is the increase in capacity raised (or in this case lowered) to the power of the scale factor:

$$C_B = C_A(B/A)^S$$

or $$C_B/C_A = (B/A)^S$$

or $$S = \log(B/A) / \log(C_B/C_A) \qquad \ldots \qquad (10.1)$$

where
C_A = cost of asset A
C_B = cost of asset B
A = capacity of asset A
B = capacity of asset B
S = scale factor less than one.

In our example, four is eight to the power of two-thirds, so the scale factor is 0.66 approximately:

$$8/1 = (24/6)^{0.66} \text{ or } \log(24/6) / \log(8/1) = 2/3$$

Of course, the larger tank would require some strengthening in the form of thicker steel, or diagonal cross-bracing, so we would expect the benefit of scale to be rather less than this arithmetic shows. The cost of the second tank will be rather higher than 24 and therefore by formula 10.1 the scale factor will be rather higher than two-thirds. You can make similar calculations for scale factors on tanks other than cubes, such as cylindrical or spherical tanks. Notice, however, that the scale factor cannot exceed one; if it did, there would be no benefit in having a large tank, and the most economic solution would be an infinite number of infinitely small tanks.

Most equipment can be conceived of as a set of cuboids, cylinders (that includes piping) and spheres, and so can be expected to have a scale factor which is a composite of those elements. There are, however, irregularities. A tank may be enlarged up to a certain threshold point before it needs cross-bracing; that is not only a significant change of design, which may raise or lower the scale factor, but it requires an additional design effort, which has a cost whether you are moving up or down the scale across this threshold. With complex plant, increases of scale may require significant changes of design at several points on the curve.

In general, with plant which is operated automatically or from control panels, increases in capacity do not require comparable increases in the control systems. This obviously applies more to industrial than to agricultural processes; in the latter, the scale factor may approach one, especially if land is included as a cost.

Moreover, there are *commercial* economies of scale; buying a bigger item, you have more negotiating power and can squeeze the profit margin of the supplier. This is a general tendency which operates to improve the benefits of scale and so reduce the scale factor.

The scale factor, power factor, or *exponent cost factor* as it is also known, therefore varies according to the type of asset, the position on the curve from which you start, and the commercial aspects. It can be studied in respect of any proposed project by looking at specific quotations, but if the analyst seeks to find it out by referring to results typical of similar projects elsewhere, only a very rough indication will be available. Many studies have found a figure around 0.6 or 0.7 and in the absence of any other indication one of these numbers can be used to estimate the cost of a plant from a known cost of a similar plant of slightly different scale. This procedure is known as the 'six-tenths rule' or 'two-thirds power rule'. Some helpful empirical studies of scale factors have been published by Bauman (1964), reprinted in Rudd and Watson (1968), and by de la Mare (1982), and Tribe and Alpine (1986). The last of these, based on sugar processing, indicates that the six-tenths rule is very effective for what it calls the intrinsic or technical scale factor, but not for commercial, managerial or financial side-effects.

Bauman's figures show intrinsic scale factors for individual components varying widely between 0.24 and 0.90. For example, 40–inch centrifuges made with carbon steel baskets showed a scale factor of 0.81, but if made with stainless steel baskets showed a scale factor of 0.63. Carbon steel tanks had a factor of 0.66; stainless steel tanks had a factor of 0.69. Naturally, a complete plant made up of several different components has a composite scale factor which is nearer the middle of the range; Bauman's results for complete plants range from 0.38 (electrolytic chlorine producing plants) to 0.90 (high pressure polyethylene plants) with the great majority clustering around the 0.6 mark. De la Mare's figures quote no source but are virtually the same. Tribe and Alpine's figures show that the scale factor varies as you go up the curve, which is also visible in Bauman's figures for individual components.

Designers and cost estimators who work in a particular specialism will know roughly what their scale factors are, from experience of earlier costings of different sizes (after allowing for inflation and currency movements at the various dates). Similar knowledge on the side of the prospective purchaser or Government is harder to obtain, though it can be requested directly. Figures published by Bauman and others tend to be confined to the chemical industries, but the indications given there in respect of individual components such as tanks can often be used for other industries, and even sometimes in handicraft or other small units using intermediate technology. Such use does, however, require detailed knowledge of the intended asset configuration. Remembering the irregularities referred to, and the Tribe and Alpine finding, such published indicators are better used as a rough guide in the early stages of project preparation, and subsequently as a rough check to validate price quotations before challenging them, rather than as a means of directly fixing prices.

STAGING STRATEGY

The smaller the scale factor, the greater the economies of scale enjoyed by larger facilities, and the longer therefore is the optimal time interval between expansions. If the scale factor is one, there is no benefit in larger plants at all, and expansions can most profitably be undertaken at the closest convenient intervals of time, normally one year apart.

When the scale factor is small, larger investments have significant economies of scale, but what weighs against them even then is the under-utilisation in early years. The larger and less frequent the investments, the costlier and longer-lasting is the idle capacity. The cost of intermittent idle capacity, when analysed in the context of an appraisal applying discounted cash flow to each individual expansion scheme, depends on the rate of discount used for the appraisal. A high rate of discount (such as 15 per cent or more) places especial emphasis on the early years, and therefore tends to favour many small increments rather than a few large expansions. This means that in determining the scaling strategy, a low scale factor pulls one way (favouring larger but fewer investments) while a high discount rate pulls the other way (favouring

Table 10.1 Optimum intervals between expansions

Scale	Discount rates (%)					
factors	2.5	5	7.5	10	15.0	20.0
0.50	20	20	17	13	9	7
0.55	20	20	15	11	8	6
0.60	20	18	13	10	7	5
0.65	20	17	11	8	6	4
0.70	20	14	9	7	5	4
0.75	18	11	8	6	4	3
0.80	17	9	6	5	3	2
0.85	14	6	4	3	2	2
0.90	8	4	3	2	2	1
0.95	4	2	1	1	1	1
1.00	1	1	1	1	1	1

the 'little but often' strategy). If we know both the scale factor and the discount rate we can calculate the optimum scaling strategy, as is shown in Table 10.1.

Table 10.1 is derived by adopting a long time horizon, of fifty years or more (sixty-five years has been adopted here), and scheduling incremental investments at various intervals of time (staging strategies) from once a year to once every twenty years. The demand is assumed to grow at an arbitrary linear rate, say 1000 tons per year, and the incremental supply capacity (in tons per year) is then calculated, viz. the annual growth multiplied by the time interval and introduced at intervals in the years preceding the dates when demand would otherwise exceed supply. The cost of each increment is then calculated, at constant prices, by assuming an arbitrary cost for an asset of given size, and scaling it up or down to suit the size required, in accordance with the scale factor, for which various values are assumed in turn. The costs of the successive investments are then reduced to a present value by discounting, using a discount rate per annum for which various values are assumed in turn (discounting is done at annual rests; continuous discounting would give slightly different results). An allowance is made for the residual value of the assets at the end of the time horizon; as it is fifty years or more away its present value can be taken as negligible if discounted at over 5 per cent, but at lower discount rates residual values do create anomalous results if not brought properly into account. The results of the various staging strategies are then compared to see which has the lowest cost in present value terms, and the answers are reported as shown. These answers are found to be the same regardless of the rate of growth of demand and of the unit cost, which are the two arbitrary figures; this can be checked by changing the arbitrary figures and recalculating the spreadsheet.

From this it can be seen that at moderate discount rates (5–10 per cent) and at normal scale factors (0.60–0.70), the optimum staging strategy is very sensitive to both factors. This 'central zone' shows optimum staging intervals ranging from seven years to eighteen years. At discount rates below 5 or above 10 per cent, it is not very sensitive to scale factors within this normal range. Scale factors in the range 0.80 to 1.00 become sensitive when the discount rate is under 5 per cent.

The upper figure of the central zone, eighteen years for projects with a 5 per cent discount rate and a scale factor of 0.60 representing fairly strong economies of scale, is a remarkably high figure. This may help to explain the frequent occurrence of so-called *grandiose projects*, which are so large that no further enlargement may be expected for many years, and which have attracted much criticism.

Higher discount rates than 10 per cent should not be considered as freakish, even though we are working in constant prices, because of project risk; higher rates should be applied to risky projects. If rates of 20 per cent or more are applied, the staging interval decreases sharply and approximates realistically to private sector commercial practice. It is arguable that the grandiose projects were approved partly because the appraisal mechanisms failed to recognise project risk and to elevate the discount rate accordingly.

In agriculture the economies of scale are likely to be much lower, as noted above, and short intervals appear in the table even at discount rates which are not heavily loaded with risk premiums. At a scale factor of 0.80 we can find a staging interval as low as five years within the range of moderate discount rates.

CAUTION

These optimal scaling intervals can damage your health unless taken with a pinch of salt. It should not be supposed that in any specific situation the investment decision will be taken based directly and exclusively on the *underlying* factors discussed above.

In specific situations, investments may be smaller or larger than their underlying optimum scale because of several local reasons. For example, one firm may incline to the larger scale in the belief that competitors are saddled with many small units, so that economies of scale offer a comparative advantage. Another firm may incline to the smaller scale because it is short of entrepreneurial capital and of borrowing facilities, and so cannot raise the finance to pay for the larger project which it knows is preferable. Yet another may consider the linear extension of market demand to be dubious in the longer term, and so may proceed by cautious small increments, or, what amounts to the same thing, may adopt a high discount rate in view of the high perceived risk, so that the optimum scale is lower than it would be in the perception of a more brash investor. Another common situation is to choose a scale which is only very roughly optimum, but is exactly what happens to be on special offer: agricultural land which comes up for sale of so many hectares, or process plant which is tendered for cheaply because it is an exact copy of a design previously made to a certain specification.

In view of these perfectly rational departures from the underlying optimum, the latter may best be regarded as useful in *sector* planning, and as a starting point in specific investment planning.

Chapter 11

Financial planning

This is a subject about which it is very easy and tempting to talk at length. There is a lack of accepted theoretical structure which if it existed might lead to determinable conclusions and put an early end to verbosity. A computerised spreadsheet system is ideal to combat this, since it insists on precision, will not accept ambiguity, bleeps at circular reasoning, and imposes limitations on words. I therefore propose to introduce this subject with a worked example. This is a case study, or exercise, which some professional students have found valuable.

BACKGROUND TO THE EXERCISE

Financial planning can be undertaken by entering hypothetical figures either into yearly balance sheets or into some kind of yearly cash flow statements. In either case it is necessary to ensure first that the pro forma income statements have already been prepared down to profit before interest and tax (PBIT) level; we cannot go further, as interest will depend on the financing, and tax will depend on the interest; so net profit after tax (NPAT), i.e. net income, cannot be completed until the financing plan is made. NPAT is to be worked out as a simultaneous calculation along with the financing plan.

We will on this occasion follow the most modern procedure and use analytical cash flow statements as a vehicle for financial planning. From the data below, we will construct draft income and ACF statements reflecting what seems an appropriate financing pattern.

THE PROJECT

The project is a typical industrial project and has a ten-year planning horizon. Its products enjoy an established brand reputation and are to be sold to consumers both at home and abroad so that it will be insulated from the effects of inflation and devaluation. It is therefore permissible to conduct the study entirely in constant prices.

FINANCIAL ENVIRONMENT

The proposal consists of an expansion of manufacturing capacity to be undertaken by a new subsidiary of an existing enterprise which is a private limited company, not quoted on any stock exchange. Equity capital can be raised by a rights issue at par, and reserves accumulated from previous operations by the parent company will contribute additional finance. According to soundings taken in conversations with the owners, the equity thus available is estimated not to exceed two billion Lire. The owners who subscribe to the rights issue will expect dividends equal to at least 15 per cent per annum per share, or perhaps an equity IRR of 15 per cent, as that has been the previous track record. When equity has been subscribed, it may not be taken out again, as reduction of equity capital is not permitted by the company laws in this country.

Bank lending is also available, both short and medium term. Short-term facilities are available with a two-year stand-by commitment and a three-year 'target' payback. The charges are variable at the bank's discretion but at present stand at 2 per cent commitment fee and 10 per cent per annum interest charge assuming that the loan is well secured by valid collateral assets. The collateral is considered sufficient when the short-term lending does not exceed 60 per cent of the current assets plus the net fixed assets minus any medium- or long-term debt which is outstanding.

Medium-term facilities consist of a five-year loan arrangement, with repayments in five equal annual instalments commencing on the first anniversary of the loan (which is to be drawn down in a single drawing). The negotiation fee is 5 per cent and interest is payable annually in arrears (together with repayments of principal) at 10 per cent per annum reckoned on the declining balance of the principal. Medium-term lending is unlikely to be negotiable in excess of 30 per cent of shareholders' funds (calculation based on maximum gearing during operating years); for the purpose of this calculation, the current portion of medium-term debt is to be included as debt.

Should the project generate temporary cash surpluses, these can be placed on deposit either with a bank earning 5 per cent per annum or with the parent company (unsecured) earning 7.5 per cent per annum.

PROJECT DATA DETERMINES THE FINANCE NEEDED

The base case requires equipment with productive capacity of 1000 tons per year. Progressive penetration of the market thanks to a steady selling effort is expected to produce sales (in million Lire) as shown in Table 11.1. No significant improvement in the rate of sales build-up could be achieved with any likely expansion of sales promotion. It would, however, be possible to slow down the build-up without any permanent loss of market.

Table 11.1 Sales (outputs) per year

	Year: 0	1	2	3–10
Sales volume (1000 tons)	0	300	600	1000
Sales revenue at 10,000 Lire/ton	0	3000	6000	10000

Table 11.2 Fixed assets and depreciation

	Cost	Life (yrs)	Annual dep'n	NBV at end of Year 10
Land	200			200
Buildings	500	25	20	300
Plant and equipment	1000	10	100	0
FFF	200	15	13	67
Vehicles	300	10	30	0
	2200		163	567

Variable costs have been assessed at 5,000 Lire per ton. Fixed costs have been assessed at 2,000 million Lire per year excluding depreciation and interest. Depreciation comes to 163 million Lire per year according to the base case study (see below). Interest depends on borrowing. Taxation is at 40 per cent of profit; interest and 100 per cent capital allowances are tax-deductible and losses can be carried forward (even though the parent enterprise may be making taxable profits at the time). The tax is payable in the year after the year in which taxable profit is made.

In the base case (the proposal made before consideration of any difficulties in financing it) figures emerged as regards fixed assets, in millions of Lire as shown in Table 11.2.

The plant and equipment is essentially a simple twin-train design. Its capacity could be halved, if only a single train were installed. The cost saving of doing so can be estimated using the six-tenths rule, however, the cost of returning to site a second time if the second train were added later would be a further 100 million Lire. The product can be readily stored so the effects of greater down-time due to single-train operation can be compensated for by a small additional investment in stock estimated at 40 million Lire.

With regard to working capital, in the study so far debtors and creditors have been estimated at ten and five weeks respectively (debtors 5/50 of sales, creditors 5/50 of variable and fixed costs other than depreciation and interest). The cash requirement is estimated at 50 per cent of creditors. Stocks are estimated to stand at 36 million Lire from the end of Year 0 until liquidation in Year 11.

From the above data we can determine the amount of finance required to get the project going, and the amount of surplus cash (if any) which it will subsequently generate and which is the primary object of the exercise so far as financial analysis is concerned. There are two ways of doing this: we can construct pro-forma balance sheets and see by how much the capital employed differs from the net assets utilised, or we can construct pro-forma cash flow statements of some kind and see how much cash has to be fed in or siphoned off to make the sources of cash equal to the uses (application) of cash. In either case, the statements are forced to balance by using the financial cash flow as a balancing item. That is simple arithmetic. There is, however, more than one financial cash flow, comprising equity capital, and borrowing, which may be short term, medium or long term, or all of these, so we have some choices to make. For this we have to devise decision rules to suit the circumstances, and that is far from simple.

For the purpose of this exercise we shall not use the balance sheet method; it grieves me to abandon the old method which is ingrained in my central nervous system, but the cash flow method is more up to date. We can always construct balance sheets afterwards, to reflect the financing flows decided upon in the cash flow statements. Incidentally, there are certain circumstances in which we need to look at the balance sheets for decision-making; this arises when the amounts which lenders are willing to lend depend on ratios which emerge from the balance sheets.

The form of cash flow statement recommended is the analytical cash flow statement (ACF). However, this particular project has been so simplified that almost any kind of cash flow statement will probably do. Since this statement is serving a temporary purpose, viz. financial decision-making, it will lead on to balance sheets and a full formal ACF statement in due course. This is therefore just a beginning. A suitable layout is shown in Table 11.3.

The last line of the table tells us that, unless financial considerations prompt us to redesign the project, we shall have to find finance amounting to 2,236 million Lire in Year 0, and 750 million more in Year 1. In fact, if any of this finance is borrowed, so that interest is incurred during those same years, the financing requirement will be a little more than those figures. In later years the project shows no further minus signs, and a healthy cash flow will be generated which will clearly be a generous payoff for the initial investments.

The next step is to consider how to blend the various possible sources of finance. In the background information of this exercise we find three sources: equity (ordinary share capital), short-term and medium-term debt.

BANKERS' APPROACH: MAXIMUM EQUITY

According to the data of the exercise, the sponsors who will subscribe to shares cannot commit themselves to more than two billion Lire. To many colleagues in LDCs and especially in Africa, this will be a familiar situation. National economies having undergone a period of crisis, no one except the multinational corporations, drug barons, footballers, and some other buccaneers

Table 11.3 Resource flows

					Million Lire in constant terms							
Year:	0	1	2	3	4	5	6	7	8	9	10	11
FIRST PASS ANALYTICAL CASH FLOW												
Sales detail												
Sales volume (thousand tons)	0	300	600	1000	1000	1000	1000	1000	1000	1000	1000	
Sales price Lire per ton	0	10000	10000	10000	10000	10000	10000	10000	10000	10000	10000	
Revenue												
Sales (million Lire)	0	3000	6000	10000	10000	10000	10000	10000	10000	10000	10000	
Variable costs												
5000 Lire per ton	0	1500	3000	5000	5000	5000	5000	5000	5000	5000	5000	
Fixed costs	0	2000	2000	2000	2000	2000	2000	2000	2000	2000	2000	
Operating profit	0	-500	1000	3000	3000	3000	3000	3000	3000	3000	3000	0
Additional working capital (changes):												
Stocks	-36	0	0	0	0	0	0	0	0	0	0	36
Debtors	0	-600	-600	-800	0	0	0	0	0	0	0	2000
Less: trade creditors	0	350	150	200	0	0	0	0	0	0	0	-700
Operating cash flow	-36	-750	550	2400	3000	3000	3000	3000	3000	3000	3000	
Additional fixed assets	-2200	0	0	0	0	0	0	0	0	0	0	
Disposal of fixed assets												2200
Total resource flows	-2236	-750	550	2400	3000	3000	3000	3000	3000	3000	3000	3536

has any money left. The capital available to indigenous entrepreneurs for serious businesses is very limited and has to be leveraged by heavy borrowing; in this environment the banks are willing to help, but try to lessen their own risks by squeezing as much equity out of the project sponsors as they can.

Those who approach this exercise from such a background will therefore tend to assume that the full two billion of equity should be put in. We will take this case and look at it first, the 'maximum equity' case.

If 2,000 million of the 2,236 million is financed by equity, that leaves 236 million to be borrowed either short or long term, plus whatever interest charge and front-end fees this may incur.

In this exercise the rate of interest happens to be the same on both short-term and five-year debt; 10 per cent has been taken for simplicity, but this is unusual. Very often, five-or ten-year money is available from official sources, viz. development finance institutions (DFIs), on a subsidised basis. The DFIs take as their collateral security private land, other fixed assets if the local law permits, and a general lien on current assets. Repayment dates are fixed in advance over a number of years, which may be preceded by a *period of grace* in which repayments of principal and/or payments of interest are deferred. Short-term money is available from commercial banks, whose security is often a shared lien on the same assets. Repayment dates may be agreed in advance over a period of a year or two, but in most cases the bank reserves the legal right to withdraw the facility at any time on demand. In the event that both DFIs and commercial banks try to foreclose on the same collateral, the commercial banks usually rank second. On the whole the DFI term loans are cheaper because of the subsidy element and because of the stronger collateral. The latter factor reduces the risk of loss by the DFIs, and so reduces the gross margin which the banker needs to take.

In most projects the short-term borrowing is to be avoided, not only because it is dearer, but because the resource cash flow is not sufficiently positive in the early years to repay the lending. A medium- or long-term loan and sometimes a period of grace is essential. In this particular project the resource cash flow is negative in Years 0 and 1, and only weakly positive in Year 2, so we have a three-year problem. Therefore, short-term lending is not satisfactory; it might of course be renewed on an annual basis, and if the worst comes to the worst we may have to take the risky course of proceeding with the project in the hope that this will be agreed when the time comes. For these reasons we must look to the five-year money in this case. The 236 million will attract a negotiation fee 'payable up-front' of 5 per cent, so we will need 248 million. This is comfortably below the limit for the five-year money, which is 30 per cent of two billion. That completes the financing pattern for Year 0, with no use of short-term money: a typical result.

In Year 1, some more finance is needed. This is because of operating losses while sales volumes are still low, and because of rising debtors, and is not unusual. From where will this extra money come? It cannot come from equity, since the two billion limit has already been reached. It cannot come from five-year borrowing, since this loan is now fixed and has already begun its repayment process (which makes the position worse). We therefore have to make up the difference with short-term borrowing, adding in the commitment fee. This is a fairly large sum of 1,020 million and the commercial bankers may not consider it to be secured adequately. It raises questions as to whether the project should perhaps be redesigned.

DIVIDENDS VERSUS SHORT-TERM DEBT REPAYMENTS

From Year 2 onwards we begin to have more choices. The equity and five-year money are fixed, but the short-term money is not. We may assume that the short-term debt is cleared as quickly as possible, deferring all payments of dividends until this has been done; if so, dividends begin in Year 3. The cash flow planning statement then appears as shown in Table 11.4.

Here the upper part of the statement contains the equity and five-year money, which we know, and the lower part contains the short-term money and the dividends, which we have to decide. We have seen that short-term borrowing in Year 0 is zero and in Year 1 is 1,020 million; now let us proceed to Year 2. If the short-term debt were maintained at 1,020, it would be possible to pay some dividend, viz. 406 million from the resource cash flow minus 102 million bank interest. The sum available is thus 304 million. However, such early payment of dividends would be imprudent, for two reasons: (a) the short-term debt is still uncomfortably high, and (b) equity has been reduced by operating losses and needs to be rebuilt, as could be seen by working out pro-forma balance sheets. It is virtually certain that the bankers would insist on debt reduction rather than dividend payouts in Year 2. The 304 million is therefore devoted to debt reduction, not dividend.

In Year 3 the cash flow permits the short-term debt to be cleared completely and a substantial further sum is available. There is therefore no conflict between the two aims here; we will assume that the short-term debt is now cleared. It is, after all, three years since it was first committed and we have no warrant to assume that it is available indefinitely.

After payment of the remaining short-term debt and interest thereon, the sum of 1,448 million remains to be disposed. It may be paid out as dividend, or kept in the company for other uses. In the latter case, if not used for other projects, it can be invested short term to earn some interest. However, we have to ignore this last feature, since we are concerned only with the financial results of *this project*, and once cash has been generated by it we are no longer concerned with the fate of that cash. Dividends paid out and retained earnings are therefore to be regarded as of equal value to the shareholders. For simplicity we have assumed that the cash arising is split 50:50 between dividend and retentions, but this makes no real difference.

In Year 4, a tax payment occurs for the first time. This timing, and its

Table 11.4 Cash planning table (preliminary version of ACF Section 3)

Year:	0	1	2	3	4	5	6	7	8	9	10	11
						Million Lire in constant terms						
Financial transfers (minus indicates payment out)												
Equity flow												
New share capital	2000	0	0	0	0	0	0	0	0	0	0	0
	2000	0	0	0	0	0	0	0	0	0	0	0
Medium-term debt service												
Debt rise/(fall)	248	-50	-50	-50	-50	-50	0	0	0	0	0	0
Interest and fees (paid)	-12	-25	-20	-15	-10	-5	0	0	0	0	0	0
	236	-74	-69	-64	-60	-55	0	0	0	0	0	0
Government and Central Bank												
Subsidies/(taxes) paid	0	0	0	0	-637	-1833	-2394	-2398	-2400	-2400	-2400	-2400
Required cash (rise)/fall	0	-175	-75	-100	0	0	0	0	0	0	0	350
	0	-175	-75	-100	-637	-1833	-2394	-2398	-2400	-2400	-2400	-2050
Sub-total	2236	-249	-144	-164	-696	-1887	-2394	-2398	-2400	-2400	-2400	-2050
Deficit/(surplus) of cash	0	999	-406	-2236	-2304	-1113	-606	-602	-600	-600	-600	-1486
Total financial transfers = resource flows	2236	750	-550	-2400	-3000	-3000	-3000	-3000	-3000	-3000	-3000	-3536
Short-term deficit/(surplus) of cash												
Short-term debt rise/(fall)	0	1020	-304	-716	0	0	0	0	0	0	0	0
Short-term debt interest/fees	0	-20	-102	-72	0	0	0	0	0	0	0	0
Dividends 50%	0	0	0	-724	-1152	-556	-303	-301	-300	-300	-300	-743
Retained earnings (increase)	0	0	0	-724	-1152	-556	-303	-301	-300	-300	-300	-743
Total as above	0	999	-406	-2236	-2304	-1113	-606	-602	-600	-600	-600	-1486

amount, have to be calculated by preparing forecast income statements to determine the taxable profits, and by special tax computations to take account of capital allowances resulting from the acquisition of fixed assets, since in most countries depreciation as such is not allowed as a cost for tax purposes. Once again we see that a cash flow statement on its own cannot be a satisfactory vehicle for cash flow planning.

In Year 5, the last of the debt repayments is made, and with it goes the last of the interest payments. From Year 6 onwards, taxable profits will be the same every year; in terms of actual payments of tax, these will be constant from Year 7 onwards. Accordingly, in Years 7–10, funds available for dividends or retentions settle down to a steady flow.

So much for the 'maximum equity' case. We can now examine an alternative, and later compare the two.

SPONSORS' APPROACH: MINIMUM EQUITY

It is evident that this project generates hefty cash yields from Year 3 onwards. The resource cash flow shows this clearly. No tinkering with interest rates or front-end fees is going to change this salient feature of the situation. The bulk of the financing requirement is therefore a three-year requirement only, not a permanent requirement. Any substantial equity which is put in will be surplus to requirements after a few years, and in most LDCs there is no way within the legal rules of taking it out again. Supposing the project is to be sponsored by its prospective equity investors, these sponsors will therefore press for the minimum equity and the maximum borrowing, especially short-term borrowing to cover Years 1–2 if the charges and collateral requirements are not punitive.

The method of applying these preferences to Year 0 is as follows. Equity is to be the lowest possible figure. The five-year money (medium-term debt) will be 30 per cent of the equity, which is the highest gearing ratio acceptable to the lenders. Short-term debt is to be fixed assets plus current assets minus medium-term debt. The total of these three must be 2,236 million plus interest and financial charges as shown in Table 11.5.

As a set of equations, these relationships may be set out as shown below. It is not suggested that the solution of a set of simultaneous equations is necessarily the best manner of proceeding; if you have a computer spreadsheet, you can often get there faster empirically by trying various values for equity until the statement balances. However, for the sake of precision the equations are as follows:

$$D = 0.3 E \text{ (gearing limit)}$$
$$S = 0.6 (2,236 - D) \text{ (collateral security limit)}$$
$$= 1342 - 0.6D$$

$$D + E + S = 2,236 + 0.05D + 0.15S \text{ (finance required including charges)}$$

or   E $= 2{,}236 - 0.95D - 0.85S$
where   E   = equity
          D   = debt
          S   = short-term debt

The financing requirement of 2,236 consists of 2,000 fixed assets and 36 current assets (stock).

This is a set of three equations with three unknowns and may therefore be solved, whether by traditional simultaneous equation algebra, by matrix algebra, by trial and error, or by computer algorithm. The results are E = 831, D = 249, S = 1192.

In Year 1, the process of paying off the five-year term loan begins. As it falls, the maximum permissible short-term debt rises. It does not, however, rise high enough to bridge the entire financing gap; additional financing amounting to 750 million is needed in Year 1, essentially to cover debtors and operating losses. Therefore, there must be a second call on equity. Shareholders will have to subscribe a further 397 million in Year 1. This is quite normal, whereas a second slice of term loan is not.

From Year 2 onwards, this minimum equity case proceeds just like the maximum equity case. We pay off in Year 2 as much short-term debt as possible, deferring any dividends. In Year 3 we pay off the remainder of the short-term money and commence to pay dividends; as before, we have assumed for simplicity that half of the available funds are distributed and half retained, but this is not important since both *accrue* to the shareholders, and belong to them. As before, there are variants in which we might adopt a policy of deferring dividends until retained earnings are rebuilt to zero, or a policy of paying off the short-term debt over three years, but these make no essential difference in this case.

COMPARISON OF TWO FINANCIAL STRATEGIES

We have looked at two very different financial strategies: maximum equity and minimum equity. The stream of cash flows from and to the equity investors are very different in the two cases. Having derived these figures in the manner described above, we can discount them and arrive at a net present value in each case; this should help to determine which is the superior strategy from the viewpoint of equity. It may not be the superior strategy from the viewpoint of the other parties involved with the financing; here we get into *beneficiary analysis*, and some compromise may have to be negotiated. This is set out in Table 11.6.

Clearly in both strategies the project itself has an IRR of 49 per cent. This is based on the resource flows and is independent of the financing arrangements. The IRR of the equity cash flow is rather lower, due to the large Government tax take, but is still high at 33 per cent on the first strategy or 40 per cent on the second. This confirms that the minimum equity strategy is

Table 11.5 Cash planning table

	Year:	0	1	2	3	4	5	6	7	8	9	10	11
Total resource flows		-2236	-750	550	2400	3000	3000	3000	3000	3000	3000	3000	3536
Financial transfers (minus indicates payment out)													
Equity flow													
New share capital	831	831	721	0	0	0	0	0	0	0	0	0	0
		831	721	0	0	0	0	0	0	0	0	0	0
Medium-term debt service	249.3												
Debt rise/(fall)		249	-50	-50	-50	-50	-50	0	0	0	0	0	0
Interest (paid)		-12	-25	-20	-15	-10	-5	0	0	0	0	0	0
Realised exchange gains/(losses)		0	0	0	0	0	0	0	0	0	0	0	0
		237	-75	-70	-65	-60	-55	0	0	0	0	0	0
Government and Central Bank													
Subsidies/(taxes) paid		0	0	0	0	-589	-1785	-2394	-2398	-2400	-2400	-2400	-2400
Required cash (rise)/fall		0	-175	-75	-100	0	0	0	0	0	0	0	350
		0	-175	-75	-100	-589	-1785	-2394	-2398	-2400	-2400	-2400	-2050
Sub-total		1068	471	-145	-165	-649	-1840	-2394	-2398	-2400	-2400	-2400	-2050
Deficit/(surplus) as below		1168	279	-405	-2235	-2351	-1160	-606	-602	-600	-600	-600	-1486
Total financial transfers to balance		2236	750	-550	-2400	-3000	-3000	-3000	-3000	-3000	-3000	-3000	-3536
Short-term deficit/ (surplus) of cash													
Short-term debt rise/(fall)		1192	397	-246	-1343	0	0	0	0	0	0	0	0
Short-term debt interest/fees		-24	-119	-159	-134	0	0	0	0	0	0	0	0
Dividends 50%		0			-379	-1176	-580	-303	-301	-300	-300	-300	-1486
Retained earnings (increase)		0			-379	-1176	-580	-303	-301	-300	-300	-300	0
Total as above		1168	279	-405	-2235	-2351	-1160	-606	-602	-600	-600	-600	-1486
Note: Max allowed STD 60%		1192	1589	1926									

Table 11.6 Analytical cash flow studies: comparison of two strategies
a) Maximum equity strategy

						Million Lire						
Year:	0	1	2	3	4	5	6	7	8	9	10	11
Financial transfers (minus indicates payment out)												
Equity flow												
New share capital	2000	0	0	0	0	0	0	0	0	0	0	0
Dividends paid	0	0	0	-724	-1152	-556	-303	-301	-300	-300	-300	-1486
Surplus cash accruing	0	0	0	-724	-1152	-556	-303	-301	-300	-300	-300	0
	2000	0	0	-1448	-2304	-1113	-606	-602	-600	-600	-600	-1486
Medium-term debt service												
Debt rise/(fall)	248	-50	-50	-50	-50	-50	0	0	0	0	0	0
Interest (paid)	-12	-25	-20	-15	-10	-5	0	0	0	0	0	0
Realised exchange gains/(losses)	0	0	0	0	0	0	0	0	0	0	0	0
	236	-74	-69	-64	-60	-55	0	0	0	0	0	0
Short-term debt service												
Debt rise/(fall)	0	1020	-304	-716	0	0	0	0	0	0	0	0
Interest (paid)	0	-20	-102	-72	0	0	0	0	0	0	0	0
	0	1000	-406	-788	0	0	0	0	0	0	0	0
Government and Central Bank												
Subsidies/(taxes) paid	0	0	0	0	-637	-1833	-2394	-2398	-2400	-2400	-2400	-2400
Required cash (rise)/fall	0	-175	-75	-100	0	0	0	0	0	0	0	350
	0	-175	-75	-100	-637	-1833	-2394	-2398	-2400	-2400	-2400	-2050
Total financial transfers	2236	750	-550	-2400	-3000	-3000	-3000	-3000	-3000	-3000	-3000	-3536

continued . . .

b) Minimum equity strategy

Year:	0	1	2	3	4	5	6	7	8	9	10	11
Financial transfers (minus indicates payment out)												
Equity flow												
New share capital	831	721	0	0	0	0	0	0	0	0	0	0
Dividends paid	0	0	0	-379	-1176	-580	-303	-301	-300	-300	-300	-1486
Surplus cash accruing	0	0	0	-379	-1176	-580	-303	-301	-300	-300	-300	0
	831	721	0	-758	-2351	-1160	-606	-602	-600	-600	-600	-1486
Medium-term debt service												
Debt rise/(fall)	249	-50	-50	-50	-50	-50	0	0	0	0	0	0
Interest (paid)	-12	-25	-20	-15	-10	-5	0	0	0	0	0	0
Realised exchange gains/(losses)	0	0	0	0	0	0	0	0	0	0	0	0
	237	-75	-70	-65	-60	-55	0	0	0	0	0	0
Short-term debt service												
Debt rise/(fall)	1192	397	-246	-1343	0	0	0	0	0	0	0	0
Interest (paid)	-24	-119	-159	-134	0	0	0	0	0	0	0	0
	1168	278	-405	-1477	0	0	0	0	0	0	0	0
Government and Central Bank												
Subsidies/(taxes) paid	0	0	0	0	-589	-1785	-2394	-2398	-2400	-2400	-2400	-2400
Required cash (rise)/fall	0	-175	-75	-100	0	0	0	0	0	0	0	350
	0	-175	-75	-100	-589	-1785	-2394	-2398	-2400	-2400	-2400	-2050
Total financial transfers	2236	749	-550	-2400	-3000	-3000	-3000	-3000	-3000	-3000	-3000	-1486

Continued . . . .

c) Financial beneficiary analysis

	Maximum Equity Strategy					Minimum Equity Strategy			
	Net Present Values			Financial		Net Present Values			Financial
	at 5%	10%	15%	IRR		at 5%	10%	15%	IRR
Equity	4693	2990	1865	33%	Equity	4658	3043	1987	41%
Debt: medium	44	12	–13	12%	Debt: medium	44	12	–13	12%
Debt: short	92	17	–39	11%	Debt: short	200	22	–115	11%
Government	11030	7461	5189	n.a.	Government	10957	7404	5145	n.a
Total project	15860	10480	7004	49%	Total project	15860	10480	7004	49%

superior for the sponsors. We can see it again if we look at the NPV of the equity cash flow using a 15 per cent discount rate, which is the opportunity cost of equity: it is again higher on the second strategy.

For the lenders, given that the nominal rate of interest is set at 10 per cent and only some small front-end charges add to this, the IRRs come out just over 10 per cent in both strategies and the NPVs come out close to zero if a 10 per cent discount rate is used.

For Government, there is no financial IRR on this project. That is because there is no subsidy but only a stream of taxes. When a cash flow is one-way only, no yield can be calculated. Of course, we must bear in mind that Government may well have to invest money in infrastructure, but these costs do not figure in the financial accounts of the project. When we deal with purely financial analysis we deliberately omit these external items, leaving them for some wider analysis such as economic or social cost-benefit analysis as a separate study. In any case, investment in infrastructure will be the same in both financial strategies.

For Government, therefore, the first strategy is superior to the second, approximately to the same extent that for the equity-holders the second is superior to the first. This must be the case if there is little to choose between the two for the other parties.

In negotiation between the two, it may emerge that while 15 per cent is the opportunity cost of equity capital having regard to the investors' assessment of the project risk, 5 per cent (say) is the Government's test discount rate, and is applied to all projects regardless of risk (wisely or unwisely). Now, at 15 per cent, the preference of the equity investors for the second strategy over the first is 122 million, while at 5 per cent, the Government's preference for the first is only 73 million. In such a case, Government may be able to make a deal whereby the first strategy is adopted on consideration of a tax concession not exceeding 49 million, or the second strategy is adopted in consideration of an environmental protection concession costing the sponsors up to 49 million.

In this particular example, since both strategies produce equity IRRs far above the minimum of 15 per cent, Government is probably in a sufficiently strong negotiating position to insist on the first strategy without any consideration. Its power to do so rests on its powers to refuse licences or to discontinue the subsidies given through the low-interest DFI loans. In many countries, Government has abandoned all centralised licensing powers and given autonomy to DFIs; even so, the bankers themselves may press for larger equity, and most banks avoid publishing clear rules about gearing so as to leave themselves room to negotiate in the direction of the preferred strategy.

BACK TO THE DRAWING-BOARD

Let us now suppose that the sponsors are in the driving seat; perhaps the other parties do not have enough information on the project to carry out the analysis as we have done. The sponsors decide that, since the project has a rather brief need for cash during the first three years only, equity will be minimised and short-term debt maximised. They indicate to the commercial bankers that they will be looking for short-term accommodation of 1,192 million Lire in Year 0 and rising, instead of 1,020 in Year 1, and that this larger figure is still within the guidelines on collateral security. Naturally enough, however, the bankers react negatively to this, considering that the sponsors themselves are now proposing to put in less money than was talked about earlier, and are being reticent about the figures. It is therefore less than certain that the short-term money will be available up to the ceiling that has been calculated. The question now arises, whether the project resource flows should be redesigned so as to smooth out this awkward peak in the financing requirement. It is known that the main machinery could be installed in two parts instead of one, with the second instalment deferred. Let us see whether this improves the situation.

The cost of the main machinery has been estimated at 1,000 million Lire. Dividing this into two is easy mechanically as it consists of two parallel units. However, the cost of each unit will be more than 500 million; we have no firm quotation on this and so will use the six-tenths rule as an estimating device. Taking the scale factor at a middle of the road 0.65, the cost of each unit comes to $1000 \times 0.5^{0.65}$ which is 637 million. The second unit attracts an extra 100 million because of the cost of returning the contractor to site. We can install the second unit in Year 2 to come on stream in Year 3 at which time output is expected to be at full tonnage; in year 2, however, output will only be possible at half tonnage, 500 thousand tons instead of the previously forecasted 600 thousand tons. There will therefore be some adverse impact on sales in Year 2. Stocks also require adjustment; to offset the unreliability of single-train operation we must add another 40 million Lire of stocks at the ends of Years 0 and 1, so stocks first rise then fall.

Entering these new figures in the spreadsheet, we discover that in Year 0 we shall require equity of 711, five-year money at 213, and short-term money at 1,020 million Lire; additional contributions of both equity and short-term money are required in Year 1 and again in Year 2. In Year 3, cash flow is sufficient to pay off all the short-term borrowing and to commence the dividend flows, as was the case in the earlier scenarios. The beneficiary analysis is shown in Table 11.7.

Comparing this scenario with the other, we find the following results:

1 It is rather better for the equity investors, showing an IRR of 38 per cent instead of 33 per cent. Although the scale factor of 0.65 was chosen arbitrarily, it is unlikely to be so far wrong as to disturb this conclusion, unless there are special factors concerning the procurement of the equipment.
2 The IRR is just about the same for the medium-term investors (12 per cent unchanged), but their gearing after Year 0 is much improved, since their

Table 11.7 Comparative beneficiary analysis

	Capital expenditure with deferred instalment			
	Net present values			Financial
at	5%	10%	15%	IRR
Equity	4188	2715	1745	36%
Debt: medium	37	10	-11	12%
Debt: short	213	19	-127	11%
Government	10422	6987	4815	n.a.
Total project	14860	9729	6422	47%

	Capital expenditure all in year 0			
	Net present values			Financial
at	5%	10%	15%	IMRR
Equity	4693	2990	1865	33%
Debt: medium	44	11	-13	12%
Debt: short	92	17	-39	11%
Government	11030	7461	5189	n.a.
Total project	10480	7004	6881	49%

stake is now 30 per cent of the initial equity required for the first instalment of fixed assets only.

3 The results work out about the same for the short-term lenders; their IRR is unchanged at 11 per cent but their NPV could be better or worse depending which discount rate they use.

4 For Government, the new scenario is distinctly worse at all discount rates; the reduced profitability in Year 2 has trimmed back the tax take.

5 For the project as a whole, IRR falls from 49 per cent to 47 per cent, and although shadow-pricing has not been attempted as this is purely a financial analysis, this does suggest that for the country as a whole the new scenario may be slightly poorer.

Summing up, the beneficiary analysis shows that the deferring of the second unit of equipment improves the yield for the equity investors but reduces it for Government and probably for the country as a whole. Whether the Government representatives, acting on their own behalf and on that of the whole country, will prevail over the sponsors, depends on what information they have and on the powers of Government.

It appears therefore that the financing pattern will be set differently in each specific situation. By a process of negotiation which as a rule is not overt and may not be comprehensible even to the support staff, a set of constraints and decision rules emerges. Translation of these to a determinate set of numbers is, however, a science rather than an art, and involves simultaneous equations which are capable of solution.

A broadly similar conclusion, though with different emphasis, is reached in Brealey and Myers (1984: 603). Brealey and Myers consider there is a virtually infinite range of solutions in financial planning, each of which may be considered an optimum in some sense, so that it is an art rather than a science. Mention is made of the Third Law of Brealey and Myers, which states that as there is an infinite set of unsolved problems in any field of enquiry, and as the number of problems that humans can bear in mind at any time is limited to ten, there will always be at least ten problems which have no formal solution, in the field of financial planning. Therefore, financial planners have to make judgemental decisions as best they may.

The negotiation between parties, the outcome of which will remain an unsolved problem until the conclusion is announced, is perhaps one of the ten problems. But even so, as has been demonstrated, some calculations are possible. Indeed it would be foolhardy to enter such negotiations without attempting these calculations first.

Computer spreadsheets are very helpful here; even though some spreadsheet programs cannot directly solve simultaneous equations, they assist the analyst to do so by trial and error. In deriving the figures given above for the case study, seven spreadsheets were used, exploring different variants of the three basic strategic ideas. In each case, not only cash flow planning tables but also income statements, tax computations and balance sheets were computed, giving certain details needed for the cash flow planning, and finally a formal analytical cash flow statement, together with some simple arithmetical validity checks, to minimise mistakes. This may seem to be making a large meal of a small project, but had we not been working in constant prices, this suite of spreadsheets would have been even larger.

The figures of the spreadsheet based on the case study with one of the financial strategies (minimum equity without deferment of capital expenditure) are given in Appendix 1. In addition to the cash planning table already exhibited, this spreadsheet contains a full set of financial statements. Such pro-forma statements can often be used to show additional implications of the strategy under consideration, since the continued soundness of the balance sheets year by year is a necessary outcome. in this case they are also necessary to determine the values of the gearing constraint and the tax flows required in the cash planning itself.

WHAT IF GOVERNMENT IS ALSO THE EQUITY HOLDER?

In the special case where all the equity belongs to Government, and the enterprise is controlled therefore by directors representing the Government, beneficiary analysis is simplified. In the ACF statement, the equity cash flow can be put into the Government section, along with taxes, subsidies, and required cash flows. The corporate planning which produces the best cash flow result in this section of the ACF will then be the best for Government in its dual capacity. Of course, this is to see Government as a financial party looking for a return, not as an agency looking for the best result for the nation as a whole.

There will still be the other sections of the ACF dealing with the debt and debt service cash flows, both long and short term, so there can still be a difference of opinion between Government and bankers as to the best corporate plan, and a negotiation between the two if necessary.

In the even more special case where the banks are also Government-owned, the entire financial section of the ACF is simplified to a single section, and the financial cash flow as an undivided whole is simply equal to the resource cash flow. This is the simplified scenario often implicitly assumed in academic 'project planning' methodology where only resource cash flows are optimised.

In this single-party scenario, Government has no reason to differentiate between debt service, dividends, and tax payments: all are controlled by Government. There is therefore no reason to distinguish between debt and equity. It might as well all be equity, if dividends can be extracted from the enterprise at any time by an order from the Ministry of Finance to its representatives on the Board.

The reader will no doubt object that this is an over-simplification. The enterprise and its Board have *a degree* of autonomy; if not, why have an enterprise with separate financial statements and separate directors? Even though appointed by Government the directors are theoretically under a legal duty of care to look after the corporation itself. The implication here is that, in a year when the Corporation has some spare cash, it can decide to retain it for future investment even though at that time the Ministry wants the maximum dividend distribution, whether for reasons of fiscal policy or because some other Government enterprise claims it has an even greater need of the money.

If indeed the Corporation does have that autonomy, then it is creating its own separate pool of capital; so the interests of the nascent equity holders on the one hand and the Government on the other do need to be kept separate in the ACF and there may be a negotiation between the two. The statutory authority for the Corporation may throw light on the legal situation. But if the degree of autonomy is obscure, and can only be found out after the event, no beneficiary analysis is possible, and only single-party financial planning is possible. This will have implications for corporate planning; it too will be simplified if capital investment programmes are not a bone of contention between different beneficiaries.

THE FINANCIAL VIEW OF THE WORLD

Brealey and Myers also state that 'there is no finance in corporate financial models'. This amazing claim rests on their assertion that:

> Most such models incorporate an accountant's view of the world. They are designed to forecast accounting statements, and their equations naturally embody the accounting conventions employed by the firm. Consequently the models do not emphasise the tools of financial analysis: incremental cash flow, present value, market risk and so on (Brealey and Myers 1984: 603).

Whether this is a fair criticism of the financial modelling methodology presented above must be left to the reader to decide. Brealey and Myers just seem to hate balance sheets, and certainly US corporate balance sheets *as published* embody very sophisticated and flexible accounting procedures which serve a range of purposes other than the communication of the truth, the whole truth and nothing but the truth. For instance, US law is quite permissive in accepting different ways of calculating depreciation. But such is not the case with the pro-forma balance sheets used for ex-ante LDC projects. Nor does the contemptible 'accountant's view of the world' place undue stress, if any, on the use of balance sheets to analyse key ratios, an exercise which is certainly rather limited in ex-ante work because dividend policy cannot be predetermined.

Brealey and Myers' exclusion of full financial statements from 'the tools of financial analysis' therefore seems rather narrow. They have their part to play.

There may be good reason to separate worm's-eye 'accounting' from eagle-eyed 'finance' but to regard the latter as superior is very questionable.

There is in fact a good deal of confusion about what is meant by the profitability of a project, confusion which the use of the ACF statement and beneficiary analysis can help to dispel. Some analysts fail to distinguish between the return to shareholders with its equity IRR, the total resource cash flow with its total project IRR, and the economic rate of return (EIRR) which is based on shadow-priced resource flows. For instance, all three are mixed up in Reimann (1990: 58):

> Central to the value-based approach is the discounting of projected cash flows to establish the economic (shareholder) value of business units and their strategies.

The term *value-based* appropriates the meaning of *value* to an increase in the assets of *shareholders*, as though there had been no other theories of value in the last two hundred years. This is really an investor's view of the world. It is indistinguishable from the 'financial view' of Brealey and Myers. It is a widely held, indeed orthodox view in the USA. In the UK there is a considerable tendency to place stress on the total project IRR, which provides the cash flow from which the beneficiaries take their various shares. The 'accountant's view' derided by Brealey and Myers probably refers to the concern of the accountant at the enterprise level, allied to other business managers at the enterprise level, to cope with the problems of survival of the underlying business activity in which they are confined.

LDC managers may be trained in either school of thought, but the perpetual problems of survival tend to bring the 'accountant's view' to the forefront even in the minds of finance staff.

Chapter 12

Inflation

In financial analysis, inflation is an enormous nuisance. Just about every LDC suffers from it, so it cannot be overlooked, but it puts a question mark over the validity of any analysis which conducts its calculations in a currency, as of course they all do. A currency is supposed to be a unit of value, and we need a currency to be a yardstick for the ex-ante measurement of inputs and outputs at different dates, in short a numéraire. If the unit keeps changing, we need to make adjustments to our calculations. The aim of those adjustments is to allow us to work in *current prices*, that is to say forecasted actual prices.

The adjustments are complicated. It is the complication, rather than the problem of forecasting the rate of inflation, which is the source of nuisance. This is not to say that the choice of rate is easy. Consider the situation of a forecaster in Brazil in the recent past. Table 12.1 shows the experience of previous years, on which a forecast for the 1990s (and beyond) might be based.

Table 12.1 Inflation in Brazil (quarterly percentage rates of change in the general price index)

	Quarter	Average monthly	Annualised equivalent
1986	Q1	10.6	235.0
	Q2	0.1	11.4
	Q3	1.0	13.0
	Q4	3.8	57.0
1987	Q1	13.7	366.8
	Q2	24.6	1300.3
	Q3	7.3	132.9
	Q4	13.9	376.7
1988	Q1	18.3	651.3
	Q2	20.2	809.6
	Q3	23.4	1246.8
	Q4	28.2	1970.9

Source: Parkin (1991: 75)

As this example shows, the rate of inflation is often quite impossible to predict with confidence, but we can deal with this by trying out different rates, in order to see how our investment proposal will fare in these different scenarios. Naturally, this means that we will have to work through the complicated adjustments many times over. Here for the first time we come to a situation where those who have to work without computers have to face the fact that they cannot cope. Financial analysis with inflation requires a large computer spreadsheet system.

AVOIDING THE QUESTION

The complexity of the problem of inflation means that analysts work in *constant prices* in all cases where a convincing case can be made that it is safe to do so. 'Safe' means that the project is very unlikely to be damaged by inflation, or that it might either be damaged or actually benefit, within a margin of uncertainty which is unimportant by comparison with other uncertainties inherent in the project.

In order to qualify as safe, in this sense of being reasonably inflation-proof from the viewpoint of financial analysis, a project must meet the following criteria:

- The initial capital costs and other costs to be incurred in the early years must be known in advance with sufficient accuracy in current price terms to permit us to feel confident that sufficient financing has been or can be arranged.
- Operating revenues must be exposed to inflation at least as much as operating costs.
- The project must be invulnerable to the effects of currency devaluation which is a normal concomitant of inflation.

Let us consider in what circumstances these requirements might be met.

The problem of arranging in advance for the financing of initial costs which are subject to inflation is confined to the period between the date of financial negotiations and the date of procurement of the assets concerned. The date of financial negotiations is not a precise date, but a period of time during which discussions are held with various likely financiers, to arrive at agreements which are all conditional on the decision to go ahead with the project. For instance, in a large project financed by the World Bank with ODA co-financing, the financial negotiations would be with (a) host Government, (b) World Bank officials, and (c) ODA officials perhaps two or three months before final approval of the project by the World Bank board of directors. The project implementation team would then be formed, consultants would be involved in design and procurement, and tenders would be invited for major items of equipment. The bidding date for each package would be different. Such a date might be a year after the financial negotiations. Even if the conditions for tendering insist on bids which embody fixed prices, in the sense that no escalation clause is to be inserted to cover inflation during the period of manufacture which follows the bid date, each bid will include an allowance for future inflation in the opinion of the tenderer, and this opinion will be formed a year after the original financial negotiations.

Supposing that the original estimate of capital costs was incorporated in a feasibility study which was the basis of project approval by Government, there is first the time taken to write that study, second the time taken to read it and pass it through the approval system, and third the time taken to reach provisional agreement with the World Bank and ODA officers. During these delays, prices will have risen. Possibly the original estimates were based on quotations with six-month validities or even longer, but these validities are very likely to expire before actual procurement takes place, and in any case there will be a procedure of competitive tendering which makes it unlikely that the original quotation will be the one selected and will survive without modification. The officers therefore have to propose loans to their boards which will be sufficient to cope with inflation throughout the process. The final loan amount may be more or less than was foreseen in the original feasibility study depending on the generosity of the contingency built into the study as a provision for this very purpose. Furthermore, the loan arrangements will stipulate that one party, usually an equity investor, should take responsibility for top-up financing if required, since supplementary loans necessitated by defective prediction of cost inflation are frowned upon by lending boards.

In smaller projects, where international lending agencies are not involved with the loans either directly or through DFI programmes as sub-loans, competitive tendering may not be insisted upon as a method of procurement. This shortens the process. Original quotations can be used as a reliable method of cost estimation and can still be within their validity periods when the time comes to place the orders.

The inflation-proofing here depends on (a) procurement and selection before finalisation of financial agreements rather than after; (b) fixed-price bids with reasonable validity periods; (c) inclusion of a high proportion of early-year costs within this framework, including not only equipment but also buildings, installation, initial spares and supplies of raw materials and consumables; and (d) use of a procedure for appraisal and approval which will not introduce delays into the project such as would exhaust these validity periods.

In general, private sector procedures are better at meeting these criteria than Government procedures, since the latter require lengthier appraisals and more formal tendering schemes. These are for good reasons, but clearly they have their costs. To some extent Governments overcome the problem by pledging equity finance in constant-price terms, that is to say, the public equity contribution is approved ('appropriated') in Year X to be handed over in

Year X + 1 with an extra allowance ('supplementary estimate') for inflation. There is often much scope for argument about the correct amount of the extra allowance, because of the complex nature of the base date to which the original costings relate, so this extra sum may hide other adjustments too.

As for inflation-proofing of operating revenues and costs, this has a different set of pre-conditions. We have in mind that the project will be operated by a team of managers who will be aware of the changing commercial conditions and will react to them with a view to safeguarding the financial integrity of the project; in short, they will put prices up. Alternatively, as happens in some LDCs, the Government committee which controls this branch of the economy will undertake that for them. Here the first pre-condition is motivation: whoever controls the prices of the outputs which generate project revenue will need to have the intention of reacting against inflation on the cost side in order to protect this investment against inflation, rather than having mixed motives such as considering the welfare of consumers or the profits of downstream businesses. Railways are prime examples of projects which are run with mixed motives; when the cost of diesel fuel rises, freight rates are often not raised proportionately, in order to protect the farmers who use the service. Again, private sector projects are more likely to meet this requirement.

It is a necessary condition also that the revenues can be raised in a manner which is linked to an index of inflation, such as the official index of retail prices, which will be a good representative index of the prices of the project inputs. For instance, if the project is to be in India, where the retail prices index is a technically good one for consumer goods, if the project outputs are a wide range of consumer goods to be sold in India, and if the project inputs are a wide range of goods and services to be bought in India, there is no reason to fear that the two will diverge. But if inputs are imported and outputs are not; if outputs are imported and inputs are not; if the official index is corrupt; if the project has only one product which may be aimed at a specific market segment; if the project has a major input of labour, which has its own index separate from that of consumer goods; then we cannot assume that managers will be able to adjust output prices to input prices without damage, though it is fair to add that the effect might be either positive or negative.

The third pre-condition for an analysis purely in constant prices is insulation from the effects of currency devaluation. Where there is movement of prices, there is bound to be movement of exchange rates between currencies; in the adverse economic and political circumstances of LDCs, this means probably a relative fall in the value of their currencies as against major world trading currencies. Many LDCs do not have freely trading currency markets but operate a system of official exchange rates, so a gradual fall in the value of the domestic currency inevitably takes the form of an occasional devaluation of the official exchange rate.

Here we have to worry about inputs, outputs, borrowings and debt service.

Devaluation will tend to raise the cost of inputs if they are imported; if they are bought locally at a price which is governed by the price of competitive imported products; or if they are manufactured locally using significant amounts of imported raw materials. Devaluation will tend to raise the revenue of outputs if they are exported, or if they are sold locally at prices which are governed by the prices of competitive imports. Devaluation will raise the cost of debt service if borrowing is denominated in foreign currency or, what is the same thing, in local currency with a fixed exchange-rate clause in the agreement.

If none of these many problems arise, it is 'safe' to analyse the project in terms of constant prices. Note that even then, individual input and output elements can be expected to drift in price relative to others; this 'differential inflation' or specific price-drift needs to be included in the analysis where it is known about, no matter whether constant prices or current prices are being used. That is why we speak of 'constant prices' rather than 'fixed prices'.

It will be painfully apparent that few medium- or large-scale LDC projects can get away safely with constant price appraisals. The projects would need to be small (thus not unduly delayed by institutional involvement), not supported by foreign currency loans, and having a good balance between inputs whose price is governed by external trade and outputs whose price is governed by external trade, preferably with little of both. *Inputs* here refers to operating inputs and replacements of fixed assets. Both inputs and outputs need to be well represented by the same index of prices, not necessarily a specific price index which is actually compiled and published but in the sense that the two are logically related to some conceptual price trend and therefore are likely to move up and down together so far as one can tell. As a broad generalisation one might sum up by saying that those projects which can safely be treated in terms of constant price analysis are probably too small to be submitted to formal analysis at all. So we must now stop ducking the problem and consider how to introduce inflation and devaluation rigorously.

THE SPECIAL CASE AND THE GENERAL CASE

Economists usually work in constant prices, and are sometimes astonished to find that financial and commercial analysts do not. The use of the terms *constant prices* and *current prices* suggests that there are two alternative approaches, which may be equally valid for their respective purposes. I disagree with that view. I argue that the first is only a special case of the second. In the real world prices do change. Every year there is some percentage change, usually an increase. Whatever this percentage increase may be, which we call the rate of inflation from one year to the next, the value *zero* has no special magic which makes it qualitatively different from any other number, except that it offers the immense convenience of permitting us to ignore inflation.

There are exactly zero situations in the real world where inflation is exactly zero, although as we have seen there are some kinds of projects (in LDCs these are mostly small and medium private sector investments which are locally financed) for which zero inflation is a *safe simulation*. Whatever may be the rationale in economic analysis for working in constant prices, it will not suffice in financial analysis except for those projects where the safety conditions are met as discussed above.

In general these conditions are not met and so inflation must be introduced into the analysis. The rate of increase in prices must inevitably be forecasted if a single prediction is to be made, or a range of forecasts must be hypothesised if a range of results ('sensitivity study') is to be undertaken. Among the infinite number of possible values for the inflation rate, two special cases may be mentioned. These are (a) the hypothesis that the year-on-year rate of inflation will be the same throughout the project life, and (b) that the rate will be zero throughout.

Along with non-zero price movements, alterations in the exchange rate arise. This is the rate at which domestic currency can be exchanged for foreign currency in order to purchase imported inputs, or foreign currency may be exchanged for local currency in order to bank the proceeds of exported outputs. Here a number of points should be noted:

1 Even if inputs are not imported, their cost may be governed by the price at which similar goods are traded in overseas markets quoted in foreign currency, so that any change in the currency exchange rate will affect the cost of inputs. This obviously arises when the major world markets are located overseas, and the local market is dominated by overseas price quotations. Similarly for outputs; even if they are not exported, the selling price may be governed by price quotations obtained overseas and converted into the domestic currency.

2 The rate used for currency conversion should be, like all forecasts, as realistic as possible. In many LDCs there are exchange control rules which require that these rates shall be whatever the central bank says they shall be, i.e. *official exchange rates*. When these are fixed at unrealistic levels, illegal currency markets develop; in most cases these handle probably a minority of the trade transactions and therefore with most projects it is appropriate to assume that the legal route will be taken. Clearly when illegal projects are being analysed, realism may dictate that illegal rates of exchange should be adopted.

3 It is unrealistic to suppose that the official exchange rate is the same for buying as for selling foreign currency: foreign exchange dealers and bankers like their profit margins as much as anyone else. On commercial transactions, there may be a spread of 1 or 2 per cent either side of the mean. We usually take the mean rate for our calculations, but include the spread in the cost of total banking services under the heading of 'other

administrative expense' or 'financial expenses'. This is a slightly inaccurate procedure and it tends to hide the volume-related nature of this cost.

4 It is too simple to suppose that there exists only one foreign currency and only one official exchange rate. What usually happens is that the official rate is determined with respect to a dominant foreign currency (US dollar, SA Rand, etc. as the case may be) and other currencies are derived from that dominant rate. Since there is always a fluctuation in world market rates, this produces a wider spread between buying and selling rates for currencies other than the dominant foreign currency; the spread between buying and selling rates, instead of being 1 or 2 per cent, is often 3 or 4 per cent. In some countries this includes an insurance premium to guard against the fluctuations on the cross-rates. The result, of course, is to favour trade conducted in the dominant currency, which is much the same as saying trade which involves merchants or banks from that dominant foreign country, and to disfavour competitors of other nationalities. The official exchange rate is therefore a structure of rates, several of which may be relevant to a project.

5 It is necessary to forecast what the foreign exchange rates will be throughout the project life. In most situations it will be sufficient to deal with one single foreign currency. Those are situations where the project is involved in world markets and the latter may be represented by the US dollar, the Yen, the Deutschmark or the Écu. Movements in cross-rates between these are assumed not to affect the project. However, there will be other situations where regional as well as world markets are important. Thus a project in north-eastern Tanzania might depend on the Kenya shilling as well as on the pound sterling. A project in Papua New Guinea might depend both on the Australian dollar and on the Yen. A project in Lithuania might depend on both the Rouble and the Kronor. This would be because the project was exporting to, or importing from, two distinct markets which do not move closely together as one.

6 It would clearly be a special case for the foreign exchange rate to remain constant throughout the project life. Clearly it is especially important to predict accurately what rate or rates will prevail during the period when the major imported plant and equipment will be bought; this will determine fixed asset costs and probably borrowing requirements. Second is debt service; if the debt is in foreign currency, devaluation can sink an enterprise even though its inputs and its outputs are evenly balanced in terms of foreign exchange components. This makes it important to predict devaluations during the period of debt service. Third are operating costs; foreign components here include inputs and outputs, not forgetting expatriate salaries if there are any, as these are typically fixed at world-price levels.

THE ARITHMETIC OF THE CRYSTAL BALL

Obviously the forecasts of inflation and the forecasts of exchange rate movements should be consistent with one another. Hyper-inflation proceeding over twenty years with no let-up and with no alteration of the exchange rate would be a scenario which it would be very difficult to defend. On this matter, circumstances vary so much from place to place and from time to time that no general rule can be enjoined other than maximum realism combined with theoretical consistency.

Where economic circumstances are not very severe, and stable conditions obtain, it may be satisfactory to assume that those conditions will continue. If inflation is at 3 per cent, there is no illegal currency market, and there is no rioting in the streets, by all means assume 3 per cent inflation indefinitely together with continuation of the existing exchange rate. Where inflation is reported at 30 per cent, and probably over 70 in fact, and where a major devaluation is under negotiation with the IMF every year, and illegal rates run at double or treble the official rates, it is not so easy – especially for the analyst in Government service. Official secrecy may require the following anodyne assumptions to be made:

- Inflation is much lower than you think.
- Within two years it will be down to 10 per cent.
- Within five years it will settle at a comfortable 5 per cent.
- The present exchange rate will remain in force throughout.
- This entire plan is based on a reliable macro-economic model.

No wonder, under these conditions, analysts like to work in constant prices and constant exchange rates. However, realistic analysis requires some assessment of the evolution and outcome of the present economic crises. Suppose the analyst's private opinions are the following:

- Inflation will run at 70 per cent for one more year before Government caves in and reaches agreement with the IMF.
- The IMF will then require a devaluation of 200 per cent (more local currency units per US dollar).
- Inflation will then run at 150 per cent for one year before fiscal restraints are made effective.
- A further very large devaluation will then be requested but only 120 per cent will be agreed.
- Inflation will gradually fall reaching 10 per cent in the seventh year.
- Exchange rate adjustments will occur once a year.
- Each devaluation will cover only half of the gap created each year by domestic inflation running ahead of US inflation (which will run at 4 per cent).
- The shortage of foreign exchange will result in implementation of the project being delayed by three years.

In the opinion of the analyst, this scenario is supposedly realistic, it is precise and can be quantified correctly on a spreadsheet, and it can be defended against any accusation of inconsistency. However, if published, this would undermine the negotiations with the IMF, and might have a bearing on party politics and factionalism too. The analyst cannot afford these consequences. The solution is to incorporate it as merely one of many scenarios in a sensitivity study. We must not say that this will happen, but if it does, the effect on our project will be such and such. Of course, the additional calculations required for multiple scenarios make it essential to use a computer spreadsheet.

The claim that the above scenario is capable of being quantified on a spreadsheet is demonstrated by the results shown in Table 12.2. Section A of Table 12.2 shows domestic inflation proceeding in the manner described in the analyst's scenario, first at 70 per cent, then at 150 per cent, then reducing to 10 per cent in the seventh year, an annual reduction of 28 per cent. Ideally this prediction of inflation should be derived from some coherent macro-economic model. An example of such a model, called neo-structuralist, together with an admission of its limitations and a good bibliography of inflation, is given by Vincent Parkin (1991). Of course in practice such predictions depend more on the consensus of hunches by experts. Either way, the analyst has settled on these predictions.

Assuming an arbitrary starting value of 100 for the price index, that index will then rise in accordance with the predicted inflation in the manner shown. The USA is proxy for the rest of the world. It undergoes inflation at a steady 4 per cent per annum and its index rises in the manner shown. That too is an assumption. The differential index obtained by dividing the local index by the US index rises in the manner shown.

We copy this differential index into Section B in the line for Implied exchange rates. Again, the starting value is an arbitrary figure representing the official exchange rate in force at the time of the study. In later years the figures shown are the exchange rates which the central bank would declare if it wanted the rate to move in accordance with the drift of inflation. By copying these figures from Section A into Section B we are implying that a 'proper' exchange rate would be one in which the trading relationship between this country and the rest of the world was not to be disturbed by inflation; any differential in inflation rates would be compensated by a proportionate movement in the exchange rate.

This is called the *purchasing power parity* principle. Of course, no sensible central bank would operate *entirely* on such a principle. In looking after its balance of payments, it would have regard to transfers and capital movements as well as trading transactions. But in the long run, inward flows of transfers and capital movements cannot be relied upon to cover weaknesses in the trade account for ever. We have to assume that the purchasing power parity principle operates as a guideline from which the central bank may diverge. In

Table 12.2 Exchange rates and inflation: effect on cost of imported goods

	Year	0	1	2	3	4	5	6	7
A:	Inflation								
	Domestic								
	Rate:		70%	150%	122%	94%	66%	38%	10%
	Index	100.0	170.0	425.0	943.5	1830.4	3038.4	4193.1	4612.4
	US								
	Rate:	4%	4%	4%	4%	4%	4%	4%	4%
	Index	100.0	104.0	108.2	112.5	117.0	121.7	126.5	131.6
	Differential								
	Index	100.0	163.5	392.9	838.8	1564.6	2497.4	3313.8	3505.0
B:	Exchange rates								
	Predicted	54.5	163.5	359.6	559.2	1043.1	1664.9	2209.2	2336.7
	Implied	100.0	163.5	392.9	838.8	1564.6	2497.4	3313.8	3505.0
	Over-valuation	84%	0%	9%	50%	50%	50%	50%	50%
C:	Project cost (imported elements)								
	Base year cost	1000	1000	1000	1000	1000	1000	1000	1000
	Revised cost	1000	3120	7139	11544	22395	37176	51303	56434

general, if the purchasing power parity principle suggests massive devaluation, it is likely to be resisted and a smaller devaluation substituted. The result will be an official exchange rate which, for trading purposes, appears to assign too high a value to the domestic currency. In Section B this excess value is labelled 'over-valuation' without intending to suggest that it should not happen. Over-valuation is defined as the number of local currency units per dollar in the official exchange rate divided by the number which would be suggested as a guideline by the purchasing power parity principle.

In our scenario, the IMF suggestion of a 200 per cent devaluation is implemented and this does away with the over-valuation briefly in Year 1. Since the exchange rate suggested by purchasing power at that date is 163.5, the official rate in the previous year must have been one-third of this figure at 54.5. The over-valuation at that time must have been 84 per cent, calculated from (100/54.5)–1.

In the following year there is a devaluation of 120 per cent and the rate becomes 359.6; compared with the rate implied by purchasing power, an over-valuation re-appears, though quite small at 9 per cent. In later years, continued heavy inflation raises the implied rate rather fast, but an over-valuation of 50 per cent holds down the official exchange rate to the figures shown in the 'predicted' line of Section B.

Finally Section C shows the effects on our project. For every 1000 rupees (local currency) of imported equipment, we have to allow for (a) increases in the exchange rate and (b) inflation in the rest of the world. If the project is delayed three years, an initial cost estimate of one thousand rupees will escalate to over eleven thousand.

THE IMPACT OF INFLATION

Under inflationary conditions the following values will increase:

1 Real resource flows which will affect Sections 1 and 2 of the analytical cash flow (ACF) statement:

- initial fixed assets, rising in value from the date or dates of their original price enquiries to the date or dates of their contract signatures during the procurement process;
- fixed assets replaced at fixed intervals (those which have a shorter depreciable life than the major asset whose life is used to determine the life of the entire project) rising in value from interval to interval;
- fixed assets disposed of at non-zero residual values;
- cost of various inputs during operating life;
- revenue from various outputs during operating life;
- stocks of various kinds, related to input costs;
- creditors (accounts payable), related to purchases of inputs;
- debtors (accounts receivable), related to sales of outputs.

2 Changes in financial transfers resulting from the above changes in real resource flows and appearing in Section 3 of the ACF statement:

- cash required for operations (required cash), usually related to inputs or to inputs and outputs taken together;
- taxation which rises because of the capital gains realised by holding stock while values are rising;
- additional finance, and additional yield, which will be distributed among the financing parties according to the formulae chosen for Section 3 of the ACF spreadsheet.

The extent to which values rise depends on the general outline of the model chosen. If the project is one which can ignore overseas trade, as might be appropriate for a canal project in central China, the index of general inflation can be used. Even if no such index is published for the remote area in question, a notional index which represents the general trend of local inflation and which the analyst feels able to predict or to use on a sensitivity basis will suffice. Taking an actual or arbitrary value for that index at the date of the principal pricing study, the subsequent annual percentage increases in the index are applied to the unit prices of the real resources. This has the effect of recalculating Sections 1 and 2 of the ACF statement. The result is that more financing is required; that has to be worked out in Section 3 of the ACF statement. This means that the financial contributions of the various interested parties should be included in the spreadsheets, not as fixed amounts taken from correspondence, but as formulae based on a structure, a financing pattern which will cope with inflation.

However, most analyses do not presuppose closed economies but introduce world prices or border prices so that the foreign exchange rate becomes relevant as well as the inflation index. In order to fit this into the model, the unit price of every input and output listed in Section 1 of the ACF statement has to be broken down into elements which bridge the price gap between the world or border price on the one hand and the price paid or received by the enterprise which is conducting the project on the other. Table 12.3 gives an example of an input and an example of an output 'decomposed' in this way.

In Table 12.3, the first column of figures gives an example for an input which is imported. The price paid by the project is governed by and starts with the border price, which we will suppose is known at the base date and subject to some kind of world inflation index thereafter. It is converted into rupees (the local currency) at an official exchange rate, which will be subjected to devaluations in the manner already described. Import duty we will suppose remains at 10 per cent. The cost of harbour dues, clearing and forwarding and transportation to the site of the project where the inputs are required are all local costs and will escalate with the local inflation index. In this way the cost of the input as experienced by the project is a composite of world inflation, local inflation, exchange rate changes, and, conceivably, import duty changes.

Table 12.3 Decomposition of input and output

	Input	Output
Border price	$5	$20
Exchange rate	8	8
Border price	Rs 40	Rs 160
Import duty	10%	20%
Import price	Rs 44	Rs 192
Port to project	Rs 11	
Cost to project	Rs 55	
Port to city		Rs 18
Price in city		Rs 210
Project to city		Rs 20
Selling price		Rs 190

The second column of figures gives an example of an output which is sold to a city market in competition with an imported rival product, supposing that the world price of the latter governs the former. We add the elements of cost which bring the imported product into the city market where the competition takes place, arriving at a price of Rs 210. In order to meet this competition after paying the costs of transport to the city, the project has to charge only Rs 190. Again we have a composite of local inflation, foreign inflation, exchange rates and possibly import duty changes, but the structure of these is different: some are added and others subtracted depending on the logic of the situation.

This logical structure of cost elements *reconciles* the border price with the project price. The structure varies according to the geography and the nature of the price competition or other constraint, so different inputs and different outputs may all have different structures. Once the structure is understood, the various elements can be subjected to inflation in the computer spreadsheets by relating them to local inflation, foreign inflation, and exchange rate changes as appropriate. These indexes and rate changes will normally be in a special section of the spreadsheet ready to be used in this way, often in a front-end section of the spreadsheet, which means that they are among the very first figures to be calculated as parameters which will affect figures calculated later.

The pro-forma income statements, balance sheets and cash flow statements will all be inflated; profit will rise, and internal rates of return will rise. They will not, however, rise in a simply predictable way; for instance, a 10 per cent inflation rate will not produce an exact 10 per cent increase in net profit nor an exact 10 per cent rise in IRR. We must remember the complexities, in particular the following:

- Inputs and outputs are inflated by a composite structure.
- Profits are inflated by holding gains on the rise in value of stocks, depending on the period of time the stocks are held.

- Tax on profits begins when early-year losses are used up, and may therefore be introduced at a different date.
- Depending on the financing structure, the additional finance required may not be spread evenly between debt and equity, so the interest expense from debt may not rise proportionately.
- The impact of inflation on replacement fixed assets may be so severe as to require additional equity or some other significant change in the financing arrangements a few years into the operating period.

In constant prices, there is normally some kind of relationship between the unit values of inputs and of outputs, based on technical coefficients, as for instance direct materials may cost 60 per cent of output at selling price, a relationship derived from experience in the trade. With inflation, decomposing inputs and outputs into their various elements each subject to a different inflation rate or exchange rate adjustment, this relationship *may* be disturbed. It depends on whether the project is basically a price-taker and everything is ultimately governed by decisions made elsewhere, or whether the project is a major actor in its various markets (or protected by Government) and so is basically a price-maker. This does not mean, however, that past experience will be disrupted by future inflation. After all, there has probably been inflation in the past too. What is does mean is that the technical coefficients must be correctly stated, as being past experience adjusted for constant prices or not, as applicable.

ACCOUNTING TREATMENT

The systems of book-keeping and accountancy have their origins in earlier centuries when a pound was a pound. Prices did change, both up and down, but relatively slowly, certainly not fast enough to cast any doubt on the validity of an accounting system that used the pound as a numéraire.

Only in the twentieth century have we experienced periods of inflation sufficiently severe and sufficiently prolonged to call the accounting system into question and provoke debate as to how best to reform it. Most South American countries have experienced severe inflation for several decades and their accountants have learned to live with it. There, the accounting system has been tweaked but not radically reformed. Only in Europe and North America, twin world centres of professional accountancy theory, has the system been the subject of attempts at thorough overhaul based on fundamental principles. Even there, the system which predominates in large businesses and is virtually universal in small and medium business is still the old system, known as *historical cost accounting*.

In most LDCs too, historical cost accounting is almost universal, although the branches of multi-national corporations will *also* work out their accounts in some more modern guise as required for incorporation into the consolidated accounts of the parent corporation overseas. In South and Central America a modified version of historical cost accounting tends to be used. Our discussion of the impact of inflation is therefore in terms of how to predict the financial statements on the assumption that they are based on historical cost accounting, while admitting that it is not an ideal system for dealing with inflation.

The characteristics of historical cost accounting are as follows:

- The value of an asset is booked at the price actually paid for it as a historical fact which can be verified by examining invoices, not at the value to which it may be judged to have risen by inflation up to the date of a financial statement.
- This is more reliable for stewardship purposes since it avoids judgemental decisions and is less open to fraud and manipulation, but is less reliable for decision-making purposes since values shown in financial statements tend to be out of date.

In conditions of severe inflation, key parts of the ex-post financial statements soon become so out of date as to be almost meaningless. In particular fixed assets and long-term foreign currency debts present a problem in this regard and these are the areas in which the system tends to be modified, as for instance in South and Central America. When fixed assets are appreciating, the calculation of depreciation in the income statements becomes highly questionable. In particular, the understatement of these assets can make an enterprise vulnerable to takeover. To counter this, companies sometimes wish to *revalue* their fixed assets, especially when they get wind of a takeover attempt. This was seen in the UK in the 1950s. It is desirable, however, that such revaluations should be regular and consistent so that they may not be used to manipulate the accounts. Provision for regular revaluation of fixed assets is the main feature of the modified systems of South and Central America. Thorough study of up-to-date values requires professional expertise and is expensive if conducted every year. Accordingly, general price indexes are often permitted to be used or even insisted upon. The analyst working in such conditions will have to structure the spreadsheets in accordance with local regulations.

For liabilities, the situation is rather different. If the liability is denominated in local currency its value will actually fall in real terms; no notice is taken of this in historical cost accounting. But if the debt is in foreign currency it may rise or fall in terms of local currency depending on exchange rate movements. Even the historical cost system has to recognise the importance of historic dollars. This occurs in two forms: whenever an instalment of debt service is paid, an additional cost will be borne, which is a *realised* exchange loss. This must be shown in pro-forma financial statements in which exchange rates are taken into consideration. The remainder of the debt is also up-valued at the then current exchange rate in anticipation of a probable further loss; this *unrealised* exchange loss should be inserted into pro-forma income statements and balance sheets but not cash flow statements of any kind. Only realised losses involve cash flows. Of course, unrealised losses become realised losses later, unless the trend of devaluations is reversed.

HOLDING GAINS

Under inflationary conditions, the profits which are derived from the underlying technical coefficients are supplemented by holding gains. For example, I trade in second-hand books and sell at twice the price at which I buy. On sales of £200 I make £100 gross profit. But now suppose inflation comes in at 10 per cent a year. I buy a book for £10, keep it for a year so it is worth £11 in the wholesale trade, and sell it at £22. I have made a gross profit of £12 in nominal pounds, a devalued currency.

In historical cost accounting, I show a gross profit of £12 in the second year (none in the first). The matching principle requires me to deduct the cost of the book, which was borne in the first year, from the revenue from the sale of the book, which occurred in the second year, and to show the difference as a second-year profit.

Under a different accounting system, *current cost accounting*, I should revalue the book at the end of the first year even though I have not yet sold it, and show a holding gain of £1, which I calculate from the 10 per cent movement in the general price index (or from a special book price index, if one exists, or from a specific valuation of the individual book). During the second year I show a trading profit of £11. The total is still £12 but the timing is different. This system is superior for decision-making, since it correctly separates gains from trading from gains derived by holding trade stock, and preserves the concept of a 100 per cent mark-up on trading which is very useful as a commercial rule of thumb in the second-hand book trade.

The use of current cost accounting has an impact on the income statements since it introduces holding gains and makes shifts of timing in the profits. It also has an impact on the balance sheets since it revalues the stocks (and other assets too) held at the end of each year. But it has no impact on cash flow statements. I still pay £10 in the first year for my book and receive £22 for it in the second year. Simplified project analyses which rely entirely on cash flow statements and do not make forecasts of income statements or balance sheets need not, therefore, bewail the failure of LDCs to introduce current cost accounting.

However, for the analyst who is seeking to make forecasts of income statements under inflationary conditions, some consideration must be given to these holding gains. Whichever system is used, they must appear some-where. Otherwise, relying as we do in LDCs upon the historical cost accounting system, what we are actually doing in our ex-ante analysis is to introduce those very errors which proponents of current cost accounting seek to take out.

In principle it would be possible to approach the problem of introducing holding gains into ex-ante financial statements theoretically, by referring to the literature on current cost accounting, listing all the adjustments which its proponents recommend, and *reversing them* so as to produce a set of historical cost statements with all their objectionable defects. In practice this is not possible, since there are many different versions of current cost accounting, and much confusion therefore surrounds that subject. ICA (1987: 424) lists eight different versions. The standard version which was officially endorsed in the UK for several years was withdrawn in 1987; the UK has the unique problem of reconciling West European harmonisation with US practice. So current cost accounting is very problematical and this is one more reason for staying with historical cost accounting in LDC project work. Nevertheless the issues raised in that literature are genuine, and any system of project appraisal based on historical cost accounting must have a satisfactory answer to them all.

HOW TO LIVE WITHOUT CURRENT COST ACCOUNTING

The main issues raised by the presence of inflation, and developed in the literature by the proponents of current cost accounting, can be accommodated within historical cost accounting for the purposes of LDC project appraisal as follows:

1 A holding gain (a non-operating profit) arises from the possession of assets other than money ('non-monetary assets') over a period of time when money is losing its value and the prices of assets are rising. Non-monetary assets for our purposes consist mainly of fixed assets and stocks (inventories).

   (a) No gain is realised unless and until the asset in question is sold off. In the case of fixed assets, some will be assigned (ex-ante) a residual value of zero and others will have a positive residual value. The latter include items which are disposed of, as a matter of policy, before they reach the end of their depreciable life, and items which come to the end of the project time horizon while still having some depreciable life left. What we must do is to inflate the non-zero residual value having regard to its date. If the sum is significant, it may be worth while decomposing it into its local and foreign elements in order to apply the various different inflation rates and exchange rates. This adjustment to non-zero residual values will be sufficient to introduce inflation correctly into the cash flow statements. So far as income statements and balance sheets are concerned, we ignore unrealised gains. In the current cost accounting system it would be necessary to revalue the fixed assets every year and to insert unrealised holding gains into statements of adjusted net income but not, of course, into *operating* profits.

(b) Stocks are assets which are purchased with an intention to sell them, so it can be assumed that holding gains will be realised in under a year. That means that we have to introduce these gains into the income statements even when using historical cost accounting. It is necessary to prepare what is sometimes called a *stock budget*. This is a small piece of a spreadsheet in which the arrival of fresh stocks, the consumption of stocks (by production or, in the case of finished goods stocks, by sales), and the quantity of stock remaining at the end of each year to be carried forward to the next year are all reconciled together. Where the nature of the stocks permit, this should be expressed in volume (physical unit) terms as well as in value, but that is not essential. The effect of this is to separate the sum spent on purchasing stocks in a given year from the cost of stocks used up in cost of sales in that year. Purchases are inflated, held in stock at their historic cost, and enter cost of sales at their historic cost; but sales are inflated separately, in effect at a later date and thus using a

Table 12.4 Holding gain from stock

1995 result	Without inflation		With 10% inflation
Stock at end of 1994	nil		nil
Goods bought in 1995	4000		4400
Stock used in 1995	2000	(half the stock is used)	2200
1995 closing stock	2000	(half carried forward)	2200
1995 Production			
Stock used	2000		2200
Other costs (say)	10000		11000
Total cost of sales	12000		13200
Gross profit	8000	(shows a 10% escalation)	8800
Sales revenue (say)	20000		22000
1996 stock budget			
Stock at end of 1995	2000		2200
Goods bought in 1996	4000	(same again but dearer)	4840
Stock used in 1996	2000	(using old stock first)	2200
1995 closing stock	4000	(half carried forward)	4840
1996 Production			
Stock used	2000		2200
Other costs (say)	10000		12100
Total cost of sales	12000		14300
Gross profit	8000	(includes holding gain)	9900
Sales revenue (say)	20000		24200

Note: The gross profit in 1995 is increased by 10% from 8,000 to 8,800 if 10% inflation is introduced. In 1996, it increases by a further 10% from 8,800 to 9,680 and then by a further 220 to reach 9,900. That 220 is the holding gain of 10% on the stock carried over from 1995 (2,200).

higher index. Table 12.4 gives a simple example. The result is to increase the gross profit. The holding gain, when realised, becomes part of the operating profit, having been deferred by the matching principle to the later year when the sale takes place. Under current cost accounting, it would not be so deferred, but would be recognised each year although not yet realised, and would be reported as a holding gain not to be confused with operating profit.

2 Current cost accounting is very concerned to ensure that the inflation of operating profit by the inclusion of realised holding gains does not lead to the distribution of excessive dividends. An excessive dividend is one that either (a) leaves the enterprise with insufficient cash to carry on, or (b) leaves the enterprise with insufficient equity to sustain itself fully. The possible shortage of cash is not a problem, since we can verify from either balance sheets or ACF statements that the required cash is present in each year of the project despite the need to meet the demands of inflated capital goods replacements and other inputs. The possible shortage of equity is more interesting. The concept here is one of sustainability. An enterprise is regarded as sustaining itself either operationally or financially. It sustains itself financially if the equity (net worth) does not fall in real terms; that is to say, if we take the shareholders' funds at two successive dates, examine the movement between the two figures as it would have been in the absence of dividends or new capital subscriptions, and adjust this 'earned' movement for the change in the general index of prices, we shall then know whether or not the operation of the business has left shareholders' funds intact. It sustains itself operationally if the equity continues to be enough to pay (with the assistance of debt) for replacement of all the non-monetary assets at their respective current prices. The difference between the financial and the operational concept is in part one of using a general price index versus specific price calculations, but in ex-ante crystal-gazing work this is not a useful distinction. More importantly it is the difference between regarding a business as being a temporary user of shareholders' funds which must be returned intact (the financial concept) and regarding a business as one which has a mission, with outputs and production, and which to be successful must maintain its ability to discharge that mission against the pressures of rising costs (the operational concept). These are two alternative concepts in the literature of current cost accounting. In historical cost accounting, how can we accommodate these two quite valid concerns? We do it first by means of the ACF statement and associated beneficiary analysis. Section 2 of the ACF statement in its with-inflation guise shows the IRR of the resource flows, and if that is satisfactory we judge that the project can carry on its mission and in that sense is *operationally sustainable* through to the end of its life. That is not the same

as saying that it is sustainable for ever; we might not wish to invest in the same product a second time, so that will be a separate decision, but at least the project will have made a net contribution to the economy of which it is a part, so the longer-term sustainability of that economy and its ability to achieve its higher-level mission will not have been damaged by this project. Second, we look at the cash flow streams in Section 3 of the ACF statement, with inflation, and check that the financial IRRs are satisfactory (exceed the cost of capital with inflation) for each of the financial participants, including the equity investors. If the returns are satisfactory we judge that the project is *financeable* in the sense that it does not leave the equity investors (or other parties) worse off. Finally, we look at the pro-forma balance sheets and examine the ratios which lending bankers would look at if called upon to invest more loans in that enterprise (to finance some other projects) in each separate year, and ensure that the balance sheets continue to meet these commercial criteria so that the enterprise will at all times be able to call on lenders to supplement the equity needed to keep the enterprise *financially sustainable* as new project opportunities appear on the horizon.

This analysis may seem wide-ranging, but it does allow us, without inconsistency, to adopt a simple 'quick and dirty' method, as we may want to do for numerous small projects, when time presses. We can construct the pro-forma income statements by inflating all the revenues and costs, and then add an adjustment for the holding gain arising from stock. This will be based on the value of stock brought forward from the previous year, assuming it to be consumed in the current year. It applies to all classes of stock alike. If the inflation index is 10 per cent per year, we simply multiply this by the value of stock brought forward (see Table 12.4 note above).

The value of stock may be seen in the pro-forma balance sheet if such exists; if not, in a schedule of working capital, itself inflated. Such an adjustment may be called stock valuation adjustment. In fact it is an adjustment to the cost of sales, but it had better not be called a cost of sales adjustment, since that term is used in current cost accounting for the correction which takes it out again and puts it elsewhere to show that it is a holding gain and not an operating profit.

The adjustment can be made on stock (inventories) alone. Other non-monetary assets and liabilities do not require it. Fixed assets are already taken care of in the gain on inflated disposals. Monetary assets such as debtors, creditors and cash do not generate holding gains or losses in terms of historic cost accounting.

ADDITIONAL POINTS OF ARITHMETIC

A few further points remain. First, a quick and dirty method has been suggested: why is it dirty and what would be a cleaner method?

It is dirty because it contains a minor inaccuracy. It takes a holding gain on the stock as it stands at the end of each year. In fact, of course, the gain accrues steadily through the year. If stock is turned over (used up and replaced) four times a year, there is a holding gain each time, reflecting a rise in the cost of stock which is *approximately* one-quarter of the annual inflation rate. These four holding gains during the year are *approximately* the same as one large gain calculated at the end of the year. In ex-post accounting this method might seem too inexact, but in ex-ante crystal-gazing it is good enough.

This near-equivalence means that the rate at which stock turns over does not actually matter in the determination of holding gains. Nor does it matter that the rate of stock turnover is an average of different classes of stock some of which move faster than others.

Second, the beneficiary analysis, which shows the distribution of the discounted present value arising out of the project among the equity investors and other financial participants, may produce a significantly different result when inflation and exchange rate movements are taken into account. Care should be used in interpreting this. A common error is to take the rate of interest on loans as fixed, according to the rate published by banks, and to use this same rate in the spreadsheets whether constant prices or inflated (current) prices are being used. The effect of this is often to produce, in the with-inflation case, a negative NPV for the bank, and a correspondingly juicy NPV for the remaining participants. But this is clearly wrong.

Third, the rate of discount used to calculate NPVs in the beneficiary analysis must obviously be higher with inflation than it would be at constant prices. LDC Governments often publish test discount rates, typically 10 or 15 per cent, which are intended to be used with constant prices. Higher rates should be used with inflation. If a test discount rate is 10 per cent under constant prices, and the general rate of inflation is 20 per cent, the adjusted test discount rate should be $(1.10 \times 1.20) -1$ which is 32 per cent. If the rate of inflation is going to differ from year to year, no single rate can be used to adjust the test discount rate, but the cash flow can be deflated by the inflation index and then discounted to see if it meets the 10 per cent criterion.

Beware of using the first five years of a project as representative of the whole. If an average inflation rate for the whole life of the project seems useful for the analysis, it should be constructed by calculating the *geometric mean* of the year-on-year increases in the general index. To calculate the geometric mean, you first calculate the *logarithms* (to any base) of the annual increases, then you calculate the arithmetic mean of those in the usual way, and find the antilogarithm of the answer.

The fourth point is validation. Every spreadsheet should have validation checks built into it, to detect possible errors in arithmetic (or if using a computer, in logic). A spreadsheet in constant prices may seem valid, but when you introduce inflation unsuspected errors appear and red lights flash all over your screen if you have built in the validation checks correctly. In other words, additional checks are needed to ensure you have dealt with holding gains and foreign exchange losses correctly.

CONSTANT PRICES AND CONSTANT TERMS

A distinction is sometimes made between an analysis in *constant prices* and an analysis in *constant terms*. The former takes all prices as fixed, apart from the price drift in one or two variables which is the manifestation of relative price movements. The latter uses current prices, but after arriving at a stream of net cash flows seeks to discount the latter, using a forecast of the general index of inflation (index of retail prices or GDP deflator). The result is a constant terms cash flow which can be discounted using a discount rate which does not contain any uplift for inflation. The constant prices NPV will not be exactly equal to the constant terms NPV because prices which are inflated under several influences including domestic and foreign price movements cannot be reduced to their original values by a single deflator. We must also remember that price movements can produce sudden changes in the timing of tax payments.

A third alternative is to take a cash flow at current prices and discount it at a rate of discount which is uplifted to allow for inflation. This will give a different result again, because an increase in the discount rate of X per cent every year is not the same as a series of specific forecasts, in which the movement may not be the same every year.

The deflator, whether based on a forecast of the retail price index, wholesale price index, GDP deflator or whatever, is normally intended to show the real value of the cash flow stream to the investor at whose request the study is being conducted. Consequently, local and overseas investors will use different deflators, and in such a case, 'constant terms' has more than one meaning.

THEORY AND PRACTICE

The recommendations above may be regarded as a counsel of perfection. The search for accurate forecasting requires frank and honest consideration of the likely course of inflation and of the movement of exchange rates and some arithmetical consistency between the two. What actually happens in practice in LDCs is quite different.

In some instances, e.g. Sudan, appraisals are made in constant prices, and the finance required is therefore understated; projects run short of finance, their implementation is interrupted while supplementary funds are authorised, and project planning generally is a shambles.

In some other cases, e.g. Nigeria, the Central Bank issues a forecast of the rate of inflation to be used. This is naturally on the low side so that it is itself an instrument in the struggle against inflation, but it goes some way to bridge the gap between predicted and actual expenditure requirements. Each project is looked at again, usually every six months, and fresh decisions are taken on up-dated information. The degree of accuracy in project plans under this system clearly depends on the severity of the inflation problem in each country. Whether in Nigeria this leads to a degree of accuracy such that one can regard project planning as effective is debatable, since some analysts would regard a 5 per cent overspend as a disaster while others are comfortable with 10 per cent.

In yet other cases, e.g. Tanzania, the Government issues a figure for the rate of inflation *prevailing at the present time* and this is assumed to be the trend for the period of project implementation ahead. In this matter there seems little difference in effect between Tanzania and Nigeria. Some projects have special features which if treated with this broad-brush 'trend' approach do lead to gross financial shortfalls.

In the private sector, analysts are of course at liberty to use any rate they please, except that when submitting their cash flow forecasts to a Government-owned bank for financial assistance they are often obliged to use the Government's inflation forecast. Bangladesh is an example. Fortunately in recent years their inflation rate has been mild and predictable, and the use of the official forecast has been in most cases not too imprudent, provided that some contingency reserves have been built in here and there.

REVAMPING THE BALANCE SHEETS

Inflation brings problems, not only with ex-ante financial statements, but with ex-post accounting too. All non-monetary assets and liabilities suffer from inflation in value as money depreciates. Balance sheets, which reflect the cumulative position reached by a business since its inception, are therefore affected more than other financial statements. In a few countries, such as Brazil, a crude form of current cost convention is used, and their law requires businesses to revalue the fixed assets in their balance sheets regularly; in other countries this requirement applies only to the larger businesses. However, determination of the current value is not a simple exercise; fixed assets are often highly specific, and not regularly traded in a market, certainly not readily marketable in the vicinity of the enterprise in question. Subjectivity in valuation is likely to be a considerable problem here. It is also necessary to revalue other non-monetary assets such as stocks, and the gains arising from these procedures must appear in income statements and in balance sheets according to fairly complex rules which have been discussed above. Even in the USA and the UK, the accounting profession has been reluctant to adopt this tough convention.

In most LDCs, unlike Brazil but including eastern Europe, the historic cost convention is used. This is presumably due mainly to the fact that the current cost convention is too complicated. The consequence of retaining the historic cost convention is that the fixed asset values as shown in the books of account diverge more and more from their current replacement costs, as inflation proceeds more or less rapidly, and so after a few years that part of the Balance Sheet no longer communicates any realistic indication of the resources tied up in the business. The merit of the Brazilian solution seems obvious, but some writers want a more radical solution. Vahcic and Petrin (1990: 67–73) in their work on the restructuring of the Slovene economy state:

> In the Yugoslav production sector there are at present over 20,000 production units employing over 5,500,000 people, and having assets whose replacement value is about $50 million ... For most of the enterprises the balance sheet data, on both liability and asset sides, have practically no economic meaning ... In any serious reform of the financial system, therefore, the existing balance sheets could in fact be scrapped.

Their concept is that all enterprises be handed over to a central state-controlled trust, which would sell them piecemeal to private owners at a price equal to the current (revalued) asset value. Each enterprise would then start again with a new balance sheet; its capital (or liability to the central trust if the enterprise were transferred without immediate payment) would be equal to its assets.

However, I do not share this radical view. Apart from the apparent over-optimism on the subject of orderly transfer, the proposal contains no indication of how the problem might be prevented from occurring all over again; rapid inflation of the local currency and the difficulties of current cost accounting will probably persist. At best it might be argued that, given a general revaluation of assets in (say) 1992, and a reduction in the severity of inflation thanks to stringent economic policies, the new balance sheets will be able to communicate quite realistic indications of the assets utilised, and liabilities, through most of the decade.

In practice, enterprises are rehabilitated, and their balance sheets restructured, one at a time, not in one fell swoop. It is true that, when the legal entity changes, the new entity absorbs the assets of the old but starts with a new balance sheet in which the asset values are current estimates of worth not necessarily taken over from the old book values; but when an existing entity is rehabilitated, the balance sheet is not scrapped. Instead, the major non-monetary items in the balance sheet should be carefully revalued, and the new values placed into the old accounting structure without destroying the integrity of the latter – as happens in Brazil. To scrap all balance sheets merely adds to the chaos. As if there was not enough already.

Chapter 13

Risk and sensitivity

What is the difference between an optimist and a pessimist? An optimist says 'Cheer up, it's not likely to happen.' The pessimist says 'Maybe not, but if it does, it will hurt.'

This is not in fact the difference between an optimist and a pessimist, but the difference between a statement of *risk* – the chance that something will happen – and a statement of sensitivity, the degree of impact it will have, if it does happen, on a given project. Actually a pessimist is just as likely to point out the range of risks which surround a given investment proposal, and an optimist might point out how little they matter even if they do happen, since many might go either way and could cancel each other out.

Taking a project to be an ex-ante *model* in the form of a number of equations in a spreadsheet based on a number of *variables* having estimated values together with relationships between variables which are used to calculate the outcome, the term *risk* refers to the fact that some of the estimates are uncertain, i.e. not known with precision and confidence. Certain particular variables may be based on especially flimsy estimates or guesstimates, or may be known to depend on the essentially unpredictable outcome of some dispute or conflict which is still in progress at the time of the study; other variables may be based on estimates which are thought to be reliable but actually contain hidden sources of uncertainty. The term *sensitivity* refers to the impact, large or small, of any given project variable upon any given measure of project worth: financial IRR, economic IRR, return to equity, tax revenue, average annual return on capital employed or whatever is being looked at as the outcome. The project analyst is concerned with discovering and communicating to decision-makers not only the amounts and timing of the expected profits (or cash flows) but also their *reliability.* No investment is quite free from risk but the aim is to determine what factors or events would cause the yield to depart from its expected value, and how responsive it is to minor or major knocks from those factors or events. In short, how sensitive is the yield to various unknowns, how unknown are those unknowns, and between what ranges of possible disastrous or excellent values may they lie?

THE FUZZINESS OF THE CRYSTAL BALL

The financial analyst's calculations usually produce several indicators of the attractiveness of the project: NPV, IRR, etc. Every one of these is subject to uncertainty; for clarity of explanation we shall look first at the uncertainty surrounding NPV, but the same remarks hold true equally for the other indicators.

If the NPV of a project is said to be one million pounds, this is its *most probable value*. It can be thought of as a probability distribution, with a mean of one million pounds and a standard deviation which is not calculated. The NPV itself is calculated from cash flows which themselves are calculated from project variables, which are technical and economic estimates each of which is itself uncertain and is merely the mean of a probability distribution. The most probable value of the NPV is therefore the outcome of a spreadsheet which uses the most probable values of the project variables. It is important to regard the latter as *central estimates* of probability distributions rather than as single numbers which are fixed and reliable.

The single 'most probable value' of NPV is not really enough information for taking the decision as to whether or not the project ought to be allowed to go ahead. It is necessary also to identify, quantify and communicate the risks and sensitivities which might cause a major departure of the NPV from its central estimate value, at any rate with projects which are large in relation to the investors' available funds.

SOURCES OF UNCERTAINTY

When a proposal is being prepared, both cost and revenue estimates may be misjudged for a variety of reasons: commercial (price trends incorrectly foreseen), economic (inflationary pressure underestimated), socioeconomic (producer response to incentive pricing misjudged), technical (process losses not anticipated), managerial (unforeseen shift in ratio of labourers to supervisors), policy (tax changes not foreseen), geographic, climatic, military, and so forth. These misjudgements may be over-optimistic or over-pessimistic. They are *errors*, which is not a pejorative term.

These errors may of course combine and interact, as when process losses rise unexpectedly (technical) because of poor maintenance (managerial skills) associated with lack of trained manpower (economic) and wrong recruitment of what little skilled manpower there is (policy). Thus each element of cost and each element of revenue is the outcome of a large bunch of assumptions which are usually too many and too complex to put in writing in full.

USE OF CONTINGENCY RESERVES TO REDUCE COST RISKS

When single-value estimates are obtained from estimating engineers (or other technical personnel) they often contain an allowance 'to be on the safe side'. The cost estimate for plant and equipment, or other fixed assets, is often made to contain such an allowance, called a *reserve for unforeseen contin- gencies*, or contingency reserve for short (or simply *contingency*). Such a sum for unknown extra capital costs may amount to as much as 10 per cent or even 20 per cent of the known costs. It is rarer for operating cost estimates to include explicit contingency reserves though elements of cost may contain hidden uplifts.

The thinking behind contingency reserves is to recognise the fact that in making a single estimate of costs on a complex project it is very easy to overlook some item of cost. It is not so very easy to overlook a revenue. The mistake of omission is more frequent than the mistake of double counting in project costs. In a recent review of capital costs in seventy-five agricultural projects, 49 per cent had overspends of 10 per cent or worse, while only 19 per cent had underspends of 10 per cent or better (FAO 1990). Thus the single estimate is *biased* unless a contingency reserve is included and many estimating engineers would consider an estimate dangerously incomplete if it did not include a contingency reserve, either explicit or hidden in the costings.

The cost which may be omitted by mistake may not necessarily be a specific item of material; it may be an increase in the quantity of a known item, e.g. additional days of crane hire, caused by an unforeseen complication arising during implementation, often associated with an increase in the duration of construction time. Such complications are very common; the opposite (saving time or materials through some unexpected windfall) is rare, because the project is designed to be efficient (perhaps using network analysis) and any change must therefore be for the worse. Hence the bias in the estimate.

In LDCs it is common to include two types of contingency reserve: a *material contingency* for unforeseen requirements as described above, and a *price contingency* in case the items which are correctly foreseen turn out to cost more than was expected. This is mostly because of poor commercial intelligence about delivered-to-site prices especially in terms of local currency. The provision of good commercial intelligence on-tap is a very costly form of infrastructure, which neither central nor local government authorities in LDCs can afford, let alone individual enterprises.

When the analyst uses the information prepared in this way, he or she should look closely at the built-in contingency reserves both explicit and hidden. If only a central value for NPV is wanted, the aim must be to make sure that the contingency reserves are adequate and reasonable. However, if a full probability distribution or a sensitivity study is to be presented to the decision-makers, it may be necessary to take the contingency reserves out of the estimates, since they will be double-counted otherwise. That is to say, the analyst's choice of the shape of the probability distribution itself deals with the twin problems of bias (omissions) and of being on the safe side ('conservatism'). It is especially necessary to take out the contingency reserves if they have been put in under the influence of a judgement of what the economics of the project would bear, i.e. allowing our judgement of revenues to affect our judgement of costs, which is an incorrect procedure.

INSURABLE RISKS

Uncertainties are reduced by arranging insurance for certain risks. When we speak of project risks we are thinking of risks which are not insurable by their nature, or are insurable but are not going to be insured against.

Insurable risks are relatively unimportant. That is to say, they cover events such as fire and vehicle damage which indeed do occur quite often but in LDCs these are much less damaging than uninsurable risks such as misjudgement of the market (low sales volume), running out of foreign exchange for regular inputs (failure of the national economy) and so on. Nevertheless, the analyst should check that the income statements do contain a realistic provision for insurance premiums. No project which does not carry normal insurance is a safe project, even though with state-owned projects insurance is commonly omitted.

IDENTIFYING THE CHIEF SOURCES OF UNCERTAINTY

It is desirable to make a *complete* list of the variables which will affect project performance. This may not be clear and obvious; for instance, annual labour costs of $100,000 (the central estimate of one variable) may hide assumptions about shift working, efficiency, skill mix, male/female employment policy, labour turnover, incentive payment policy, housing provision, medical care, and so forth. All of these are actually separate variables. For instance, in the construction of the Panama Canal, in many ways the grand-daddy of all post-Renaissance projects, labour cost came in within budget in the final phase while under the control of the US army, but was totally out of control in the earlier phase under de Lesseps and the French engineers, largely because of a change in the provision of *medical care*: the role of mosquitoes in spreading yellow fever had just been discovered (Martinez 1978: 115–16).

Having identified all the project variables which are subject to uncertainty in the most comprehensive manner possible, a calculation is made to determine which are the most sensitive variables. To do this, you can vary each variable in turn up or down by 10 per cent (or some other arbitrary percentage) of its central value and see the percentage impact on NPV which this change makes in each case. It will then be possible to *rank* the variables, which means, to write them in an ordered list with the most sensitive at the top. This is called a *sensitivity study* and it reveals which are the most crucial assumptions. We often find that there is a group of four or five rather sensitive variables at the top of the list, and then a clear gap before other less sensitive variables appear, followed by a tail of many variables which are not significant at all in terms of sensitivity.

Note that such a study looks at the sensitivity of each variable in turn, while all the others are kept at their central values. It therefore cannot measure the total riskiness of the project, but it is a good start.

COVARIANCE

If all the variables are independent from one another, we may expect that some will turn out better than predicted, others worse, without systematic bias. Unfortunately, however, some variables are associated with others. Louis Pouliquen in his World Bank study on risk analysis (Pouliquen 1970) gives an example from a harbour construction project in Somalia which was particularly sensitive to two project variables: (a) the efficiency of dock labour, and (b) the capacity utilisation of the dock. However, when capacity utilisation rises and a port becomes congested, labour efficiency falls. Thus the two variables are associated. They do not move totally together, but nor are they quite independent. The two extremes (treating them as totally correlated or as totally independent) give widely differing NPVs for the entire project. This is a serious mathematical difficulty which can only be resolved by combining the two variables into one broader variable ('port efficiency'). Of course, the fewer and broader the variables, the less penetrating the analysis, and the harder it will be in due course to contrast the out-turn with the prediction and explain the differences.

SOME CATASTROPHIC COVARIANCES

One situation which is sadly common is that a foreign exchange crisis hits the project in several ways: imported spare parts are difficult to obtain so maintenance is postponed and output falls; power supplies become intermittent due to lack of imported fuel; project administration becomes less cost- effective due to poor communications; transport in and out becomes slow and costly; and so forth. Thus a foreign exchange crisis will hit almost every element of cost adversely. In these circumstances, the variables move together, for the worse.

Similar but often worse still is the impact of war or destruction of personnel and equipment by armed forces. This will normally be accompanied by a foreign exchange crisis also. Of course, these are especially ruinous to those projects which in other circumstances would be very beneficial, i.e. ambitious projects having extensive linkages with other projects and disseminating new skills.

Project appraisals do not usually consider these disastrous covariances. This is because in countries where the operating environment is as threatening as this, the project planning will tend to be rough and ready. Either the project will be dismissed at a much earlier stage of appraisal on the ground of unacceptable 'country risk' or it will be required to have a very quick payback period, which is another way of dismissing it. Or, predatory forces may compel the analysts to turn a blind eye to the risks and go ahead regardless. In any event, there is no attempt to deal with these problems on a mathematical basis.

THE MATHEMATICAL APPROACH TO PROBABILITY ANALYSIS

In a companion volume to Pouliquen's study, Shlomo Reutlinger (1970) looks at the underlying mathematical basis of uncertainty in a variable such as NPV which is itself the aggregate or outcome of many separate uncertainties. If the NPV can be expressed mathematically as a function of separate elements (cash flows) in a project, and if each element can be expressed as the mean of a probability distribution with a definite shape (itself a function) and a known standard deviation, then the shape of the probability distribution of the NPV with its mean and standard deviation could be computed. Then instead of a single central value for the NPV, we could see for instance that the expected value (mean) of NPV was $1,000,000, and also that the probability that NPV would be at least $500,000 was 79 per cent. This is much more meaningful for decision-taking, assuming of course that those responsible fully understand probability distributions, NPV, and so on.

As Reutlinger demonstrates, the mathematics required to aggregate the separate probabilities into one overall NPV probability function are not too difficult *if the costs and benefits are the same every year*, and if investment takes place at one time only. Sadly, they are too difficult in any more realistic case. Therefore, this particular mathematical technique is never or rarely used. However, it is important for the analyst to appreciate the theoretical framework, and in particular, that measures of project worth such as NPV are of this nature.

THE MONTE CARLO TECHNIQUE

Besides the problem of defining the variables so that they are independent of each other, and the necessity to get the relationships between variables right in the spreadsheets so that the NPV and the other measures of project worth correctly reflect the values of the variables, there is also the need to ascertain the probability distributions of all those project variables which are subject to uncertainty. This is needed not only for the impractical mathematical probability technique discussed by Reutlinger but also for the alternative, more practical Monte Carlo technique described below.

Chapter VII of Pouliquen's book describes some of the probability distributions which can be chosen for each of the sensitive variables. Each has a distinctive shape when plotted on a graph. These are step-rectangular, uniform, beta, discrete, trapezoidal, normal, and triangular. Which shape to choose requires discussion with the same professional experts who provided the single (mean or modal) value in each case. The choice is inevitably subjective and unreliable, but better than a central value only, which amounts to a normal distribution with zero standard deviation, or indeed is equivalent to any of the other shapes but with zero standard deviation. It is the zero standard deviation, which refuses to contemplate any risk of deviating from the central figure, which is objectionable.

Suppose a project's NPV depends on five sensitive variables, that is, five variables whose values are uncertain and which are known to have an appreciable impact on NPV, alongside all the other variables of which this is true to a lesser extent. Suppose that each of these five sensitive variables has been looked at by the estimators and mathematically defined as a probability distribution with a particular shape, then the Monte Carlo technique provides a practical way to arrive at the shape of the aggregate probability distribution of the NPV.

The Monte Carlo technique takes its name from the famous gambling casino at Monte Carlo and is sometimes called the stochastic simulation technique. If one were to try a small gamble many times over on a roulette wheel, one could eventually find out the probabilities of various numbers coming up on the wheel. In other words, the characteristics of the whole wheel are disclosed. Similarly by calculating hundreds of possible NPVs using different values for the five variables one can observe the outcomes and so find out the characteristics of the whole structure. At least a hundred and preferably several hundred 'trials' are required. The different values used in these trials have to be randomly representative of the five shapes. This produces several hundred NPVs, one from each trial. These are themselves plotted on a graph, representing a frequency distribution with a mean, a mode, and a range. The distribution of results around the mean will be found to be statistically normal, approximately.

It is important to understand that the mean NPV found by this Monte Carlo method will not be identical to the NPV found from a single trial with the central (mean) values of the same five variables. There may be a big difference between the two results. This is because the Monte Carlo technique brings out the way that the variables work together. Two variables each with only a slight chance of falling within given ranges may when they do so have a major effect upon NPV by their joint reinforcing effect. This will influence the Monte Carlo mean but will not show at all in the single-value mean. This is a strong argument in favour of trying to use the Monte Carlo technique.

A computer is needed for sensitivity analysis because of the extra calculations which arise when the single values are altered. Generally speaking, any computer capable of running spreadsheet software will suffice. If there are twenty project variables, the spreadsheet will have to be changed and recalculated twenty times to determine the sensitivity ranking. However, the Monte Carlo analysis requires a spreadsheet to be changed and recalculated hundreds of times; typically three hundred, according to

Pouliquen. Each time, the values for the sensitive variables have to be chosen in a way which reflects the shapes of their probability distributions. Unfortunately ordinary spreadsheet software cannot easily handle these two additional requirements. Indeed, a special computer program may have to be written for each project. Fortunately, however, a program once written (in a human-readable computer language such as BASIC or FORTRAN) can be modified quite quickly to suit a second project, so this is a good investment of time. Major bureaux like the World Bank project departments have developed 'chunks' of program code which analysts can put together to suit their particular projects, and so build up a complete model of a project ready for Monte Carlo analysis.

Some considerable computer programming skill is needed for Monte Carlo analysis. The programmer should be very careful since an error in the output will not be readily noticed among all the other changing values.

The computer memory requirements are large, and mainframe or mini-computers are generally used for Monte Carlo analysis rather than micro-computers. This puts LDC analysts at a disadvantage. However, add-on software to enhance the facilities of standard spreadsheet packages are becoming available for the more powerful micro-computers.

When using Monte Carlo analysis, the output from the computer is a graph. The vertical axis measures probability up to 100 per cent. The horizontal axis shows NPV (or IRR or whatever indicator of project worth is on test). If one point on the graph shows an NPV of $40,000 with probability of 30 per cent (on the horizontal and vertical axes respectively) this means that there is a 30 per cent chance of NPV being below $40,000 and a 70 per cent chance that it will be above $40,000. Many users will be especially interested to look at the point below which cash flows would be so bad that debt service as well as dividends would be damaged; in the USA this is known as leverage-related risk. However, no one point is especially emphasised by Monte Carlo analysis, except the mean value of the NPV trials, which is marked as such. The entire curve is shown. The risk that NPV will fall short of whatever value is regarded as a hurdle can be read off from the graph. Looking at the up-side risks, the probability that the NPV will exceed its single-value or mean figure can also be read off.

This is intended to communicate the whole risk situation. It combines (a) the uncertainties inherent in the most critical project variables with (b) the sensitivity of NPV to alterations in the values of those variables. It is therefore a complete statement of risk.

As an exercise in communication the presentation of such a graph does depend on the mathematical understanding of the reader. What it gains in content it loses in intelligibility. Decision-makers should be trained in handling risks.

INVESTOR REACTION TO RISK

If the project risk is communicated in this way to decision-makers who are responsible for providing funds (whether loan or equity) it will affect their yes/no decision on the project. Obviously if two projects are competing for the same funds, and both offer the same NPV and IRR but one has greater risk than the other, the first will be chosen (if financial criteria alone are used). The interesting trade-off arises, however, when one project offers higher mean values on the indicators of project worth, but another project offers lower risk.

Some decision-makers will reject all projects where risks are high, no matter what trade-off is available to compensate. This applies particularly to LDC government projects in low-technology sectors where past projects have been routinely successful. I consider this attitude to be irrational except in terms of *individual* survival strategies. Some decision-makers will accept high-risk projects only if the trade-off from extra high mean NPV or IRR is very great. This is known as risk aversion and is not irrational though there should be some reason for it. Some others are less concerned with risk and will accept investments in a reasonable spread of business situations in exchange for single-value IRRs varying by only 4 or 5 per cent or even less, according to some US data (Gale and Swire 1988) though this behaviour is not substantiated for private sector LDC managers. The investors' aversion to risk thus varies considerably.

Many analysts attempt to deal with risk by raising the hurdle rate of IRR, inserting a *risk premium* element in the cost of capital, but this must be highly subjective both because of the variability and irrationality in the risk aversion and because of weaknesses in the data concerning the probabilistic estimates of uncertainties surrounding the key variables. Let us turn to a consideration of what might be a sound theoretical structure to illuminate what should be the rational response of an LDC investor (or an approvals committee) to a proposition which is known to contain risk. This will be of limited interest to the project analyst whose work is done when the risk has been faithfully reported, but will be of major interest to the analyst who is concerned with the profitable investment of funds rather than with any one project.

PROJECT RISK AND COUNTRY RISK

A sophisticated investor such as an international bank will have a strategic policy towards each country as well as towards the project-specific risks connected with each project in that country. Thus, any application for funds has to pass a double test. The country risk is associated mainly with the prospects that the country will run short of foreign exchange, or will suffer insurrection and change of government with the usual damage to assets, or that assets may be nationalised or otherwise confiscated under some new policy of the present or a new government. Less common considerations in country risk are war, climatic change, and epidemics. Clearly if any of these risks materialise, virtually all projects in the country concerned will be hit and financial yields will be affected.

In the same way, a sophisticated investor who chooses to be limited to projects within a single country still faces country risk, but in this case it will not be perceived as country risk, rather as the general and common level of risk which attaches to all business projects and which derives from the ambient conditions, which are perceived as primarily economic and political, and perhaps social. This is over and above the specific risks which are characteristics of each project and which can be investigated by a Monte Carlo analysis of uncertain project variables. In that case, should general economic variables such as the rate of inflation be included among the project variables for economic analysis? The investor who is prepared to accept the general level of country risk, and who stipulates a minimum IRR accordingly, might ask for a Monte Carlo analysis based only on those other variables which are specific to this particular project. These are of two kinds: genuinely project-specific variables such as the cost of equipment or the level of material wastage in operations, and variables such as wage costs which, while general in the sense that they affect the whole country and are part of the ambient conditions, may affect this particular project more than most, because let us suppose it is a very labour-intensive project, or less than most, because it uses little labour.

Variables therefore fall into two classes: those uncertainties which beset this particular project but not others, and country risk variables, which may hit this particular project harder or less hard than all other projects, or more precisely, represent a greater or a lesser degree of risk than the investor perceives as covered by the general risk premium and are therefore acceptable. Note that the latter depends on the subjective assessment of the investor. All economic and other country risks will affect a project to some degree and it is not possible to say in respect of each variable whether or not that degree of risk is covered by any given hurdle rate of return. The only rational procedure therefore appears to be to include both types of risks in the Monte Carlo analysis, even though they may affect other projects, and to consider whether the mean value of IRR that emerges from that analysis does or does not compensate for the aggregate risk by being sufficiently high above a hurdle rate for completely risk-free investment.

In LDCs the typical investor in the great majority of investments, by number if not by value, is a head of family engaged in peasant farming. The typical investment decision will be relatively small in value, to do with a calf, a building, a ditch or an implement. Each involves difficult imponderables and therefore risk. The consequence of a bad investment is reduction in family income, where income is already low and living is precarious. Even one cow, if it dies, may cost a year's personal income to a person who only had two cows.

The result may be one which entirely alters the style and quality of life, or in extreme cases endangers life itself. Faced with such severe consequences on the down-side, and no gigantic opportunities on the up-side, risk aversion is strong. It is not surprising that peasant societies have the reputation of being conservative rather than progressive. An LDC government if it sought to represent the will of the people as regards risk-taking and if it had to put as many eggs in one basket as a poor family does would also have to behave very conservatively.

It is interesting to note that because of the imponderables mentioned, project-specific risk is likely to be much more of a consideration than country risk in these numerous cases. It is also interesting to note that in many cases the out-turn of the risk will be known in a year or two, so that risk aversion here is not a function of time and cannot readily be associated with a higher discount rate.

A THEORETICAL MODEL FROM THE USA

A much more impersonal kind of investment is available to that minority of investors who can buy, and if necessary sell, a stake in an enterprise operating on a larger than family scale. Turning to the opposite extreme, in the USA most investment decisions (by value and perhaps by number) are by quoted corporations. Private individuals can buy equity shares, and also loan stocks (loans evidenced by certificates which can be traded second-hand like shares) through a ubiquitous financial market. This is known as a capital market although only a small fraction of its work is to contribute new capital and most of the transactions are in second-hand securities. The decision to invest is thus split into two: the decision at the business level, taken by managers who may not be owners, and the decision by the investor purchasing securities on the capital market, who may have little or no detailed knowledge of the projects which are in the minds of the managers in the corporate enterprises concerned. Neither the manager nor the capital market investor is subject to quite the same kind of down-side risk as the LDC peasant farmer, but if the sum risked is sufficiently large in proportion to the annual income of the corporation or the investor, the consequences can certainly be damaging to life-style. The corporation lives under a special threat which is that cash flow may be damaged so severely as to bite not only into dividends (which are recognised to carry some risk) but into debt service as well. Should this happen, managers are liable to be laid off.

Just as most companies are financed by a mixture of equity and debt so they have a cushion against bad risks in the equity, so investors in the capital market, if they are corporate investors but many individuals too, will be financed by a mixture of equity and debt and they too live under the threat of inability to meet debt service maturities if a bad risk damages their planned cash flow by more than enough to reduce the return on equity to zero.

Insolvency, receivership, and personal bankruptcy loom in the background, though they are not life-threatening.

When investors are linked together by a capital market in the manner described, the market prices of risky securities reflect the consensus of risk-aversion in the market as a whole. It is then rational for each investor to adopt a degree of risk aversion which reflects (a) their own debt-equity gearing, and (b) the spread of market prices which of course reflects the market's consensus view on risk. For investors who are themselves financed by a normal gearing, it pays to invest in a spread of securities which is typical of the whole market. In short, the mechanism of supply and demand which governs the prices of securities evens out the differences among investors so that the market's consensus on risk aversion tends to be the adopted behaviour of each individual investor. This is a standardising effect. It does not provide a rationale for risk aversive behaviour in the whole market, but it does provide a rationale for the behaviour of individual portfolio-holders, a micro-rationale as it were.

This model of investor behaviour, thus summarily described and oversimplified, is the capital asset pricing model (CAPM). Together with related propositions on the distorting effects of taxation, CAPM in the USA has come to acquire the status of orthodoxy. It is eloquently summarised in Brealey and Myers (1984), Franks, Broyles and Carleton (1985), Kitchen (1986), Reimann (1990) and elsewhere. Some commentators comment on the outcome of attempts to prove or disprove CAPM by statistical observations on the US capital market; Reimann expresses concern that practising managers feel uncomfortable with it.

Contrary to what has been argued above, a basic assumption of CAPM is that risks can be classified into business-specific and ambient-condition risks, the latter referred to as *market risk*. A second assumption is that investors spread their risks by investing in a diversified portfolio, very different from the poor peasant with two cows. Investors therefore assume the burden of those risks which affect the market as a whole (market risk), but risks of the first category, which are specific to the particular businesses and their underlying particular projects, are assumed to be ignored by the investor. This is because the specific risks have already been taken into consideration by the market mechanism of supply and demand in determining the reduced price at which those securities can be bought by the investor. Any errors in this process can be taken care of by the spread of the portfolio.

In CAPM the risk borne by the investor is therefore market risk only. For any particular security, the risk is increased or diminished to the extent that the security is likely to be affected in the same way as is the market as a whole. This is measured by studying the past behaviour of a security in terms of its earnings (dividends and capital gains, after tax) and comparing the movement of these earnings with those of the entire capital market. This is done by regression analysis, producing a regression line by the usual statistical methods, with the formula $y = \alpha + \beta x$, where β (pronounced *beta*) is the slope of the regression line and measures the association, strong or weak, between that security and the entire market. Any separation between the particular and the general, giving a beta of less than one, is assumed due to the risks of the first category, business-specific risks, and is reflected in the market price of the security.

According to CAPM, only an investor in the *new issues* market needs to be concerned with looking at specific project risks in any detail. This is, of course, not at all the situation of a government or financial institution in an LDC, where the financial analysis of projects is almost exclusively concerned with new money rather than with second-hand securities.

The investor seeking to determine a minimum acceptable rate of return should therefore begin with the existing yield on shares, which can be found in statistics published by the stock exchanges, and which includes a risk premium which is enough to cover the usual market risk, add or subtract an adjustment for the beta of any particular offering, and make various adjustments for gearing and tax effects. In this way the cost of capital for enterprises wishing to offer more securities (of the same riskiness as before) is determined. It is above the level which would apply to risk-free investments. In this way the market defines pragmatically how much extra return is needed to compensate for market risk.

Although some writers such as Kitchen (1986) have explored this model's usefulness for LDC applications, it clearly has several weaknesses, some of which have been pointed out by Kitchen and by Reimann. These weaknesses can be summarised as follows:

- LDCs mostly do not have developed capital markets.
- LDC investors mostly do not have portfolios.
- LDC investors mostly have entrepreneurial links to projects.
- LDC securities mostly do not have long past histories (needed for calculation of β by regression).
- LDC development is concerned with *first-hand* risks.
- Every new project has a new riskiness, not the established beta of its business enterprise.
- Individual investor behaviour is explained, but that of the market as a whole is not.
- Monte Carlo mathematics do not logically support the concept of two distinct categories of risk.
- Compensation for risk by way of a higher minimum rate of return places undue emphasis on later years of project life.

There are therefore objections both on theoretical grounds (the last four items) and on the ground that conditions pertaining in the USA are so different from those in LDCs that certain necessary assumptions cannot realistically be satisfied to apply CAPM in LDCs (the first five items). Taken together, these objections must be strong enough to resist the incursions of CAPM into LDC training programmes.

HOW SHOULD RISK BE COMPENSATED?

The last of the nine objections is a weakness that CAPM shares with some alternative models and it is difficult to find an altogether satisfactory solution to the problem. The problem may be posed like this: suppose the hurdle rate of discount on risk free investments is 5 per cent, and that is the minimum acceptable to investors given their risk aversion, whether they are rich or poor, families or corporations, and whatever may be the sociological background to their motives. We have a project which displays some elements of uncertainty; we have done the necessary sensitivity studies and a Monte Carlo analysis, and we find that the mean value of the IRR on several hundred Monte Carlo trials is 8 per cent with standard deviation of 2 per cent. The enterprise which is to serve as a vehicle for the project is a well-established enterprise, the biggest in the country. So we know everything there is to know about the risk and about the attitude to risk. Should it go ahead on the figures given? If not, is there any mean IRR which would just suffice? Does it actually make sense to regard a higher mean as compensating for a standard deviation?

The results of Monte Carlo trials are distributed about the mean with a roughly normal distribution. This means that if we multiply the standard deviation by three on either side of the mean we can be 99.5 per cent confident that we have a range within which the IRR will fall. The range is thus from 2 per cent to 14 per cent. If we insist on 99.5 per cent confidence of achieving a minimum of 5, we require a mean of 11 per cent. The range of possible outcomes then would be from 5 to 17 per cent. Taking an even tougher line, to be 99.9 per cent confident we would require a range from 5 up to 18.2 per cent with a mean of 11.6 per cent. In principle, we need to know the risk-aversion. This may be seen as a mathematical function which somehow relates the increase in the mean (the risk premium) to the standard deviation. For instance, a standard deviation of 1 (per cent IRR) might be acceptable in exchange for an increase in mean of 0.5 percentage points. That would be a linear function. Or, a standard deviation of one or two might compensate for an increase in mean of one or three respectively. That would be non-linear. Or, a standard deviation might be regarded tolerantly down to the point where IRR becomes zero, at which point a very heavy compensation might be accepted. That would be a discontinuous function.

We must remember, however, that IRR is not the only indicator of project worth. Applying Monte Carlo analysis to NPV will also give us a mean and a standard deviation. It may be that a disastrous down-side NPV would be regarded more severely than a large down-side IRR, while a fantastic IRR would be regarded as more attractive than a large up-side NPV. It may be that within a lower and middle range of outcomes the most accurate compensation for extra risk would be an addition to the mean of the NPV, while in up-side areas the trade-off should be extra IRR. Thus any rational translation of rational risk aversion into a mathematical function is likely to be complicated, with more than one explanatory variable, and one or more discontinuities. Clearly there will be severe problems of empirical validation.

We also need to look at the other side of the coin and ask, what will be the effect on project approvals if investors insist on raising hurdle rates of (a) IRR and (b) NPV to compensate for risk?

If the minimum IRR payout is raised, this means that the project must pass the test of an equivalently increased discount rate, a test which bears with especial severity on projects which have a long deferred payoff. This includes projects with lengthy construction periods, therefore all really large projects; lengthy operating periods, including all irrigation and forestry (especially hardwood) projects; and most R & D projects. This means that a 10 per cent uncertainty (with equal probabilities up-side and down-side) might knock out a twenty-year hardwood project but leave a ten-year softwood project on the approved list.

Is this really rational? Well, if the uncertainty comes in on the selling price of timber, it may well be, since the uncertainty does increase when we predict further ahead, so indeed the hardwood revenues are more uncertain than the softwood revenues. But suppose the uncertainty is on the initial cost of the land? That arises in Year 0 in both cases. But if it puts up the discount rate and thereby hits the PV of remote hardwood revenues, that is not rational. So we need to distinguish between risks which increase with time and those that do not. This is a weakness in CAPM because it assumes that all risks increase with time (Franks, Broyles and Carleton 1985: 272).

Risks increase with time, generally speaking, if near-term forecasting is more accurate than long-range forecasting and if project management cannot be relied upon to make regular fresh forecasts and to adapt the project to changing conditions. In other words, if the project is a cannon-ball and not a guided missile. Alternatively, if the ability of the management to make these in-flight corrections is itself a feature which can be depended upon less and less in the more distant future, this runs counter to the proposition that management will improve its performance as it gains experience.

Those risks which are not a function of time ought not to generate a risk premium in the form of a higher discount rate, but rather should be treated as a notional penalty in Year 0. This is a reduction of Year 0 revenue, or an increase of Year 0 cost, which adjusts the single-value estimate to a certainty-equivalent on some sort of probabilistic basis. This adjustment will hit the NPV equally at all discount rates. It will also hit the IRR but in a way which does not discriminate against long-term projects.

We have been speaking of IRR and NPV as though these were unique, whereas we really need to distinguish between that cash flow which measures real resource inputs and outputs, and the financial cash flows of shareholders and the various other financial beneficiaries. Each of these has its own NPV and IRR (except for Government which will have NPV only if the flows are unidirectional). But having arrived at the concept of a notional penalty in Year 0, we are free to put it where it belongs. If for example it is an adjustment for uncertainty in the cost of fixed assets, it must first go into the resource flow statement (Sections 1 and 2 of the ACF) as though it were an additional fixed asset. In fact it is indistinguishable from the old-fashioned contingency reserve which is normally included in the cost estimate for fixed assets, though this does not help us to determine how big it should be. Then it must find its way into the financial flows statement (Section 3 of the ACF, which must balance with the other sections), appearing in rows and columns wherever the spreadsheet equations dictate. If this additional cost does occur, who will finance it and what will be the repercussions? There will certainly be interest and tax consequences. It may well affect the cash flows of all the financial beneficiaries, over several years. Therefore, there is no reason to suppose that the impact on project NPV or IRR will be the same as the impact on investor NPV or IRR. The translation between the two will only work if we regard all financial beneficiaries as one entity. That happens in CAPM where the investor represents a typical mixture of debt and equity and where government is perceived not as an important beneficiary in its own right but merely as a tax collector necessitating some arithmetical adjustments to the behaviour of the rational investor.

There remains the difficult question of how much compensation to give for a given risk, whether by way of higher hurdle rate or by way of notional adjustment in Year 0. We cannot use the investor risk aversion as a means of determining the amount by way of compensating the investor, if we lose the direct translation between project adjustment and investor adjustment as we must if we forsake CAPM; in any event CAPM does not prescribe market behaviour, but only micro behaviour. The only alternative is to derive the adjustments from past project experience.

Here we have a choice between two techniques. If, for instance, we have a large number of irrigation projects which have undergone ex-post evaluation, and if we find that on average working capital (a notoriously difficult item to forecast) was under-estimated by 20 per cent, then (assuming the present project contains working capital which was estimated by those same defective techniques) we can add 20 per cent. In fact, that is a crude technique, with nothing very probabilistic about it. We are correcting for a known bias in our estimates. But a second technique is to correct for both bias and uncertainty. Past estimates were not all equally 20 per cent out; there was a range, and a standard error. Adding 20 per cent to the new forecast corrects the bias, but it could still be above or below out-turn, because of the standard error. We can deal with this by applying confidence limits. That means adding a further upward adjustment which will be a multiple of the standard error depending on how sure we want to be of coming in within budget on this item.

This might be described as the engineering approach, as opposed to the investor approach. It is the basis of a methodology called project evaluation and review technique (PERT) which is popular in large manufacturing projects, though not found often in LDCs because of the lack of past history data.

There are hazardous processes in manufacturing industry, especially in chemical plant, where managers require a very high degree of confidence in the chemical and physical outcome of processes and therefore over-design the equipment for the sake of safety. This leads to prudent over-estimation of the funds required for the equipment. Accordingly, the engineering approach is favoured in this type of project. Stipulation of confidence limits on the basis of *investor* risk aversion could lead to accidents.

A very good account of the engineering approach, not using PERT but a simplified system which can be applied in LDCs, is given by Rudd and Watson (1968: 332). The massive world-wide expansion of the US chemical industry in the 1960s and 1970s, much of it in imitation of existing plants, produced much empirical evidence of standard errors of estimation and of their impact on project profitability. Much of the early work was due to Bauman (1964) but it has been updated through the 1980s. Bauman found, for example, that plant and equipment cost showed forecast errors ranging from −10 to +25 per cent, whereas start-up (commissioning) costs ranged from −10 to +100 per cent. These are indications of risk in that kind of project at that time, and show an under-estimating bias which was characteristic of that expansionary phase and has at least to some extent been corrected since.

Rudd and Watson take these uncertainties, assuming that they would continue complete with their built-in bias, apply Bayesian decision-making criteria to these problems and show how, under suitable assumptions, the compensating risk premium can be calculated, as an addition to the cost of capital over and above the risk-free rate of return. But they go further; forecasting errors in sales, operating costs and other variables are also translated into IRR (minimum discount rate) adjustments by some simplifying assumptions such as a ten-year project life. Finally (1968: 359) they distinguish between new projects (highest risk category), expansion projects (moderate risk, involving new customers but old techniques) and cost-saving projects (lowest risk, involving no new customers and only marginal adaptation of techniques).

This engineering approach gives some frighteningly high values for the risk premiums, especially with new projects. It would appear that when the IRR or cost of capital on a cost-saving project is 13.5 per cent the corresponding rate for an expansion project with its enhanced risks should be 20 per cent, and for a new project a staggering 46.8 per cent. This may well be satisfactory in a financially mature industry, but in LDCs at the early stages of indigenous economic development virtually all 'development projects' are new projects in the Bauman sense. This is particularly true when diversification out of traditional livelihoods is national policy. It suggests that, in the chemical industry at any rate, very few LDC projects would go ahead if the true risk premium were known.

The empirical project-based approach seems a useful one even if the uncertainties can be challenged as being valid only for one particular kind of project in one country at one period of evolution. To develop similar data for a broad range of LDC projects might perhaps be possible within large institutions such as the World Bank if the engineering approach were accepted there, and if it were acceptable to ignore those many projects which are too small in size to come within the purview of those institutions.

However, there are still problems with the theory. Empirical ex-post investigations lump together two different factors: the bias of consistent over-optimism and the irreducible uncertainty of unbiased estimates. The former should be self-correcting, given good estimating procedures which look back over earlier projects; where costs have been previously under-estimated, the source of error can be identified and eliminated, or failing that, a contingency reserve can be introduced to recognise an unidentified source of extra cost. But when this has been done, and up-side risks made equal to down-side risks, there remains an uncertainty, which has ill effects and requires to be accounted for. The ill effects fall on the project beneficiaries and it must be their aversion to uncertainty, not that of project engineers or project designers, which ought to determine the amount of compensation which is equivalent to any given uncertainty.

ANALYTICAL UNCERTAINTY AVERSION

Here we come to my own recommendations. We have noted that there are different financial beneficiaries, although the CAPM tends to treat them as one. They may have different aversions to uncertainty. A bank, itself highly borrowed, may have a strong aversion to cash flow uncertainty during the period of its lending. Government, mindful of its future expenditure plans but not committed to them beyond a year ahead, may have only a moderate aversion to uncertainty on the Government cash flow values, but may have a strong aversion to uncertainty in total project resources, and for bureaucratic reasons a Permanent Secretary might require 99 per cent confidence that total resource IRR will not be negative. Equity investors may have very little aversion to IRR uncertainty and even less to NPV uncertainty, remembering that the central prediction may equally well be high or low, but it is perfectly possible that an individual investor facing specific cash flow scheduling difficulties might have a strong aversion to uncertainty over a particular time period and a weaker aversion at other dates. In financial negotiations, these concerns should emerge separately. Using the analytical cash flow (ACF) statement, which distinguishes the cash flows of the parties concerned as well as the total project (resource) cash flow, we can cope with all of these, in principle. The appropriate procedure would thus appear to be as follows:

- Eliminate estimating bias, using contingency provisions if necessary.
- Prepare ACF statement with NPVs and IRR for each party.
- Enquire of each party what are the indicators whose uncertainty concerns them.
- Run Monte Carlo studies for each party concentrating on those indicators which concern them.
- Inform the parties of the results of the Monte Carlo analysis.
- Let the parties decide whether the project is attractive or not.

This means that the financial participants define their areas of concern, the project analyst measures the degree of uncertainty in each area, and the financial participants assess for themselves whether the play is worth the candle. The expression of uncertainty aversion in terms of linear functions, non-linear functions, functions with multiple terms, and plain irrational cussedness, is left entirely to the party concerned for self-interpretation. This avoids the necessity for a theoretical framework in which risks inherent in the project design and aversion to risk inherent in the standpoint of the investor must be understood together, quantified and reconciled. And it avoids the requirement that the parties concerned should agree on a common consensus of risk aversion, which is clearly unrealistic.

For many medium and large projects in LDCs, whether governments are involved or not, implementation of the above recommended procedure should not be too ambitious a goal. For smaller projects which cannot justify the expense of computerised financial analysis, it will not be practicable.

A CLUTCH OF SIMPLER TECHNIQUES

One simple calculation which can readily be made with revenue-earning projects is the return on sales (ROS), defined as profit after interest but before tax, divided by sales revenue and expressed as a percentage. The calculation is normally made on the average of the operating period years: it is difficult to think of a typical or normal year in this context because interest expense which changes from year to year is involved.

The ROS shows by how much the selling price might fall before profits turn into losses. Selling prices are often driven down by pressure of competition, and ex-ante forecasts may under-estimate the determination of competitors in reacting against the proposed new investment which threatens their market share. Note that sales *volumes* can fall further than sales prices before a break-even point is reached, since a fall in volume leads to some saving in costs too, but a fall in prices has no saving graces for the seller. ROS therefore indicates how robust the plan is in terms of competitive commercial considerations, which can be very 'iffy'; it is a measure of sensitivity rather than of risk.

A second technique looks at sales volume and its effect on profit over the average of the operating lifetime. Here we have to bring in the cost savings associated with a fall in volume. This means assuming that costs fall into two categories, those ('variable costs') which vary with volume, and those ('fixed costs') which do not, though they may vary with other things and are therefore not constant from year to year. This assumption is rarely accurate and some arbitrariness is required; moreover over a long operating period we can regard *all* costs as variable, so to make the technique work we have to class as fixed all those which would be fixed in the short term.

Revenues in any given year vary directly with hypothetical volumes, while costs are partly fixed and partly varying with volume. The selling price per unit of output clearly must be higher than the variable cost per unit, so as to leave a contribution towards fixed costs and profits. A larger volume will make a greater contribution than a small one. There is therefore a level of volume which produces a contribution just enough to cover fixed costs without any extra for profit; this is the *break-even volume*. Any greater volume will generate profits and any less will produce losses. The break-even volume is calculated as fixed cost per year divided by net contribution per unit (selling price minus variable cost). The forecasted volume is compared with the break-even volume; the difference between the two is called the *margin of safety*. If this is large it indicates that the investment is robust in that sales volume might fall considerably before profits turn into losses.

This break-even technique is another long-established technique to test the commercial robustness of a competitive revenue-earning investment and, like ROS, the danger-point is defined in terms of profit or loss to owners in an average year. Among the costs treated as fixed are depreciation and interest, though not repayment of loans (which are not costs). As with ROS, interest varies from year to year and normally disappears completely in the later years, so an average volume over the life should be used.

In some cases, output volume is hard to measure, because the output consists of several different products at once. A railway, for instance, delivers freight as well as first and second class passenger-miles. In such a case we must resort to using revenue as a proxy for volume. The formula then is revenue multiplied by fixed costs divided by (revenue minus variable costs) = break-even revenue. Note that we can only take revenue as a proxy for volume if (a) the mix of different products is assumed to remain the same at different levels of total sales, and (b) the selling price of each product is unaffected by its volume.

There are other related techniques, equally valid but not so often used. One is to calculate the sales volume at which some measure of cash flow, rather than profit, becomes critical, i.e. the surplus cash at any balance sheet date falls to zero. This is called *cash* break-even as opposed to *profit* break-even. This technique requires taking depreciation out of fixed costs and putting in capital repayments instead. Clearly the break-even volume in this cash sense will be much higher in the early years than later; since cash shortage can cause sudden death, the year-by-year figures are important, which is not the case for profit break-even. Over the life of the project as a whole, we might regard the break-even volume as that which reduces the resource cash flow to a net present value of zero at some appropriate test discount rate, or better still, that which reduces the financial flow of any one of the financial parties to an NPV of zero at their particular hurdle rate. Such calculations must also bring in the pre-operating cash flows. Computer spreadsheets obviously help in working out these indicators, since the sales volume can be made to depend arithmetically on some multiple, initially set at one, which can be experimentally reduced in steps until the break-even point is empirically reached.

This entire approach to volume rests on some crucial assumptions. To assume that revenue is a linear function of volume is actually an assumption about price determination. To assume that variable costs are a linear function of volume requires a similar supposition, together with the assumption that larger volumes should not be associated with any technological shift, nor any change in storage facilities, nor any change in management structure. In short you have to take a short-term view, or a series of short-term views over the long term.

Take for instance the managerial salaries of a provincial bus enterprise. You do not hire and fire the bosses because takings go up and down from week to week; these are *fixed* costs. Yet over the fifteen years or so of operating lifetime of such a project, you would indeed enlarge or reduce the management staff if passenger-miles were significantly above or below plan levels. So when we calculate the break-even passenger-miles over the average of the project life, we are saying that the margin of safety in any one year is on average such and such, though for the project as a whole it would be significantly greater.

Break-even analysis is therefore imprecise, and gives only a broad indication of robustness.

A further problem is that these calculations can be made either in constant prices or with inflation. Deriving as they do from the short-term approach, they are invariably presented in constant-price terms in western textbooks of cost accounting. However, for LDCs this can give a grossly over-optimistic result. This is because inflation is associated with exchange rate movements, giving rise to currency losses when servicing foreign debt. If a loan is denominated in a harder currency, interest (and repayment of capital) will be inflated by exchange losses. These do not vary with volume and are therefore fixed costs. The effect on interest is to raise the break-even volume, both in profit and in cash terms; the effect on loan capital repayment is to raise the break-even volume in cash terms only.

Sadly, it follows that break-even analysis cannot be more precise than is permitted by forecasting of changes in foreign exchange rates – where foreign loans are involved. Fortunately most small projects are not affected.

Chapter 14

On the fast track

Fast-tracking in this context means producing financial appraisals very quickly by short-cut methods. It is not possible to undertake financial *planning* by using accelerated methods, but appraisal can sometimes be cut short. A critic once wrote of a piece of classical music which was being performed for the first time that it had taken more time to play than the Viennese audiences were prepared to devote to it, and even he himself could not comment on the closing passages of the piece. That was a classical piece of fast-tracking, quite possible for the appraiser, but never for the creative artist.

Essentially there are two avenues open to us here. One is to deal with complex projects simply, knowing that we may be missing important points but trying to cover as much as we can in the limited time available. The other is to deal with simple projects simply and very quickly, relying on their similarity to a standard project which has already been fully appraised. Use of either technique is really a matter of degree, and indeed both may be said to be applicable to some extent in virtually any project, if the truth be told.

WHY CUT CORNERS?

You may ask what justification there is for taking short cuts in project appraisal when you are dealing with other people's money. The fact is that a time limit will very often be imposed. In commercial projects, there is usually a *window of opportunity* which will close if you leave it so late that competitors get in first. Any product has a market of limited size, and each time a business makes its presence known as a committed supplier to that market the attractiveness of the market to other potential suppliers is reduced. The late bird does not get a worm. A financial analyst who damages the market opportunity of the project under review by delaying it too long will certainly incur criticism: what we want is financial analysis, not financial paralysis.

We must also remember that project data has an expiry date. When you obtain an estimate for capital goods, you must not mull over it so long that its validity expires. Putting together the various facts, designing and redesigning the project, preparing the appraisal report for submission to a decision-making body or bodies, and then allowing time for decision, all these processes must be achieved within the validity period of the major cost and revenue estimates. That sets a very approximate but severe time limit on the work of the financial analyst.

Finally we must remember that any delay in the analysis of a meritorious project means delay in deriving the net benefit. In discounted terms this is an absolute loss. Such a loss may be hidden from exposure to criticism by the twin practices of using a movable Year 0 as the base year for discounting and excluding the cost of project planning and appraisal from the project costs. Nevertheless it is a real loss. It is especially onerous in disaster relief projects such as post-hurricane rehabilitations, and in some such cases the financial analyst may have hours rather than weeks in which to work.

When reduced to literally a few hours, the financial analyst must function on an emergency basis. In such cases the decision to proceed must have been taken already. Who authorised it and to what value? Is the scope of the project properly defined in terms of intention and duration? What is the relationship of the project to what was there before? Are the managers and those who will have powers of expenditure identified and have they a track record of competence in similar work? When will the first expenditures be required, and is everybody briefed and standing by? Can we log everything that happens for sorting out afterwards? These few questions can be asked and the answers noted.

This amounts to emergency financial controllership rather than financial analysis. The latter is concerned with appraisal. This does not mean that the financial analyst has no work to do in cases where the decision to proceed has already been taken. Indeed, many projects, especially internationally aided projects, are the outcome of *programmes* decided upon in principle at the ministerial or ambassador level. The problem this poses for the analyst is raised by Bridger and Winpenny (1983: 15) who say

> It should be re-emphasized that the purpose of an appraisal is not just to help decide whether a project should or should not be implemented; it can also help to improve the design of a good project or suggest ways in which an unacceptable project can be redeemed. That is why it is undesirable to rush project appraisal, or take short cuts, even if the appraiser believes that the project would go ahead anyway.

If there is time, then, even a project which is approved in principle can be subjected to fruitful analysis. In this respect the ex-ante scrutiny of public expenditure is paralleled in private sector practice where capital investments which have been endorsed to the extent of incorporation in a five- or ten-year business plan have to be reviewed again in greater detail when it comes to obtaining specific approval for fixed assets.

PROJECTS WITH MANY COMPONENTS

Granting then that even complex projects may have to be reviewed within a time constraint, what ought to be the approach of the financial analyst to this job?

First, it is necessary to divide the project into its component parts, which are really separate projects being proposed together but capable of separate decision and separate appraisal. A vertically integrated agro-industrial project might include a water component for irrigation, some estate production, smallholder production, a nursery unit, a vehicle maintenance unit, a complete village for workers to live in, a factory producing an intermediate product, further equipment producing two or three finished products in bulk, a packaging unit producing retail quantities, a printing unit and so forth. Similarly an integrated rural development scheme or an urban small-scale industrial estate has many component parts. These are set forth as complementary elements of one single project but may really be several sub-projects being considered together. It sometimes happens that the design of the overall project can be improved by excluding some components which are not genuinely complementary, or by placing them in different ownership, and the examination of this possibility raises useful questions about the prices at which goods and services are passed from one component to another.

A project with many components is not necessarily large in terms of total proposed outlay. For instance, it is characteristic of projects supported by the Sri Lanka Export Development Corporation that they are small but complex. Even the simplest coconut matting enterprise requires its own power supply or power connexion, its own small road, its own water and sewerage, and because of difficulties with the utility corporations it has to construct these itself with all that this implies in terms of interaction with local communities and with related small enterprises.

It is tempting to say that the way to simplify is to select the large core components and ignore the small ones, or to select the core components and ignore the peripheral ones. Either of these procedures carries the danger that the components which are ignored will introduce losses into the total. The magnitude of such losses depends in part on the prices at which resources are transferred between components. It is therefore necessary to look specifically at these.

If the cost allowed for water, for instance, is set 30 per cent above the standard public utility price per thousand litres, that will be a contingency reserve which should provide some reassurance for the analyst who has not got time to look further – provided that the project location is defined and the capital cost estimate for fixed assets also includes some considered amount for the water connexion, storage and subsequent disposal. It will not then be necessary to check exactly what financial arrangements will be made for the water, or whether the water component will itself be profitable; there may be several options, the best of which can be chosen later, knowing that adequate funds will almost certainly be available. The analyst is then free to look into the more serious question of whether the main project is likely to be delayed by the physical unavailability of water at the date at which it will initially be needed.

A similar problem arises with agro-industrial projects which rely on independent smallholders to alter their cropping pattern in order to deliver the new crop to the proposed factory. Often such projects fail because the incentive package offered to smallholders is unattractive. The price may be too low, or other aspects of the package inadequate: payments may be late; transportation arrangements unreliable; quality damage may be inflicted by peak-season queuing; fertiliser and other necessary inputs may be too expensive and related finance may be hard to get; seasonal labour requirements may conflict awkwardly with subsistence crops; and in general the long-term prospects for such a major shift may seem too precarious. In such a case, even a factory gate price with a 30 per cent contingency built in may not provide reassurance; some indication of serious institutional arrangements providing some accountability to the smallholders would also be required.

Such an indication is often absent. Even though the raising of smallholder incomes may be identified as a goal of such projects, the smallholders rarely have a major input into the project design, and even more rarely endorse the project design to the extent of voluntarily becoming shareholders. The analyst faced with a time constraint of months rather than years can neither initiate consultations leading to smallholder endorsement nor investigate small-holder economics, so the attractiveness and acceptability of the smallholder component cannot be proven. This component may be seen as peripheral if the factory occupies centre stage, and it may be seen as small in terms of total investment outlay, but it is essential to the financial (and economic) success of the factory and indeed of the goals of the entire project. All the analyst can do in such a case is to point to the history of past attempts along these lines and identify the basic weakness of the scheme.

A possible way out of the time constraint problem in projects with several components is to work on them simultaneously as though they were separate projects, assigning staff to each. This must be faster than dealing with them one at a time.

SIMPLIFICATION OF COMPLEX PROJECTS

Let us now turn to the case of a project with a single major component which has its own complexities, as for instance several kinds of fixed assets with different lives, some requiring replacement, a construction period of more than one year, more than one product, a progressive build-up of output volume, two or three sources of finance, various kinds of stocks (inventories), and assorted risks and uncertainties including exchange rate risk. Suppose that, for whatever reason and unsatisfactory though it may be, the time allowed for full financial analysis is cut short, how should we react and how can we best deal with such a situation?

In practice you go for the essentials and proceed onwards until stopped, as does a bull at a gate. But if you knew just how much time was available and just how long each piece of analysis would take, would there be any better way of using your time?

Taking an Olympian view of this, I would say that once you have set out the techniques of financial analysis in a sequence for the purpose of exposition, from the most basic concepts of net income and net worth through to the arcane refinements of analytical uncertainty aversion, you should be able to work backwards, peeling off each layer in turn and considering, what is lost by omitting this? how dangerous is such an omission? can the omission be partly compensated for by some cruder technique? – until you reach an irreducible core which you cannot sacrifice without abandoning the main concerns of financial analysis.

CUTTING OUT RISK AND SENSITIVITY ANALYSIS

To omit all risk and sensitivity analysis is to end up with a report that says the IRR will be so much and the debt service cover ratio will be so much, which as an unqualified prediction is inherently unbelievable and may be professionally damaging. On the other hand, to undertake a rigorous sensitivity analysis so that all variables are tested for their sensitivity, followed by a Monte Carlo analysis on the main indicators of concern to the several financing parties takes a good deal of time and care just at the end of the available time when your dead-line is raising your blood-pressure and you feel you ought to be writing your final report. Monte Carlo analysis is particularly onerous if computing facilities are not set up for it and pre-tested in advance.

One obvious cut is to confine the Monte Carlo analysis to the indicators, or to one indicator, of concern to one party, which naturally means the party who is paying for the financial analysis. When working for the World Bank, stick to the economic internal rate of return.

The Monte Carlo analysis works by changing the values of several sensitive variables many times, to observe the effect on the indicator. Those values must be representative of the shape of the probability distribution for each variable. In principle every project variable could be included after making enquiries about its probability distribution, but when time presses, the number of variables could be reduced, say to three, without losing the essential properties of Monte Carlo analysis and still producing a meaningful and useful result. It would of course be necessary to use the three most sensitive variables, and this means making a serious sensitivity study first to determine which they are.

Cutting down further by producing a sensitivity ranking of the variables without meaningfully analysing their sensitivities separately or together would not be a sensible form of reporting. To say that a shoe factory project is more sensitive to the price of shoes than to the cost of leather is to say nothing at all. If time does not permit a Monte Carlo study, it is better to report the sensitivities of a few variables separately. This is quite easily done if a computerised spreadsheet is used; all that is necessary is to build up the spreadsheet foreseeing that this will be needed, so that the values which are to be varied are grouped in a recognisable part of the spreadsheet from which they are taken into the other cells by regular formulae. This means that when you change one figure you change them all and you do not need to examine every cell to see whether the alteration has spread through all the financial statements or not, which is very wasteful of time.

Many LDC projects are assessed out without computers, however. This particularly applies in India and Pakistan where the national policy of appropriate technology restricts the use of capital-intensive techniques such as computerisation of work which in the past was done by clerks. Of course, very large projects are computerised in every country, and very small projects are largely done manually in most countries, so the policy of appropriate technology bears mainly on medium-sized projects. For manually analysed medium-sized projects in India and Pakistan the methods are close to those used in the UK and the USA in the late sixties and early seventies before mainframe computers became available. The procedure is as follows:

- The analyst uses common sense and judgement to select two or three variables which are likely to be the most sensitive.
- In Government work and in large corporate institutions, certain variables are prescribed as necessary to be included. For commercial projects these will be selling price and capital cost.
- The effect of these on NPV and on IRR is calculated; if economic analysis is being offered it will be the effect on shadow-priced NPV and shadow-priced IRR only, without spending time on the financial impact (FNPV and FIRR).
- For variables such as selling price which have an impact on the cash flow of more than one year, some short-cut method is adopted.

The short-cut method referred to is usually based on the fact that a 10 per cent cut in revenue *every year* will produce a 10 per cent cut in the present value of that revenue stream. It does not matter whether you cut and then discount, or discount and then cut, you get the same answer; the arithmetic is commutative. If you already discounted in the base case, you simply cut the present value. The implications for profits tax can be ignored if only EIRR, not FIRR, is reported.

Ex-post evaluation experience shows that projects do have unexpectedly sensitive variables which may be overlooked by this kind of crude routine. I remember a chemical plant in which I underestimated the sensitivity of the start-up date. Marketing commenced ahead of start-up so that the plant would be well loaded, demand being met temporarily by imports. But start-up slipped two months, and the imports became very heavy. This was an unforeseen cost. Worse, the additional transportation imposed heavy work-loads on drivers, and there was a fatality which remains on my conscience after twenty-five years.

When there is no comprehensive sensitivity study, variables such as start-up date (length of construction period) are easily overlooked. But also, the impact of obvious variables such as capital cost on results other than NPV and IRR can be overlooked. Chief among these is the impact of a cost overrun on the financing scheme. It is important to indicate to those who accept responsibility for putting in additional finance (known as *end-finance*) if it should be needed how great this requirement might be and under what circumstances it will arise, so that they have every opportunity to plan ahead to meet the need. It seems more than likely that failure to consider this, and the habit of quoting a central estimate only, for the financing scheme leads to the position that when a cost overrun arises it is often necessary to react by reducing the scope of the fixed assets and so of the project as a whole. In particular when a cost overrun arises because it is found that an item of scope has been overlooked, such as water for workers' housing, then the bureaucratic response is to proceed with that item missing. This may be remarkably harmful to the project in later years, to say nothing of the harm done to the people immediately concerned. Whether the more appropriate response would be to cut out some other item or to raise more money is a decision which is precluded by failure to put the financiers on stand-by, and the single estimate rigidly prevails.

CUTTING OUT INFLATION

Also common in non-computerised systems is the omission of studies in current prices. The use of exclusively constant prices is common even in countries where inflation is significant.

Oddly enough, in countries which have hyper-inflation, i.e. prices rising at more than say 50 per cent per year, the use of current prices tends to fall away, because the numbers become quite astronomical in a fifteen- or twenty-year project. A common alternative is to use a foreign currency which is fairly stable, such as US dollars. Very often such projects are undertaken by multi-nationals who will in any event wish to view the ex-ante results in their own currency. This is particularly true with US multi-nationals because of USA accounting rules which require the translation of overseas subsidiaries' accounts into dollars along certain lines. The expenditure on fixed assets has to be translated at the rates ruling at the dates of expenditure, giving so-called historic dollars. It is clearly quite useful to them to have ex-ante studies made in the same way, so that they can see how the results will appear when duly translated and consolidated into the parent company accounts.

The assumption that local currency financial statements can take care of themselves in these circumstances is not so surprising as it may seem. First, hyper-inflation tends to generate a contempt for 'Monopoly money' and a feeling that local currency financials mean very little. Second, there is a perception that the sustainability of the enterprise in local currency terms is not essentially a financial matter at all, but one of smart management, influence with government, and relations with banks. These are the arcane arts required for pricing changes, renegotiation of contracts, alterations of collateral security valuation, purposeful revaluation of assets, and general maintaining of business confidence. This is all expected to happen under an aura of controlled corruption. The financial analyst may well feel that his or her work can add little to this that will be helpful and so may wish to keep at arm's length from it.

Coming back to the other scenario of inflation which is significant but not severe, there are one or two useful possibilities lying intermediately between a full inflationary study and a fixed-price study. One is to look at inflation at a single rate instead of taking a range of rates into a sensitivity study. Another simplification is to assume the same rate of inflation every year; often a round number such as 8 or 10 per cent is chosen. This indicates the direction of change; inflation sometimes makes a project worse and sometimes stronger, and this itself is useful to know. It also gives an acceptably reliable indication of the inflation during the early years for the purpose of arranging finance in sufficient quantity. This is required because, with the exception of Government appropriations, all financing arrangements are expressed in current terms. The inclusion of a *price contingency* in the fixed assets costing is not sufficient to achieve this requirement. There is also working capital to be considered, and early-year loss financing. The total finance needed, including end-finance, has to be arranged for, including the extra money needed because of expected inflation.

SIMPLIFYING THE SOURCES OF FINANCE

The smallest adjustment to the financing pattern with the biggest saving in analysis time is to do away with short-term financing altogether. If you increase the equity and/or the long-term debt you can provide a safety margin for cash flow blips without assuming any short-term borrowing. The blips in question arise at year-ends when revenue is low, typically in the early years of operation, and at other times of the year for seasonal requirements. Of course, no commercial enterprise would wish to forego the safety-net of having a short-term facility on stand-by, for these situations, but the calculation of interest and other charges in the ex-ante analysis is onerous. It often requires forecasting at intervals of less than a year. It introduces the danger of circularities in the spreadsheet calculations. It requires an extra line in the balance sheets. It raises complicated questions of the hierarchy of rights in the pledging of collateral securities. All this is very time-consuming.

Since the omission of short-term borrowing involves the omission of short-term interest, it would be prudent to replace this by assuming more long-term debt rather than more equity, but that of course disturbs the gearing ratio, and in most LDC projects the ratio of debt to equity is already at its highest acceptable level. The usual arrangement therefore is to bump up both debt and equity to a total which is 5 to 15 per cent higher than the asset figures (maximum net assets utilised) appear to require. This precaution produces an apparent flow of surplus cash right from the beginning of the project, which is unrealistic and possibly generates unrealistic expectations on the part of shareholders. However, the 'equity flow' calculation offsets this against the equity investment, which is higher than is actually intended if in fact short-term borrowing will be taken.

Another simplification which saves much time and does little harm is to assume that all the long-term debt is drawn down in a single tranche. We must remember that interest begins and commitment fees cease on draw-down, so the timing we choose to assume for that notional single tranche is important. It must be conservative, that is to say, it should err on the early side. This does not mean assuming that the closure of the loan facility, which is also the beginning of the repayment period (or grace period), occurs early. In other words, if there are eight drawings over two years and then the debt is frozen and repayments begin six months into the fourth year, we can simplify this into a single notional drawing of the full amount at the end of the first year followed by a repayment schedule which is not affected. To be more accurate than this requires knowledge of the implementation schedule and in particular those milestones in the achievement of fixed asset construction which will trigger the signing of certificates for payments to suppliers. Since the terms of payments to suppliers probably have not been decided yet, unless the financial analyst has the authority to decide them, a simplifying assumption is inevitable.

At an earlier stage in the project preparation, such as the pre-feasibility study, there might be very little indication of what will be the sources of finance. In that case the conservative assumption is that everything is financed by debt, with interest at a high level. This is of course unrealistic in terms of gearing. A method sometimes used in private sector work is to assume that everything is debt-financed but at a rate of interest which reflects a mixture of the cost of borrowing and the cost of equity. This is an estimate of the composite cost of capital, sometimes called *controller's cost of capital*. Since the opportunity cost of equity (based on market rates) is higher than the cost of debt, this is fully conservative. On this basis any net profit which is left after paying the notional interest on this assumed debt is a super-profit; one does not seek to produce a market rate of return to equity as well. Indeed there is no equity in this method. As mentioned, this is unrealistic, but when you do not yet know how a project is to be financed, and reserve the right to change the financing pattern anyway during the life of the project by divestment or takeover, it is better to make an assumption which generates the necessary cash flow in all possible circumstances than to choose a single estimate of the most likely financing pattern and work to that. For public sector projects, if they are fully in the state sector, the split between public equity and public loan will not affect the government cash flow anyway, and it makes sense to copy the private sector technique, work on the basis of 100 per cent public debt finance, and apply a controller's cost of capital.

Of course any such simplification needs footnoting. Colleagues down the line have to take the matter further in due course. It is often useful to adopt an unrealistic assumption when you wish to be prudent without attempting to pre-empt an actual decision, but this can be baffling if it is misunderstood as a genuine forecast.

CHOICE OF TECHNIQUE AND OTHER OPTIMISING CHOICES

Choices within the project include the choice of technique, choice of scale of production (which may be seen as a staging decision), choice of scale of storage and other reliability costs, choice of location, how far to go in the direction of spending on health, safety, pleasant working conditions and environmental protection generally, marketing decisions, and the balance between ruthlessness and equity in holding down labour costs. The exploration of these various options is normally the work of specialists other than the financial analyst. When more than one alternative has been explored, and its costs, benefits and risks assessed, the financial analyst can and should advise on the financial implications of the choice. That means working out which option is best for the various financing parties; it may or may not be the same answer for all of them and for the project as a whole, which is where beneficiary analysis comes in.

However, where only one alternative has been explored, the financial analyst should enquire why this is so and list the omissions. This is more likely to be the situation when time is short and corners must be cut. If some important options have not been investigated, or they have been investigated but the results have been suppressed, it is highly likely that the overall project design is not optimal and that changes will have to be introduced during the implementation period or during a rehabilitation phase after a short unsuccessful operating period. The duty of the financial analyst, knowing this, to blow a warning whistle at least in the form of a simple list of omissions can scarcely be denied.

A difficulty of another kind arises when there is a reasonable but not generous time for financial analysis, and some investigation into design choices is possible, but the full range of all the choices and their permutations and combinations is not possible. The latter never is possible, since it always takes much too long. Something has to be sacrificed. What should it be?

There is no research base from which a convincing general answer could be penned to this very hypothetical question. Research on what happened is hard enough; research on what might have been, the counter-factual, is impossible. One must be very tentative here.

From my own experience I can only say that the choice of location often appears to be irrational, having to do with the personal background of the sponsors. There is no doubt some rationality in choosing to operate in a location where one has business contacts and good information, even though it may be known that another location would be superior in the long run. However, to stick to one's home base in the face of overwhelming evidence that it is a hopeless location seems irrational, and for lenders to support such a project doubly so. Maybe the tributes given to grand business leaders in their own communities are their own reward, or perhaps the adoption of that rôle is naïvely expected to be self-sustaining regardless of the vulgar mechanics of the actual project itself. If such is the case, the financial analyst does not need to spend much time delving into the merits of other locations, and what is needed is a tactful statement such as, that there is no evidence to support the proposition that the local market is large enough for the project.

Choice of scale, apart from grandiose projects using other people's money which may also derive partly from self-aggrandisement, seems to be more rational, albeit sometimes mistaken. An asset may be coveted because one of that type and size is seen to work well in the hands of a neighbour, or overseas, or because it is known to be on the list of items approved by the rural credit bank. These are inadequate but rational criteria. Often the size is the smallest available, owing to lack of finance, even though this leads to some imbalance in the complete configuration of assets and from the national point of view is inefficient. This is particularly true of private investors with brief or small-scale track records, who are not attractive to lenders. Frequently the sponsor is aware of being constrained in this way and cannot benefit by comments from an analyst to the effect that a larger investment would be better, unless those comments contain new suggestions as to from where the finance might come.

The question of reliability is worth raising, however, in terms of perhaps buying good quality equipment at a slightly higher price than the very cheapest, and in terms of installing storage facilities for raw material, intermediate product stock, and finished goods stock. An enterprise which is so starved of finance that it has to deny itself all of these may well be so far from an optimum design in other respects too that it is unlikely to be competitive, or if a public service, unlikely to be reasonably efficient. Unfortunately the impact on revenue of a given investment in reliability is difficult to quantify, and impossible to quantify with certainty, so this is not an area in which much time ought to be spent. Most analysts confine themselves to determining whether or not a considered judgement has been made on what is a good working configuration. Too many will let pass without comment a configuration which is patently deficient both in storage and in parallel-train operation, on the unsophisticated basis that the configuration has been duly quoted for by a specialist manufacturer of plant and equipment. Two or three pro-forma invoices or quotations may be attached running into many pages, and yet these define the cost of a configuration which would be unsatisfactory to operate without supplementary expenditures to make good the deficiencies. In some notorious cases, even when foreign consultants were used, the resulting plant proved to be quite inoperable. One way an analyst can save time while facing up to the dangers of bare-bones specification is to make a very prudent assumption as to the number of days of operation of such facilities, such as 250 rather than 365 days per year. Or this can be taken into the sensitivity study as an important and sensitive factor the value of which has not been closely estimated, and the facts can be described in the discussion of sensitivity, leading to a brief warning in the executive summary of the report.

We sometimes see projects which exhibit insensitivity to ecological and environmental issues to an extent that even financially it seems unlikely that such an impudent design can succeed. I have on my desk a project document, not unusual, describing an estate agriculture scheme in a sparsely populated province, intended to produce the political benefit of demonstrating firm government control in a previously ungoverned area, following a change of government. European taxpayer 'aid' was invested in this scheme and European technical assistance was given on the basis that it would be a pilot scheme providing a model for other estates and smallholders to emulate on the soils of the area which were largely unknown to western agriculturists. There was no environmental impact assessment, and no attention was paid to ecological or societal damage to the native people's habitat. No attention was paid to employment opportunities for male, female and juvenile labour, and indeed no statistics of these were reported even ex-post. There was no beneficiary analysis and the question of who was supposed to be benefitting from all this development somehow fell between the two stools of economic and financial appraisal. The local residents were to be employed seasonally at a wage which, though never specified in either project design or ex-post reporting, turned out to be too low. Though not as low as the casual wages paid on some other projects to 'tribal' labourers, this wage was evidently unattractive. Too few labourers joined the scheme and many of them quit after a time. Foreign immigrant labourers then had to be used to make up the requisite number of workers. At the same time international rates of pay and allowances were provided to a relatively large number of expatriates, with housing and airstrip, in addition to a foreign consultancy fee, and while domestic beneficiaries received little, the project income statement was hopelessly overburdened with these exotic elements. The project made losses and went through a series of cash crises. Everyone except the consultants and the crop marketing agents lost heavily for some years, after which by good luck a positive operating cash flow appeared because of unforeseen technical developments and product price increases.

This was unquestionably a poorly designed project. The fault which led to the non-cooperation of the local people is, however, not classifiable under the headings of scale, location, marketing, and so on. By modern standards the absence of local participation in project design would be recognised as a design failing, though there is no guarantee that participation through existing social institutions would have fully explored the full package of pay and conditions, seasonal shifts, ecological damage, medical impact, and cultural destruction, or that agreement would have been reached on the appropriate incentive wage level. The absence of local participation in project design is not, of course, a mistake in the financial design of the project, but both financial and economic analysts ought to have been aware and ought to have pointed out that this project faced severe financial and economic risks, in relying upon a necessary major input (unskilled or more precisely deskilled labour) on terms which as a package had never been agreed, and where the negotiation of satisfactory terms would inevitably be made difficult by the gigantic range of incomes on the site. But neither consultant felt it came within his remit.

This illustrates that design failures in project areas which at first sight have little to do with finance do have financial implications and the financial analyst is entitled to draw attention to them on grounds of logic and common sense despite perhaps being at variance with received wisdom or ideology in the other professional area concerned. Even when time is short, too short to explore alternative designs, the high risk ought to be pointed out, which may not take ten minutes of word-processing or shorthand dictation once the problem has been appreciated. That is a corner which should never be cut.

SIMPLIFYING SIMPLE PROJECTS

The example above involved an integrated estate project with a long period of implementation and all kinds of difficulties. By contrast, the sinking of a rural tube-well by an Indian Government team takes under a week. Each team has a Land-Rover and moves from farm to farm on a programme in which each well is allowed four days on average to complete. That is a simple project, comparatively speaking. The work is always conducted in areas where hydrological surveys have shown that the underground aquifers are appropriate. From other surveys we know that the climate in these areas is such that rainfall is inadequate for farmers' needs, and the soils are such that additional yields can be produced, given additional water. Specialised banks offer credit for the purchase of these tube-wells and associated costs, on terms which are standardised packages, with repayment over a year or two. The borrowers are individually known to the bankers. What could be simpler?

When you have many identical projects you can regard them in aggregate as a single project, which, however, we call a *programme*. To be more precise, the projects are identical *in major respects* but not in all respects. In the tube-well example, each farmer will have different ideas about the change in cropping pattern which will develop after the tube-well provides water for irrigation. Thus each project will have its specific revenue benefits. Since different crops require different complementary inputs such as sprays, each project will have its specific operating costs. Even the capital cost will differ, because although the tube-well may cost the same every time, the facilities needed to distribute the water from the well to the various fields will depend on the distances and possibly on the gradients, and these will vary from farm to farm.

So when we consider how to simplify and speed up the appraisal of seemingly simple projects, we have to consider the common features and we have to consider the specifics.

The procedure with a programme is to plan and appraise the entire programme first. In the case of a programme like tube-wells, which goes on for years, the shifts in cropping patterns in each region are surveyed, a typical or representative farm studied in depth, and the whole project can be assessed, including such items as the head office costs of the Land-Rover teams, the selling of surplus water from the farms, the efficiency of the banking service, the loan default rate, and so on. If the programme as a whole is viable, then the typical project is viable, provided only that the tube-well is correctly priced so as to link the part to the whole.

That typical project has figures, for asset cost and so on, which are averages for the programme. Besides calculating the averages, the central authorities also need to look at the variability, using a statistical measure such as range or standard deviation. This exercise will no doubt be computerised, and will introduce shadow-pricing to determine the economic internal rate of return (EIRR).

If a region has a number of distinct types of agricultural practice or cropping pattern, typical figures for each type can be computed centrally. For each one there will be financial and economic rates of return corresponding to the average fixed asset cost, and a range of other rates corresponding to higher or lower than average values. This resembles a sensitivity analysis, except that the values are not mutually exclusive possibilities but a range of coexisting situations on different farms. This report can be copied to the bankers.

From the point of view of the lending bank, differences in details from client to client are merely differences which are distributed with a limited range on either side of the average. Since the average is a typical project which is known to be satisfactory, the portfolio of loans as a whole will be satisfactory. The only investigation which needs to be made, and this will determine the time taken by the bank to appraise the loan request from the client, is to see whether the request falls within the terms of the scheme, whether the fixed asset cost falls within the range for asset cost, and perhaps one or two other variables. This can be discussed during a short interview, after the client's past banking history has been checked out for outstanding arrears. Once it is confirmed that the request falls within the scope of the scheme, the expected FIRR and EIRR can be noted. This produces a very rapid appraisal without the use of computers in the bank branches.

Programmatic appraisal such as this concentrates on the points of commonality and ignores the differences by leaving them to the laws of averages. In this respect the behaviour of a rural credit bank, making decisions in the manner outlined above, shows some similarity to that of a wealthy investor in the US capital market, behaving in accordance with the capital assets pricing model by looking for an acceptable return on the overall portfolio while leaving project-specific details to be looked after by the prices at which the various securities can be bought.

However, even though the bankers may confine their attention to portfolio results, the client farmers have to attend to project-specific features. What will be the optimum cropping pattern in each case? What will be the best way of distributing water? What about water storage? Is the water liable to theft? What about working capital for the new crops? Will more fencing be needed? Will more labour be needed? How will the new crops be marketed? Will there be an opportunity for catch crops during the change-over? Would it be better to wait another year before undertaking this investment? These are all problems of project design, to be solved by detailed appraisal of the various options. This kind of problem-solving is of course a permanent characteristic of farming, and takes place constantly; without computers, farmers think about these things through the changing seasons. These decisions are certainly as important as those of external appraisers such as lending bankers but discounting and IRR probably do not figure prominently in these calculations.

SMALL INDUSTRIAL PROJECTS

Small industrial projects do not lend themselves to programmatic treatment as readily as small agricultural projects. A one-man garage for the repair of motor-cycles differs only slightly from a one-man garage for the repair of motor-cars, in terms of the structure of its financial statements and in terms of its marketing concepts and its risks. A two-man enterprise is significantly more complicated, with the introduction of incentives and supervision. Add on a 'mobile mechanic' and a breakdown tow-truck and you have considerations of idle capacity, man-machine balance, and break-even levels of activity with quite high fixed costs. Add the sale of parts from dismantled vehicles, the rebuilding of writeoffs, a petrol pump, a paraffin concession, provision for bad debts, and a spot of illegal transportation, and you have a complex, unique, yet still very small business.

The owner asks for three hundred dollars to finance an air compressor to inflate tyres after repairing punctures. How can you appraise it as though it were typical of a programme? The cynical may say that tube-well farmers are just as distinctive as small garage proprietors and it is only our determination to turn a blind eye to the specifics that allows us to construct the image of a typical tube-well. I would not agree. The inputs and outputs of agriculture are standardised, and despite quality differences, can be quantified and aggregated, and so can be treated statistically. With repair shops, the output is a combination of goods and services. Indeed, it is the failure of the vehicle-owners to standardise the servicing of the vehicles that creates much of the demand for one-off maintenance and repair work. Certainly we can aggregate the output in monetary terms, by saying that the annual income consists of so much for parts and so much for labour or fees. But the commercial relationships between the complementary activities, essential for success of the enterprise and therefore figuring prominently in any well-structured financials, disappear under this aggregative approach. Commercial success depends on project-specific detail, not on conforming closely to the ideal project.

Of course, if the central authorities produced a programme to subsidise the garage counterpart of a tube-well, such as car hoists or air compressors, then conformity to the ideal would become important and it might be worthwhile stripping off some ancillary activities in order to conform and become eligible for that input. But that never happens in industry.

When appraising a request such as that for the air compressor in a small but complex enterprise, the appraisal must be simplified not only to save time but also to save cost. A three-hundred-dollar compressor may be a major expansion of the business which can make or break the entrepreneur, but it cannot stand an appraisal expense exceeding twenty or thirty dollars. That may pay for three hours' work for an accountant without a computer. Have calculator, will travel; client to supply cold Fanta. What can you do in three hours?

I should make it clear that what is involved here is not the 'rapid project appraisal' that Bridger wrote about in 1986 which is a quick judgemental overview of inputs, outputs and conversion of inputs to outputs in the very first phase of project identification, but a specifically financial appraisal at a late and possibly final stage of decision-taking. However skimpy the treatment may be, there will be no more of it later.

It will be necessary first to decide whether it is reasonable to appraise this project, which is for the extension of an existing business, in isolation without considering the business as a whole. If not, most of the three hours will be taken up with the business as a whole, projecting the cash flow (or income) of the existing business. If it can soon be established that the existing business is financially self-sustaining, and that its site is owned or is on a long and secure lease, then the compressor can be appraised incrementally. Now, compressed air is paid for only in connexion with (a) the sale of new tyres, (b) the repair of punctures, and (c) spray-guns for paintwork. As there is no compressor yet, none of these activities yet exist. These represent new market segments, of which only (b) is intended at present. The existing business provides knowledge that an unsatisfied demand exists, and provides a means of communicating with the potential customers. In no way is the new service a substitute for an existing service. No significant extra management effort is needed, though an extra labourer will be employed and trained. Everything is set clear for us to appraise the extension without looking further into the existing business.

Next, two more basics (technology, management) can be immediately disposed of as mere preliminaries, and we get down to the fixed asset configuration and cost. We ask the obvious questions: is the compressor new or second-hand? Is it in dangerous condition likely to explode, and who will be hurt if it does? Where is the compressor going to be placed? Who owns that space? Is the space adequate? Will there be fumes? Is the floor adequate for the weight? Does it have its own motor, or does it use mains electricity? If mains, how many volts, amps, phase? Where will the switchgear be? Is there an existing supply, not too often disrupted? What about the hose connexion to the tyres: will the connexions fit all the tyres? Will the tubing perish in the heat? What about the equipment for removing tyres from wheels, which will also be needed? What maintenance does the equipment need? Does the price include delivery to site and operating guarantee? – remembering that in LDCs laws about quality of goods and product liability do not operate very well. By these questions we check that the full configuration has been included in the quoted cost.

The next big question is revenue. How many punctures per day and at what price each, for car tyres and for bus or truck tyres? The owner will have looked at similar businesses, to know this; in three hours you cannot double-check this data, only the arithmetic.

Costing involves the wage of the labourer, the depreciation, maintenance and interest expense of the equipment, power, and a nominal allowance for space, supervision, insurance if any, allowance for kick-backs and bribes if necessary, and bad debts. We will leave taxation out of consideration for the moment. Once the cost of the equipment and the bank charges are established, the crucial figure will be the depreciable life of the equipment, which should be a prudent estimate, and the wage, which will probably be exactly known. In a typical case the depreciable life, and the project life, might be ten years, with a bank loan for two years, covering 85 per cent of the equipment. Revenue in the first year might be prudently put at half the normal level, allowing time for the operator learning curve and for the existence of the business to become known by word of mouth. So we have all the data.

Next we have to decide whether to draw up a cash flow statement, an income statement, whether to calculate IRR or pay-back period, or in short what indicators we need to support a yes-no decision, in what is left of three hours. Needless to say we shall have to work in constant prices.

The financial internal rate of return, and sensitivity analysis, cannot be computed in the time available and in any case would not support decision-making unless the owner understood those techniques, which is most unlikely. I would therefore opt for some easy and simple proxies. In these particular circumstances I would recommend the following.

First, estimate the profit before tax in an average year. In an average year, revenue will be 95 per cent of normal, since it is half of normal in the first of ten years. Depreciation and other operating expenses will be normal. Interest will be one-tenth of its maximum, since it runs for only two years which is one-fifth of the time, and the average principal sum during those two years will be one half of its maximum. So we quickly find the profit after interest before tax in an average year.

If this is negative, we advise against the project and stop wasting time. Otherwise, we continue. What about tax? Tax on profits in most LDCs is negotiable and therefore problematic. It may be officially a very high rate but in practice substituted by more modest sums by way of bribes. Most small enterprises pay little or no taxes. Some keep double or even triple account books to evade taxes. Clearly consultation with the owner is necessary to arrive at a prudent percentage, without bothering with capital allowance computations. It may be that zero is appropriate.

The next question is whether the net profit after tax in an average year is high enough to be acceptable. It has to be seen in relation to the equity employed, which in an average year is half the fixed assets (because of straight-line depreciation) plus the whole of the working capital (in this case a small stock of tyres), minus the average debt. This gives us the average return on investment (ROI). Twenty or 25 per cent might be considered acceptable, though in this case 15 per cent might be good enough if bearing in mind the potential of unexploited growth points, namely the use of the compressor to support the sale of new tyres (as distinct from new and repaired inner-tubes) and for spray-painting.

Next comes cash flow. As time does not permit a full ten-year scheduling, and there is absolutely no sense in scheduling for an 'average year' as there is with income statements, we need to look at that year or years in which cash flow will be critical. Clearly the first year, with its low revenue and full debt service requirements, will be the most difficult. If the project cannot survive this first year, there is no point in looking at the later years; if it can survive this first year, it can survive all the other years. We shall not discount the cash flows, for the reasons given; cash flow analysis is used here not to find out if the project is attractive but to see if it can survive.

In the first year we have the full capital outlay, defrayed as to 85 per cent by bank lending; we have perhaps three quarterly instalments of debt service. If the equal-instalment form of debt service is used, the amounts of the instalments will need to be calculated, either by using a special calculator with financial functions or by printed sheets of financial tables. Other costs (excluding of course depreciation) arise in full, ignoring the possibility of trade creditors, and revenue comes in at half volume, ignoring the possibility of trade debtors. What is the cash flow balance of the first year? If positive, that is fine, and suggests that the whole project will be remarkably profitable. If negative, which is much more likely, we have to ask whether the owner can find that cash deficiency from other sources, and if so, we can look at the second year to see whether that produces a positive cash flow. The third year obviously will do; we know that from our ROI calculations. The worst case is a negative flow for two years, to be financed by the owner from existing savings or (as to the second year) from the unused surpluses of existing operations. It is necessary to make very clear that these injections of cash will be required, and what the lending bank is likely to do if debt service falls into arrear.

In fact, the cash flow of the following eight years will be the same every year if we ignore taxes and if we ignore the liquidation at the end of the project, so with the aid of discount tables and other financial tables we are not far from estimating the complete financial NPV and IRR. Another fifteen minutes may do the trick. If time allows, and if the proxy investigations have produced a non-borderline result, this may permit the analyst to make a recommendation one way or the other. Not up to World Bank standards, perhaps, but good value for thirty dollars.

Appendix 1

The minimum equity spreadsheet

This shows the figures computed for the purposes described in Chapter 11. It contains the following:

1 A cash planning table, called 'first pass analytical cash flow', into which various figures were placed in order to experiment with different financial strategies by a process which in part was one of trial and error, though a more rigorous algebraic procedure is described in Chapter 11. In this case since equity and medium-term debt were pre-determined, short-term debt and dividends were placed in a special part of the table for decision-making.
2 Pro-forma balance sheets showing the effects of the equity and borrowing assumptions used in cash planning.
3 Pro-forma income statements incorporating the interest and financial charges arising from the financial arrangements; calculating profit taxes as needed for cash flow planning; and calculating retained earnings as needed for the balance sheets.
4 Formal analytical cash flow statements in which all financial flows are included in their normal places in the table regardless of the sequence of decision-making.
5 Financial beneficiary analysis, in which discounting is applied to the various financial components of the ACF to arrive at present values and IRRs.

The order in which they are exhibited on the computer spreadsheet is not necessarily the order in which they are calculated, nor the order in which they are reported here. Spreadsheets are flexible and various layouts are possible.

Table A1.1 First pass analytical cash flow

							Million Lire in constant terms					
Year:	0	1	2	3	4	5	6	7	8	9	10	11
Sales detail												
Sales volume (thousand tons)	0	300	600	1000	1000	1000	1000	1000	1000	1000	1000	
Sales price Lire per ton	0	10000	10000	10000	10000	10000	10000	10000	10000	10000	10000	
Revenue												
Sales (million Lire)	0	3000	6000	10000	10000	10000	10000	10000	10000	10000	10000	
Variable costs												
5000 Lire per ton	0	1500	3000	5000	5000	5000	5000	5000	5000	5000	5000	
Fixed costs	0	2000	2000	2000	2000	2000	2000	2000	2000	2000	2000	
Operating profit	0	-500	1000	3000	3000	3000	3000	3000	3000	3000	3000	0
Additional working capital (changes)												
Stocks	-36	0	0	0	0	0	0	0	0	0	0	36
Debtors	0	-600	-600	-800	0	0	0	0	0	0	0	2000
Less: trade creditors	0	350	150	200	0	0	0	0	0	0	0	-700
Operating cash flow	-36	-750	550	2400	3000	3000	3000	3000	3000	3000	3000	
Additional fixed assets	-2200	0	0	0	0	0	0	0	0	0	0	2200
Disposal of fixed assets		0	0									
Total resource flows	-2236	-750	550	2400	3000	3000	3000	3000	3000	3000	3000	3536

continued . . . .

Year:	0	1	2	3	4	5	6	7	8	9	10	11
Financial transfers (minus indicates payment out)												
Equity flow												
New share capital 831	831	721	0	0	0	0	0	0	0	0	0	0
	831	721	0	0	0	0	0	0	0	0	0	0
Medium-term debt service												
Debt rise/(fall)	249.3	-50	-50	-50	-50	-50	0	0	0	0	0	0
Interest (paid)	-12	-25	-20	-15	-10	-5	0	0	0	0	0	0
Realised exchange gains /(losses)	0	0	0	0	0	0	0	0	0	0	0	0
	237	-75	-70	-65	-60	-55	0	0	0	0	0	0
Government and Central Bank												
Subsidies/(taxes) paid	0	0	0	0	-589	-1785	-2394	-2398	-2400	-2400	-2400	-2400
Required cash (rise)/fall	0	-175	-75	-100	0	0	0	0	0	0	0	350
	0	-175	-75	-100	-589	-1785	-2394	-2398	-2400	-2400	-2400	-2050
Sub-total	1068	471	-145	-165	-649	-1840	-2394	-2398	-2400	-2400	-2400	-2050
Deficit/(surplus) of cash	1168	279	-405	-2235	-2351	-1160	-606	-602	-600	-600	-600	-1486
Total financial transfers to balance	2236	750	-550	-2400	-3000	-3000	-3000	-3000	-3000	-3000	-3000	-3536
Short-term deficit/(surplus) of cash												
Short-term debt rise/(fall)	1192	397	-246	-1343	0	0	0	0	0	0	0	0
Short-term debt interest/fees	-24	-119	-159	-134	0	0	0	0	0	0	0	0
Dividends 50%	0	0	0	-379	-1176	-580	-303	-301	-300	-300	-300	-743
Retained earnings (increase)	0	0	0	-379	-1176	-580	-303	-301	-300	-300	-300	-743
Total as above	1168	279	-405	-2235	-2351	-1160	-606	-602	-600	-600	-600	-1486
Max allowed STD 60%	1192	1589	1926									

Table A1.2 Balance sheet projections

						Million Lire in constant terms							
Year:	0	1	2	3	4	5	6	7	8	9	10	11
Fixed assets at original cost												
Land (freehold)	200	200	200	200	200	200	200	200	200	200	200	
Buildings	500	500	500	500	500	500	500	500	500	500	500	
Furniture, fixtures & fittings	200	200	200	200	200	200	200	200	200	200	200	
Plant and equipment	1000	1000	1000	1000	1000	1000	1000	1000	1000	1000	1000	
Motor vehicles	300	300	300	300	300	300	300	300	300	300	300	
	2200	2200	2200	2200	2200	2200	2200	2200	2200	2200	2200	
Less: Provisions for depreciation	0	−163	−326	−489	−653	−816	−979	−1142	−1305	−1468	−1631	
Fixed assets at net book value	2200	2037	1874	1711	1547	1384	1221	1058	895	732	569	
Current assets and liabilities												
Stocks (various)	36	36	36	36	36	36	36	36	36	36	36	
Debtors 10 weeks	0	600	1200	2000	2000	2000	2000	2000	2000	2000	2000	
Cash (needed)	0	175	250	350	350	350	350	350	350	350	350	
Sub-total, current assets	36	811	1486	2386	2386	2386	2386	2386	2386	2386	2386	
Less: Creditors 5 weeks	0	350	500	700	700	700	700	700	700	700	700	
Current taxation	0	0	0	589	1785	2394	2398	2400	2400	2400	2400	
Short-term debt	1192	1589	1343	0	0	0	0	0	0	0	0	
Current portion of medium-term debt	50	50	50	50	50	0	0	0	0	0	0	
	1242	1989	1893	1339	2535	3094	3098	3100	3100	3100	3100	

continued . . .

Year:	0	1	2	3	4	5	6	7	8	9	10	11
Net current assets	−1206	−1178	−407	1047	−149	−708	−712	−714	−714	−714	−714	
NET ASSETS REQUIRED	994	859	1467	2758	1398	676	509	344	181	18	−145	
Surplus cash	0	0	0	379	1555	2135	2438	2739	3039	3339	3639	
NET ASSETS UTILISED	994	859	1467	3137	2953	2811	2947	3083	3220	3357	3494	
Ordinary shares	831	1552	1552	1552	1552	1552	1552	1552	1552	1552	1552	
Retained earnings	−36	−843	−185	1535	1401	1259	1395	1531	1668	1805	1942	
Subtotal: equity	795	709	1367	3087	2953	2811	2947	3083	3220	3357	3494	
Long-term debt	249	199	150	100	50							
Less: current portion	−50	−50	−50	−50								
Provision for unrealised exchange losses	0	0	0	0	0	0	0	0	0	0	0	
CAPITAL EMPLOYED	994	858	1467	3137	2953	2811	2947	3083	3220	3357	3494	

Table A1.3 Profit and loss account (income statement) forecasts

| | Million Lire in constant terms | | | | | | | | | | | |
Year:	0	1	2	3	4	5	6	7	8	9	10	11
Sales detail												
Sales volume (thousand tons)	0	300	600	1000	1000	1000	1000	1000	1000	1000	1000	
Sales price Lire per ton	0	10000	10000	10000	10000	10000	10000	10000	10000	10000	10000	
Revenue												
Sales (million Lire)	0	3000	6000	10000	10000	10000	10000	10000	10000	10000	10000	
Variable costs												
5000 Lire per ton	0	1500	3000	5000	5000	5000	5000	5000	5000	5000	5000	
Fixed costs	0	2000	2000	2000	2000	2000	2000	2000	2000	2000	2000	
Operating profit or loss	0	−500	1000	3000	3000	3000	3000	3000	3000	3000	3000	
Expenses: depreciation		−163	−163	−163	−163	−163	−163	−163	−163	−163	−163	
interest: medium term 10%		−25	−20	−15	−10	−5	0	0	0	0	0	
interest: short term 10%	0	−119	−159	−134	0	0	0	0	0	0		
negotiating fee 5%	−12											
commitment fee 2%	−24											
Extraordinary items												
Unrealised exchange losses	0	0	0	0	0	0	0	0	0	0	0	
Gain/loss on disposals	0	0	0	0	0	0	0	0	0	0	0	
Profit before tax	−36	−807	658	2688	2827	2832	2837	2837	2837	2837	2837	
Taxation at 40%	0	0	0	−589	−1785	−2394	−2398	−2400	−2400	−2400	−2400	
Net income (net profit after tax)	−36	−807	658	2099	1042	438	439	437	437	437	437	

continued . . . .

APPROPRIATION ACCOUNT

Year:	0	1	2	3	4	5	6	7	8	9	10	11
Retained earnings brought forward	0	−36	−843	−185	1535	1401	1259	1395	1531	1668	1805	
Net profit before tax, current year	−36	−807	658	2688	2827	2832	2837	2837	2837	2837	2837	
	−36	−843	−185	2503	4362	4233	4096	4232	4368	4505	4642	
Provision for current taxation	0	0	0	589	1785	2394	2398	2400	2400	2400	2400	
Dividends 50%	0	0	0	379	1176	580	303	301	300	300	300	
Retained earnings carried forward	−36	−843	−185	1535	1401	1259	1395	1531	1668	1805	1942	

Table A1.4 Tax computation

	Year:	0	1	2	3	4	5	6	7	8	9	10	11
						Million Lire in constant terms							
Profit before depreciation and extraordinary items (e.g. unrealised exchange losses)		-36	-644	821	2851	2990	2995	3000	3000	3000	3000	3000	0
Tax allowances:													
Brought forward		0	2200	2200	1379	0	0	0	0	0	0	0	0
Fixed asset acquisitions		2200	0	0	0	0	0	0	0	0	0	0	0
Less: disposals		0	0	0	0	0	0	0	0	0	0	0	0
Allowance available		2200	2200	2200	1379	0	0	0	0	0	0	0	0
Allowance used		0	0	821	1379	0	0	0	0	0	0	0	0
Carried forward		2200	2200	1379	0	0	0	0	0	0	0	0	0
Taxable profit		-36	-644	0	1472	2990	2995	3000	3000	3000	3000	3000	0
Cumulative taxable profit		-36	-680	-680	1472	4462	5985	5995	6000	6000	6000	6000	0
Tax liability at 40%		0	0	0	589	1785	2394	2398	2400	2400	2400	2400	0

Table A1.5 Analytical cash flow

	Year:						Million Lire in constant terms					
	0	1	2	3	4	5	6	7	8	9	10	11
Real resource flows (minus indicates input)												
Operating profit	0	−500	1000	3000	3000	3000	3000	3000	3000	3000	3000	0
Additional working capital (changes):												
Stocks	−36	0	0	0	0	0	0	0	0	0	0	36
Debtors	0	−600	−600	−800	0	0	0	0	0	0	0	2000
Less: trade creditors	0	350	150	200	0	0	0	0	0	0	0	−700
Operating cash flow	−36	−750	550	2400	3000	3000	3000	3000	3000	3000	3000	3536
Additional fixed assets	−2200	0	0	0	0	0	0	0	0	0	0	2200
Disposal of fixed assets	0	0	0									
Total resource flows	−2236	−750	550	2400	3000	3000	3000	3000	3000	3000	3000	3536
Financial transfers (minus indicates payment out)												
Equity flow												
New share capital	831	721	0	0	0	0	0	0	0	0	0	0
Dividends paid	0	0	0	−379	−1176	−580	−303	−301	−300	−300	−300	−1486
Surplus cash accruing	0	0	0	−379	−1176	−580	−303	−301	−300	−300	−300	0
	831	721	0	−758	−2351	−1160	−606	−602	−600	−600	−600	−1486
Medium-term debt service												
Debt rise/(fall)	249	−50	−50	−50	−50	−50	0	0	0	0	0	0
Interest (paid)	−12	−25	−20	−15	−10	−5	0	0	0	0	0	0
Realised exchange gains /(losses)	0	0	0	0	0	0	0	0	0	0	0	0
	237	−75	−70	−65	−60	−55	0	0	0	0	0	0

continued . . .

Year:	0	1	2	3	4	5	6	7	8	9	10	11
Short-term debt service												
Debt rise/(fall)	1192	397	-246	-1343	0	0	0	0	0	0	0	0
Interest (paid)	-24	-119	-159	-134	0	0	0	0	0	0	0	0
	1168	278	-405	-1477	0	0	0	0	0	0	0	0
Government and Central Bank												
Subsidies/(taxes) paid	0	0	0	0	-589	-1785	-2394	-2398	-2400	-2400	-2400	-2400
Required cash (rise)/fall	0	-175	-75	-100	0	0	0	0	0	0	0	350
	0	-175	-75	-100	-589	-1785	-2394	-2398	-2400	-2400	-2400	-2050
Total financial transfers to balance	2236	750	-550	-2400	-3000	-3000	-3000	-3000	-3000	-3000	-3000	-3536

FINANCIAL ANALYSIS (REPARTITION OF DCF)
Standard analysis reflecting project accounts only
Based on flow equality principle

	Net Present Values at 5%	10%	15%	Financial IRRs
Equity	4658	3043	1987	41%
Debt: medium	44	12	-13	12%
Debt: short	200	22	-115	11%
Government	10957	7404	5145	n.a.
Total project	15860	10480	7004	49%

Appendix 2

The multiple project situation

An enterprise may be started to carry out an investment in order to derive a benefit (i.e. a project) but, as it develops a management culture and a momentum of its own, it subsequently undertakes additional projects which become an infinite series unless the enterprise dies. At any given moment a mature enterprise has a *set* of fixed assets and a *set* of working capital items generating a *set* of benefits some of which will be revenues and others will be cost savings. Only the most sophisticated management accounting procedures, not normally found in LDCs (outside some trans-national corporations), will itemise these sets project-wise so that managers can see the ex-post costs and benefits of individual projects.

Occasionally management may demand that the accountants or controllers itemise the sets on an estimated basis, by product if not by project. This task comes under the heading of controllership.

For a single product or project it is relatively simple to identify the assets involved, and so forth, and produce a statement of its ex-post profitability or FIRR. But when you examine the entire enterprise, and make sure that every asset is allocated or apportioned to one or more products or project, and likewise every liability, every cost and every revenue, then you require a much more rigorous treatment of the subject. Naturally the profitabilities and cash flows of the various products have to add up to the profitability and cash flow of the whole enterprise.

Sadly, you often find disappointments when you apply this rigorous treatment. You may find that the overall profitability is 10 per cent on capital employed whilst every one of the underlying projects had been accepted on the basis of a hurdle rate of 15 per cent on capital employed. Then the question is, how could this happen, and which of the many project predictions was at fault? To answer this question, which is asked only occasionally, requires a sophisticated computerised system of management information to be in place at all times, which is expensive and difficult. That is why it is rarely done in LDCs.

The financial analyst is concerned both with individual projects, to assess their wisdom, and with the enterprise as a whole, to assess its viability. It is the projects, not the enterprise, which produce the benefits, but they will fail if the enterprise is a frail vessel which sinks under their weight. The almost total absence of ex-post project accounts makes it vital for the financial analyst to be very clear indeed about the impact which a proposed new project will have upon its enterprise, i.e. upon the existing set of projects which make up the enterprise at the time the new one begins.

To throw some light on the concepts involved here, three typical situations are given below.

SHARING THE OVERHEAD COSTS

An enterprise is running Project A which is a newspaper with printing press, selling into a city. It is proposed to undertake also Project B which is another newspaper, of identical format and number of copies, to be sold into another city. The same printing press can be used, as it has idle capacity. An expansion of the editorial team will be required but some of the material can be used in both newspapers, so team A + B will be smaller than twice team A. Similarly premises, transport, and general labour costs will be subject to a modest expansion.

The result will be double the revenue while costs, assets and liabilities will increase by less than double. Risks and uncertainties are considered insignificant. In such a case the analyst should prepare two reports.

First, on the incremental or 'with and without' basis. With the new newspaper, results will be A + B. Without it, results will be A. The net result B is the difference between the two. This is an incremental benefit in exchange for an incremental investment; there is an incremental cash flow, an incremental income statement, and an incremental balance sheet projection. If B is unattractive, it should be abandoned, even though the total picture A + B is attractive. (Sometimes, of course, a financially unattractive option has to be accepted for reasons of corporate planning strategy, e.g. to prevent competitors from getting there first.)

Second, on the full-cost basis. The analyst should take the scenario A + B with its projected financial statements and break them down into A and B, not on the basis of attributing all existing items to the existing project A, but on the basis of an equitable apportionment. For instance, on the full-cost basis the salary of the Managing Director will probably be split 50:50 between A and B as will his or her duties, whereas on the incremental basis the existing salary would be charged wholly to A, and B would be charged only with the salary increase which is likely to accompany the expansion of the business. The purpose of the full-cost study is to answer the following question: once B is in place, and is no longer regarded as an increment to A but as a separate product in its own right, will it make a satisfactory contribution to the profit and to the cash flow of the enterprise as a whole? The concept is that a healthy enterprise is the sum of its parts each of which contributes positively.

In general one would expect the following:

- If proposal B is to be accepted, B must be attractive both incrementally and full-cost, and A + B must also be attractive (for A + B there is no distinction between incremental and full-cost results).
- If B is attractive on full costing, it will be even more attractive incrementally. The full-cost test is the more stringent.

The word *attractive* is used here to refer to the several indicators discussed elsewhere, both accounting measures of profitability and measures based on discounted cash flow. The same rules apply to economic criteria if shadow prices are used. They do not hold good, however, to measures which reflect the risks of A and B, such as Monte Carlo results.

NEW PROJECT INFLICTING DAMAGE TO EXISTING PROJECT

Another very common situation arises when the lapse of time between the starts of Project A and Project B introduces technical improvements so that with hindsight Project A seems relatively inefficient.

Suppose the enterprise contains Project A which is a brick factory with adjacent clay pits. Proposed Project B is a new brick factory thirty miles away adjacent to some other clay pits. B is a carbon copy of A except that its variable costs are lower (either because it is more modern or because it is bigger). Typically when a new factory is opened the first four or five of its (say) fifteen years of life are spent increasing the sales and the production up to the level of full-capacity working. Project A has already gone through its build-up period and is working at full capacity. But if B goes ahead, A will drop back while B goes straight to full capacity; that is because it has lower variable costs per brick (including variable transportation costs) for all delivery points which are within a certain radius, cutting deep into the potential customer area of factory A. Therefore, B will inflict idle capacity on A. How is this to be reflected in the studies?

On an incremental basis, the cost of the idle capacity in A should be a charge against B. In terms of balance sheets, this means adding to the assets of B that proportion of A's assets and liabilities which is the percentage of idle capacity in A for each year ahead until full working is resumed. A corresponding deduction is made from the balance sheets of A, so that A + B is not affected. In terms of income statements, it means debiting B (but not crediting A) with the corresponding proportion of A's lost revenue, less the associated saving in variable costs, year by year. This transfer is identical to the proportion of A's expected profit before tax and fixed costs, including depreciation and interest, year by year (since revenue minus variable cost equals contribution to fixed costs and profits). In terms of cash flows it means debiting B (but not crediting A) with the reduction in revenue, reduction in variable costs, and associated reduction in working capital, year by year. However, the notional transfer of idle fixed assets and related liabilities from A to B should also be recognised in the cash flows, debiting B and crediting A; if this is not done, B's cash flows will not agree with B's balance sheets.

From the standpoint of B, these adjustments internalise what would otherwise be external costs, viz. the damage inflicted on A. It is interesting to reflect that this is shown up only when A and B are under the same ownership, and the total A + B is important. The damage inflicted on a hundred small shops when a new supermarket opens under separate ownership is never internalised in financial analysis. Of course, externalities are supposed to be dealt with in *economic* analyses.

As for the full-cost study, this will not show the transfers, but will leave the damage entirely in A. Here the concept is: this is a factory which has become partly superseded before its original advocates supposed it would; let the accounts reflect what has happened. The fact that B is under the same ownership is accidental, and may not be permanent. Under separate ownership, the analysts working on B will neither know nor care about the damage done to A.

In the previous example with the two newspapers, it was assumed that paper B would assist paper A, with no loss of customers to A. Depending on the distance and transport facilities between the two cities, this may not be wholly true; A may suffer some idle capacity. Thus some of the aspects of the brick example may have to be introduced as complications into the newspaper example.

NEW PROJECT EXTINGUISHING OLD PROJECT

It may also happen that A suffers not just temporary idle capacity but complete termination under the impact of B.

Suppose A is an old airport. It is overcrowded, dilapidated, but profitable with a positive cash flow. Project B is a much larger airport on virtually the same site, financed by overseas aid. If it goes ahead, A will be bulldozed, or be relegated to an outbuilding of zero value having no revenue of its own. For simplicity we will assume that it has no remaining long-term liabilities: Project A dies with its assets.

In the incremental study, the 'without B' case is the continuation of A alone. The 'with' case is normally A + B but in this situation is B alone. The incremental study is normally B with adjustments for the impact upon A, but in this special case is simply B – A. Thus the incremental study must include on the debit side the loss of profits and of cash flow which would have come from the continuation of A. This means making a study of the hypothetical future operating results of the old airport. Since everyone knows it is closing down, this is likely to be a more difficult exercise than the projections of 'without' cases in Newspaper A and Brickworks A, where management has a secure future.

The full-cost study is B without the adjustments and is identical to that of the enterprise as a whole, since B will be its only project.

Since the old airport is profitable, the full-cost study will be more attractive than the incremental study. Those who advocate B may play down the importance of losing A, and emphasise the hypothetical nature of its continuing profitability and the unreliability of data coming out of so difficult an exercise. There may even be pressures not to attempt or not to publish the incremental study.

The question arises, since the new airport is deemed attractive in spite of the loss of revenue from the old airport, how can its ex-post performance be measured to see if it keeps its promise, when the old airport has been extinguished? There ought to be some notional debit in the cash flow of the new project which will reduce its FIRR and allow us to see what the incremental FIRR is under this influence.

There has been a study of A without B, we will suppose, heroically withstanding any pressures to the contrary. For simplicity it might assume a further ten years of constant cash flow and constant profit, with fixed assets being written down over the same ten years on a straight-line basis without any replacement to a zero residual value. To insert such simple figures into the ex-ante incremental case B – A is easy enough. But a year later, in the ex-post B-only situation, if we wish to look at the incremental FIRR of B then, are we to repeat the same figures? The cost of aviation fuel has changed, tourist patterns have altered, and the commercial situation of the old airport had it still been in use might have been very different.

We are faced with a choice of procedures:

- Assume no change in A (except inflation). This we know is unrealistic.
- Revise the forecast for A. This carries the horrendous implication that all dead projects have to be re-forecasted annually – a necrophiliac procedure which is totally impractical.
- Ignore A and treat B as a new project. The weakness of this is that it does not protect the *enterprise* from a series of projects treading on the heels of predecessors, and violates the principle that an enterprise is the sum of its projects.
- Debit B with a once-for-all capital charge or lump sum representing the damage to A. This should in principle be the arm's-length market valuation of A at the time of its demise. Since there is no active market in defunct airport out-buildings, we have to substitute the prospective ten-year cash flow discounted to a single present value at a rate of discount which is the average cost of capital in B having regard to the riskiness of A's cash flow.

Clearly the last of these is the sensible route we must follow. When an existing project is to be wound up, we have to value its assets either by arm's-length valuation (net of disposal costs such as auctioneers' fees) or by discounting the cash flows deriving from a hypothetical study.

This situation arises more often than might immediately appear. In project rehabilitation situations, the existing project sometimes has to be rebuilt, re-oriented or cannibalised to such an extent that it is in effect closed down and replaced by Project B even though the latter is promulgated as a rescue of Project A. The terminal valuation of A's assets and liabilities can then be seen as a starting point for B.

Appendix 3

Double accounting in public utility undertakings

In general the formats used for financial statements should be modern commercial formats, i.e. those used in modern profit-seeking undertakings. However, much LDC investment is conducted by organisations which adopt other conventions. Some investments take place within government departments directly, and it is worth remembering that some quite large enterprises such as certain railways operate that way. Others are undertaken by village councils. Governments and villages typically do not produce balance sheets at all.

The main purpose of public authority accounting is to prove that all expenditures were on objects duly approved by the appropriate authorities and on none other. A secondary purpose is to prove good stewardship of cash, which means that all cash is accounted for in great detail, though other assets are often neglected. This is of course linked with the theory of public finance (monetary and fiscal policy) in which monetary assets are assigned a rôle which is denied to fixed assets.

In unincorporated publicly-owned undertakings, the accumulation of capital is not demonstrated, since any surpluses or losses are held by the larger organisation; the enterprise itself has no right to retain reserves and no balance sheet to show them in anyway. International loans intended to help unincorporated enterprises present intractable problems, as some of my banking acquaintances have told me. In a dynamic sense they can scarcely be regarded as enterprises at all.

Such a framework as that, worthy as its objectives are in other respects, fails to provide an adequate management information system for projects which by their revenues are intended to be wholly or partly self-sustaining. Unless both Government and commercial accounting systems can be introduced to work in tandem, this is stony ground in which to plant such projects and the likelihood of success is slim.

There are, however, certain organisations which occupy a middle ground between Government and commerce. These are typically publicly-owned utility undertakings whose fixed assets have a long working life: water, railways, municipal housing, and the like. They do have their own balance sheets and their own retained reserves. Over the decades they have developed a distinct set of accounting conventions.

Public utility accounting derives its concepts and its customs from the practical experience of early public utilities in the nineteenth century. Sometimes new borrowings are made conditional on the adoption of modern commercial accounting systems, and temporary hybrid systems arise. One cannot therefore predict from the nature of an enterprise what kind of accounting system it will have. The analyst preparing ex-ante financial statements must enquire of an existing organisation, or consider in respect of a proposed brand new organisation, what accounting conventions are to be accepted, in order that correct financial statements can be drawn up. There is, however, a sufficient cluster of enterprises using a recognisable convention developed for public utilities, called *double accounting*, to justify special consideration here, as follows.

THE CONCEPT OF DOUBLE ACCOUNTING

In double accounting, the operating account is kept separate from all capital transactions, and is usually entitled the *revenue account*. Not to be confused with double-entry accounting, double accounting is so called because it presents its balance sheet in two halves, the *current account* and the *capital account*. It can be readily understood if thought of in terms of a nineteenth-century railway seeking share subscriptions from the public. Investors wanted assurance that their money would be devoted solely to the purposes described in the prospectus, viz. the further development of the railway in terms of land acquisition, permanent way, stations, locomotives and rolling stock. They did not want their money to be swallowed up as an operating subsidy to the revenue account, though if existing operations turned out to be profitable they would have no objection to the revenue account contributing to the capital account.

Consequently the accounts have to demonstrate that the capital liabilities – share subscriptions and loans received – are equal to, or less than, capital expenditure on fixed assets. The capital receipts can be less than the capital expenditure if there is an operating profit to make a contribution to the capital account. Taking this so-called revenue contribution into account, the two halves of the capital account have to be equal. In designing this system it was also hoped that this would demonstrate that no capital expenditure had been applied to fixed assets not in the prospectus, such as unauthorised branch lines, which were a problem with some early railway managers.

The balancing of the capital account – the equality between capital assets and capital liabilities – has meant that the lifetimes of the liabilities have to match the lifetimes of the assets. Thus fixed assets which in the nineteenth century were regarded as virtually permanent were to be financed by virtually permanent capital receipts, that is, by shares. No depreciation of such assets was entered in the accounts. Any wear and tear on the assets was to be made good by 'proper maintenance' which was an operating cost, and the Directors had to certify that it had been done.

Those assets which were financed by long fixed-term loans were depreciated over the lives of the loans. It was not recognised that this might lead to a set of unrealistic depreciable lives for the assets, but rather, it was considered prudent that realistic lives for the loans should be negotiated to suit the assets. The outcome of this correspondence between the life of an asset and the life of the associated loan is that the annual depreciation expense of an asset becomes equal to the redemption (repayment) of the loan, excluding interest of course. This is quite different from commercial accounting in which the annual depreciation has regard to the useful life of the asset regardless of any loans.

The other half of the balance sheet is the current account. This shows current assets and current liabilities. Profits from operations are seen as producing additional current assets, such as cash, however, any surplus of current assets over current liabilities is either distributed as dividend and taxation, held in revenue reserves, or transferred as a contribution to the capital account. By these entries, the current account always remains balanced.

We may compare the double-accounting surplus in a public utility revenue account with the single-accounting profit of a commercial income statement as follows. Take the commercial net income (net profit after interest and tax). Add back commercial depreciation and substitute loan repayments (redemption of capital, not interest). Add back also interest capitalised, if any. The result is the annual surplus in the public utility revenue account, and if cumulated, will give the revenue reserves in the current account part of the balance sheets. Subtract the current assets from the current liabilities (the latter including these reserves), and anything left is the revenue contribution to the capital account.

Current assets should include cumulative expenditures on uncompleted projects, known as capital work in progress, which is not capitalised until the project enters its operating phase, at which time the asset becomes a capital asset, and its associated finance likewise ceases to be a current liability and becomes a capital liability. This too differs from modern commercial practice though it can be defended.

A WORKED EXAMPLE

Tables A3.1 and A3.2 show the first five years of a twenty-year project which was a water supply scheme for a small town in India. Finance for the reservoir, main pipes, pumping system and initial house connections was to come partly from the International Development Agency (IDA) and partly from the Government of Tamil Nadu (GTN). Subsequent additional house

TableA3.1 Forecast balance sheets (commercial format)

	Rupees at year-ends ('000s)				
	1982 −1983	1983 −1984	1984 −1985	1985 −1986	1986 −1987
ASSETS UTILISED					
Fixed assets					
at original cost	3312.0	3388.0	3400.0	3412.0	3425.0
Less: provisions for depreciation	0.0	0.0	88.0	176.5	265.5
Net Book Value	3312.0	3388.0	3312.0	3235.5	3159.5
Current assets					
Stock Weeks: 0	0.0	0.0	0.0	0.0	0.0
Debtors Weeks:12	0.0	31.1	33.6	36.2	41.9
Cash float Weeks: 0	0.0	0.0	0.0	0.0	0.0
Cash surplus	0.0	19.3	50.9	87.9	0.0
Subtotal	0.0	50.4	84.5	124.2	41.9
Less: current liabilities					
Creditors Weeks: 6	0.0	−10.4	−11.0	−11.6	−12.4
Net current assets	0.0	40.0	73.5	112.5	29.5
Total net assets utilised	3312.0	3428.0	3385.5	3348.0	3189.0
CAPITAL EMPLOYED					
GTN grant	1769.0	1809.0	1809.0	1809.0	1809.0
IDA loans	1616.3	1809.3	1981.1	2169.3	2129.3
Reserves	−73.3	−190.3	−404.7	−630.3	−749.2
Total capital employed	3312.0	3428.0	3385.5	3348.0	3189.0

connections receive no capital finance, and depend on the 'revenue contribution' for their capital.

Table A3.1 shows the pro-forma balance sheets in conventional format, Table A3.2 in the format of double accounting. Both take their data from separate spreadsheets, not shown, in which capital expenditures, funding patterns, revenues and costs (there is no taxation) have been previously worked out. The cash flow statements are calculated subsequently; they too have two alternative formats (not shown here).

In these tables, operating subsidies have been previously calculated and included in revenue, and when this results in a cash surplus at any date, it is shown as retained in the balance sheet rather than repaid to central Government. This is analogous to the assumption of a no-dividend policy in a commercial analysis. The cash surplus is not to be confused with the cash float (petty cash required for operations) which in this project was mistakenly budgeted as nil.

TableA3.2 Forecast balance sheets (public authority format)

	1982 −1983	1983 −1984	1984 −1985	1985 −1986	1986 −1987
	Rupees at year-ends ('000s)				
CAPITALACCOUNT					
Fixed assets in operation	0.0	3618.3	3802.1	4002.3	3975.3
Financed by:					
GTN grant	0.0	1809.0	1809.0	1809.0	1809.0
IDA loan	0.0	1809.3	1981.1	2169.3	2129.3
Revenue contribution	0.0	0.0	12.0	24.0	37.0
	0.0	3618.3	3802.1	4002.3	3975.3
CURRENTACCOUNT					
Capital work in progress	3312.0				
Working capital	0.0	40.0	73.5	112.5	29.5
Revenue contribution	0.0	0.0	12.0	24.0	37.0
	3312.0	40.0	85.5	136.5	66.5
GTN grant	1769.0				
IDA loan	1543.0				
Revenue reserves	0.0	40.0	85.5	136.5	66.5
Deficit (if any)	0.0	0.0	0.0	0.0	0.0
	3312.0	40.0	85.5	136.5	66.5

The line 'deficit if any' shows where the deficit would appear if this spreadsheet were calculated without any operating subsidies. Note that the subsidies themselves do not appear in either form of balance sheet. They appear in income statements and in cash flow statements, and are a vital outcome of the analysis. Regrettably, a Government when it accepts a proposal in which subsidies are shown does not thereby commit itself to providing those subsidies. This is because of the system of annual appropriations with annual accountability. One of the principal concerns of financial analysis is to check that the enterprise which undertakes the project will survive the attempt; this is defeated in cases where the accounts rely on unpromised subsidies. Of course, a government department will not be bankrupted, but enterprises which are partly Government and partly commercial may occupy a very uneasy ground.

NOTE

The mechanics of double accounting are explained in detail in Sidebotham and Page (1960) and briefly in older textbooks such as the first edition of

Carter's Advanced Accounts (undated). For the situation of Government and public authority accountancy in relation to the whole set of accountancies, see Enthoven (1973). For the historical origins and development of double accounting, Edwards (1989) is highly recommended.

Ratio analysis in ex-ante statements

It is obvious that the calculation of a number can lead to a sound judgement about a proposed investment *only* if that number can be judged to be high or low in relation to some other number or *norm*. For example, a figure for current assets of five million dinars is meaningless on its own, but compared to current liabilities of twenty million dinars it can be judged to be bad. The ratio between the two numbers is unsatisfactory, because as a general norm current assets should be larger than current liabilities, to avoid imminently running out of cash.

However, it is also obvious that the number of ratios which it is possible to calculate is almost limitless. It is therefore necessary to be quite clear what aspect of the proposal is being investigated and which are the most useful ratios for that aspect.

NORMS FOR INSIDERS AND NORMS FOR OUTSIDERS

You will find in any accounting textbook some 'common' ratios concerned with profitability, liquidity, efficiency, and gearing. An example is the so-called current assets ratio: current assets divided by current liabilities, which is supposed to be three or greater. This kind of ratio is no good for development projects. First, it is a rule of thumb with a considerable safety margin built in because it is intended to be used by bankers (potential lenders) who have no detailed inside knowledge of the business. In ex-ante work, however, we have much more detailed information (albeit less reliable) than is given in published financial statements. We have the full *inside story*. No one knows anything we do not know. We can break down the current assets (assets realisable within one year) into various different sections of differing liquidity; we can break down the current liabilities into a diary of maturity dates. Above all, being experts in the business in question, we can use our past experience to derive norms which are more accurate than the safe 3:1 rule that you can apply when you do not even know what kind of business it is. If we intend to run a retail fruit business based on wholesale trade credit, we might well have current liabilities exceeding current assets, as a matter of specific policy.

So can we eliminate from our enquiries all those crude ratios which are designed for outsiders looking in, without the benefit of inside knowledge? Unfortunately not. If our project will require investment by a bank which adopts the blunderbuss approach, and always insists on a current ratio of three or more, and a debt-equity ratio of 60 per cent or less, throughout its client portfolio regardless of the nature of the business, we will have to comply with these norms too.

ASPECTS OF INTEREST

Liquidity is certainly important, at any rate in an enterprise which is a legally separate entity, not merely a department of Government. If an enterprise, in its forecast accounts, is predicted to pass through a period when its liquid assets are low in relation to current liabilities or in relation to expenditures, this represents a 'near miss' or 'near disaster' situation. We must remember that all predicted numbers are the central estimates of implicit probability distributions; they are not completely accurate. Thus a predicted near disaster has a distinct probability of turning out to be an actual disaster. If the enterprise even temporarily runs out of cash and cannot pay its bills, this will have repercussions on customer confidence, on lender confidence, and on investor confidence. This will disrupt both production and sales. It may lead to a management upheaval, re-orientation, or downsizing. Thus a predicted near-miss lasting through just one or two year-ends (in the ex-ante balance sheets) may turn out to be a medium-term crisis threatening to bring the entire activity to a halt. That is why we need to look at liquidity. For further discussion of ratios useful in predicting catastrophes, see Tamari (1978).

Ratios showing the yield or profitability of the proposed investment are in many cases central to the whole appraisal. Only investments undertaken on a non-profit basis, such as charitable, philanthropic, military, and environmental projects can afford to draw out of the pool of capital without asking how much will be put back in. Profitability criteria include ratios which operate one year at a time (the so-called *accounting criteria*), and those which cover an activity through its life (*discounted cash flow measures*). The latter set includes items such as IRR which can only loosely be called *ratios*. Both types are considered indispensable in modern accounting practice. In advanced economies where shares are quoted on stock exchanges, *earnings per share* is one of the key ratios.

Where an investment will be managed and controlled by X but financed partly by Y, additional special ratios are needed to reassure Y that X is not misbehaving. The two dangers are (a) using borrowed finance to pay for a protracted nosedive (and perhaps unearned dividend payouts) instead of expansion, and (b) appropriating the cash required for servicing the debt to pay for those same undesirable activities. The first of these can be dealt with by limiting the ratio of debt to equity, the so-called *gearing ratio*; the second, by setting an ex-ante lower limit to the ratio of cash flow to debt service, the so-called *debt service cover ratio*.

Where an investment is to be undertaken by a public enterprise, acting according to government directives as well as possibly pursuing commercial goals, some extra ratios are probably needed to measure the efficiency of the enterprise in terms of the aims and objects of the directives. Sometimes it may be possible to divide the accounts into commercial and non-commercial activities, confining the application of profitability ratios to the former, and devising norms of effectiveness or efficiency for the latter (Turk 1984: 44–51).

Finally, where some activity within a section or department of the enterprise is particularly crucial for the success of the investment, or particularly in need of monitoring for some other reason, special ratios can be added to the list. For example, in a difficult competitive trading environment, ratios which assess the performance of the marketing function may be added (Bonoma and Clark 1988). Tamari cites the example of freight carried divided by carrying capacity, in the marine cargo shipping trade; this is a key *technical coefficient*. In the hotel business, bedroom occupancy rates are a familiar benchmark of the same kind.

Also in this special section might come ratios or norms of environmental protection. These might include for example the ratio of toxic discharge (of a specified nature) to volume of product, or more specific measures as specified in permits and licences. It is even possible that *general purpose* environmental protection ratios might ultimately emerge in the manner of general purpose liquidity ratios, as for instance energy consumed per rupee of revenue, or energy radiated per rupee of value-added. However, with environmental ratios, as with economic measures such as EIRR, we are straying too far away from financial analysis, which is our subject.

Figure A4.1 offers a list of some useful ratios. In each case the ratio is calculated from a pair of indicators. To be useful, the result should be compared with some standard or norm of what is satisfactory. Here, however, the figure is silent as to what that norm should be. As discussed above, it must vary widely according to detailed circumstances. Norms must be derived from past experience of closely similar investment projects. Regrettable though that may be for countries in a very early stage of development, since it may entail the cost of employing an international consultant, it is better than using inappropriate   norms.

In making a list of ratios for financial analysis it is perhaps useful to think where our topic begins and ends. Suppose for example we are concerned with performance in a transport undertaking; performance is certainly relevant to financial results, and reasonable performance standards must be set in the ex-ante phase. We might look at revenue divided by carrying capacity, as an indicator of marketing performance, and we might look at carrying capacity divided by the asset cost of the carriers as an indicator of purchasing performance. Carrying capacity does not appear in any standard financial

YIELD OR PROFITABILITY

Profit before interest, dividends and tax	Net assets utilised	Return on capital employed, at each year-end and for average of all operating years.
Profit after interest, before dividends and tax	Shareholders' funds i.e. equity plus preference shares	Return on equity or ROSF, at each year-end and for average of all operating years.
Contribution (revenue minus variable costs)	Unit of sales volume	Contribution per unit, each year.
Profit after interest, before dividends and tax	Revenue	Return on sales (ROS) shows margin by which prices may fall before loss arises.
Present value of cash receipts measuring resource outputs	Present value of cash outgoings measuring resource inputs	Benefit/cost ratio at a given rate of discount. If the rate of discount produces a B/C of one, that rate is the IRR, and the NPV is zero.

LIQUIDITY

Current assets	Current liabilities	Current ratio, at each year-end and for average of all operating years.
Net working capital	Revenue (output)	At each year-end and for average of all operating years.
Sources of cash predicted in short run (e.g. three months ahead)	Uses of cash predicted in short run	Superior form of current ratio.

Figure A4.1   Ratios for financial analysis

DEBT SECURITY

Specific mortgaged assets (less estimated cost of collection)	Secured debt or total debt	At each year-end, for each lender.
Shareholders' funds	Net capital employed	May also be expressed as debt:equity ratio.
Equity	Total capital employed	Recognises short-term debt, shows gearing (leverage) in full.
Cash flow before debt service	Cash flow required for debt service	Debt service cover ratio.

PERFORMANCE (see also Figures 3.1 and 3.2 p. 36 and 37)

Revenue (output)	Gross fixed assets (unsuitable where inflation is strong)	Average over asset life. This is a hybrid ratio (see text below).
Revenue (output)	Employee	Including full-time equivalent of part-time employees.
Value added	Employee	As above.
Expenses	Revenue (output)	Regards expenses as a burden to be kept to a minimum.
Trade debtors at year-end	Annual revenue divided by days in year	Collection period for debtors, in days.
Trade creditors at year-end	Purchases of materials divided by days in year	Payment period for creditors, in days.
Selling expense	Sales (or annual increase in sales)	Should be adequate but not wasteful.

ADDITIONAL PUBLIC SECTOR PERFORMANCE INDICATORS

Profitability and performance indicators as above, adjusted for:
(a) effect of state-administered pricing
(b) taxes payable on profits, or subsidies receivable
(c) tax deductions from wages and other personal incomes
(d) cost of training schemes provided for benefit to others.

Figure A4.1   Continued

statement; we rely on our access to the full project data. If we used financial data only, we would have to use revenue divided by asset cost, which would be a hybrid, a mixture of the two performances. It would be an inferior ratio. Being a mixture, it would be hard to set as a standard for operation, and it would be difficult to ascertain an industry-wide norm to determine the appropriate ex-ante ratio. So financial analysis does not disdain non-financial data but its aims are limited to the drawing of conclusions which directly or indirectly affect financial flows.

Bibliography

Argenti, J. (1989) *Practical Corporate Planning*, rev. edn, London: Unwin Paperbacks.

Bauman, H.C. (1964) *Fundamentals of Cost Engineering in the Chemical Industry*, New York: Reinhold.

Bonoma, T.V. and Clark, B.H. (1988) *Marketing Performance Assessment*, Harvard: Harvard Business School.

Brealey, R. and Myers, S. (1984) *Principles of Corporate Finance*, 2nd edn, Tokyo etc.: McGraw-Hill.

Bridger, G.A. (1986) 'Rapid Project Appraisal' in *Project Appraisal*, Vol. 1, No. 4, December.

Bridger, G.A. and Winpenny, J.T. (1983) *Planning Development Projects*, London: HMSO.

Carter, R.N. First edn undated, *Advanced Accounts*, London: Pitman.

Cole, S. (1987) *Applied Transport Economics*, London: Kogan Page.

Conatser, K.R. (1991) 'Trends and Spends' in *Lotus Computing for Managers and Professionals*, May, London: IDG Communications.

Cracknell, B. (1991) *Lessons from Evaluation Findings* in Kirkpatrick 1991.

De la Mare, R.F. (1982) *Manufacturing Systems Economics*, Eastbourne: Holt, Rinehart, and Winston.

Development Academy of the Phillipines (1978) *How to Develop Project Feasibility Studies*, Manila: Sinag-Tala Publishers.

Edwards, J.R. (1989) *A History of Financial Accounting*, London: Routledge.

Enthoven, A.J.H. (1973) *Accountancy and Economic Development Policy*, Amsterdam: North-Holland.

FAO (Food and Agriculture Organisation of the United Nations) (1984) Investment Centre, *Guide to Financial Analysis*, mimeo, Rome: FAO.

FAO (Food and Agriculture Organisation of the United Nations) (1990) *The Design of Agricultural Investment Projects: Lessons from Experience*, Investment Centre Technical Paper, No. 6, Rome: FAO.

Finney, C.E. (1990) 'A Consultant's Criteria for the Economic Ranking of Public Sector Projects' in *Project Appraisal*, Vol. 5, No. 1, March.

Fitzgerald, E. (trans.) (1909) *Rubáiyát of Omar Khayám*, London: Heinemann.

Fok Kam, A.E (1988) *Management Accounting for the Sugar Cane Industry*, Amsterdam: Elsevier.

Franks, J.R., Broyles, J.E., Carleton, W.T. (1985) *Corporate Finance: Concepts and Applications*, Boston, Mass.: Kent.

Gale, B.T. and Swire, D.J. (1988) 'Business Strategies that Create Wealth' in *Planning Review*, March/April.

George, S. (1988) *A Fate Worse than Debt*, London: Penguin.

Griffiths, L. (1986) *Arthur Daley's Guide to Doing It Right*, Glasgow: Fontana/Collins.

Gunatilleke, G. (1989) 'Enhancing Social Responsibility for the Future' in *Marga*, Vol. 10, No. 1, Colombo: Marga Institute.

Harvey, C. (1983) *Analysis of Project Finance in Developing Countries*, London: Heinemann.

ICA (Institute of Chartered Accountants in England and Wales) (1987) *Accounting Standards 1987/88*, London (biennial).

Kalecki, M. (1954) *Theory of Economic Dynamics*, London: Allen and Unwin.

Keynes, J.M. (1936) *The General Theory of Employment Interest and Money*, London: Macmillan.

Killough, L.N. and Leininger, W.E. (1987) *Cost Accounting Concepts and Techniques for Management*, 2nd edn, St Paul, Minnesota: West Publishing Co.

Kirkpatrick, C. (ed.) (1991) *Project Rehabilitation in Developing Countries*, London: Routledge.

Kitchen, R.L. (1986) *Finance for Developing Countries*, Chichester: Wiley.

Lee, G.A. (1974) *The Funds Statement*, Edinburgh: Institute of Chartered Accountants of Scotland.

Lee, G.A. (1975) *Modern Financial Accounting*, London: Nelson.

Marshall, V. (1990) 'The Management of Disasters', public lecture, University of Bradford, 24 April.

Martinez, O. (1978) *Panama Canal*, London: Gordon and Cremonesi.

Miller, M. and Modigliani, F. (1961) 'Dividend Policy, Growth and the Valuation of Shares' in *Journal of Business*, Vol. 34, No. 4, October.

Muro, V.T. (1975) *Preparing Project Feasibility Studies for Philippine Business Enterprises*, 2 vols, Manila: Business Technology Corpn.

Parkin, V. (1991) *Chronic Inflation in an Industrialising Economy*, Cambridge: Cambridge University Press.

Pouliquen, L.Y. (1970) *Risk Analysis in Project Appraisal*, Baltimore and London: Johns Hopkins for IBRD.

Ray, A. (1984) *Cost-Benefit Analysis – Issues and Methodologies*, Baltimore: Johns Hopkins for World Bank.

Reimann, Bernard C. (1990) 'Why Bother with Adjusted Hurdle Rates?' in *Long Range Planning*, Vol. 23, No. 3, June.

Reutlinger, S. (1970) *Techniques for Project Appraisal under Uncertainty*, Baltimore and London: Johns Hopkins for IBRD.

Rosenkranz, F. (1979) *An Introduction to Corporate Modeling*, Durham, N. Carolina: Duke University Press.

Rudd, D.F. and Watson, C.C. (1968) *Strategy of Process Engineering*, New York: John Wiley.

Sidebotham, R. and Page, C.S. (1960) *Accounting for Local and Public Authorities*, London: Gee.

Stiles, K.W. (1991) *Negotiating Debt, the IMF Lending Process*, Boulder, Colorado: Westview Press.

Tamari, M. (1978) *Financial Ratios Analysis and Prediction*, London: Paul Elek.

Thornton Baker Audit Manual (1983), London: Oyez Longman.

Tribe, M.A. and Alpine, R.L.W. (1986) 'Economies of Scale in Sugar Production' in *Engineering Cost and Production Economics*, Vol. 10.

Turk, I. (1984) *Accounting Analysis of the Efficiency of Public Enterprises*, Ljubljana: International Center for Public Enterprises in Developing Countries, Monograph 19.

UNIDO (United Nations Industrial Organisation) (1972) *Guidelines for Project Appraisal*, New York: UNIDO.

UNIDO (United Nations Industrial Organisation) (1978) *Guide to Practical Project Appraisal*, New York: UNIDO.

Vahcic, A. and Petrin, T. (1990) 'Restructuring the Slovene Economy' in *Slovene Studies*, Vol. 12, No. 1.
Wells, G.L. (1980) *Safety in Process Plant Design*, London: George Godwin.

Index